Ed Brisson    Lisandro Estherren    Niko Guardia

# the Last Contract ™

BOOM!
STUDIOS

**THE LAST CONTRACT, May 2017.** Published by BOOM! Studios, a division of Boom Entertainment, Inc. The Last Contract is ™ & © 2017 Edmond Brisson & Lisandro Estherren. Originally published in single magazine form as THE LAST CONTRACT No. 1-4. ™ & © 2016 Edmond Brisson & Lisandro Estherren. All rights reserved. BOOM! Studios™ and the BOOM! Studios logo are trademarks of Boom Entertainment, Inc., registered in various countries and categories. All characters, events, and institutions depicted herein are fictional. Any similarity between any of the names, characters, persons, events, and/or institutions in this publication to actual names, characters, and persons, whether living or dead, events, and/or institutions is unintended and purely coincidental. BOOM! Studios does not read or accept unsolicited submissions of ideas, stories, or artwork.

A catalog record of this book is available from OCLC and from the BOOM! Studios website, www.boom-studios.com, on the Librarians page.

BOOM! Studios, 5670 Wilshire Boulevard, Suite 450, Los Angeles, CA 90036-5679. Printed in China. First Printing.

ISBN: 978-1-60886-962-6
eISBN: 978-1-61398-633-2

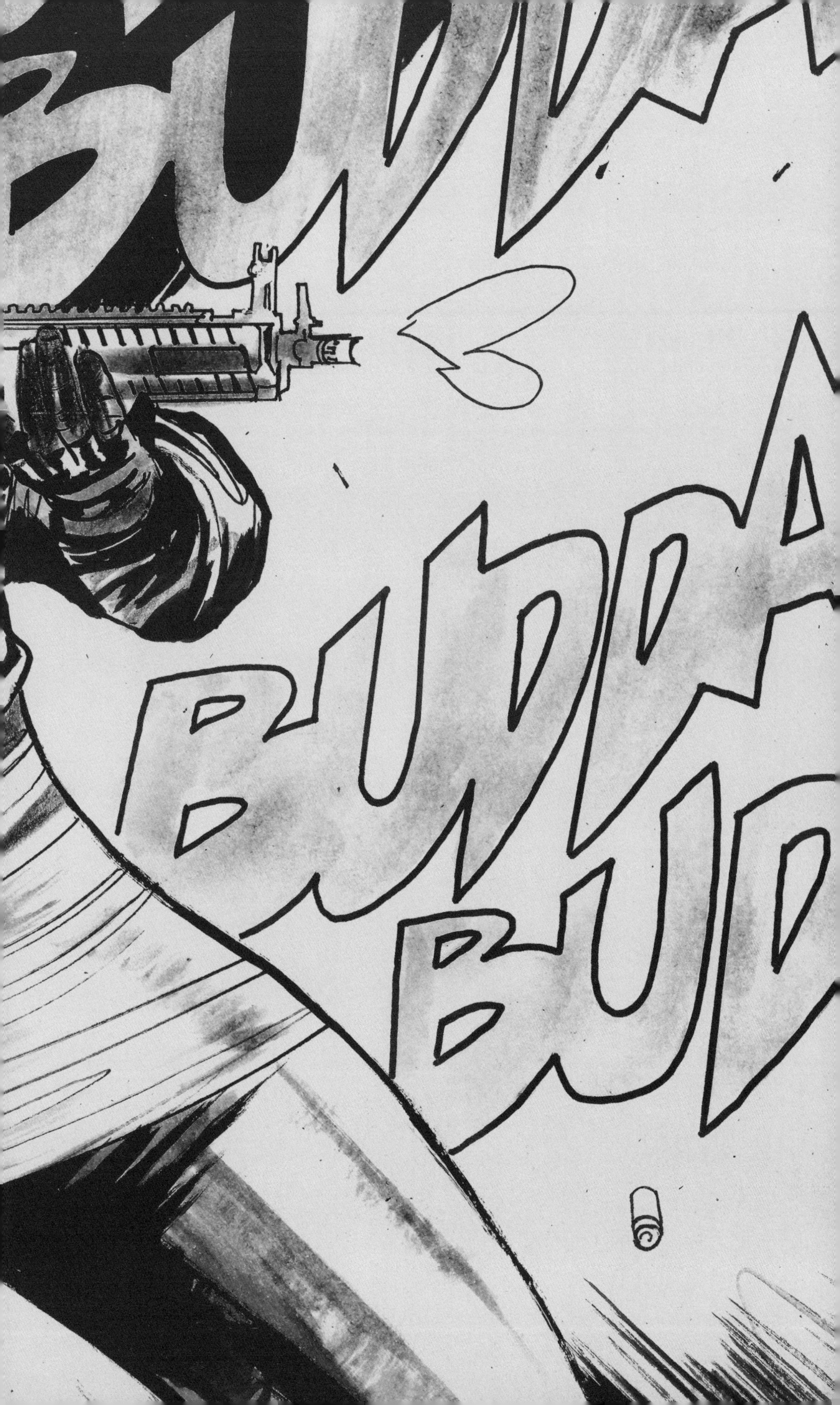
BUDD
BUD

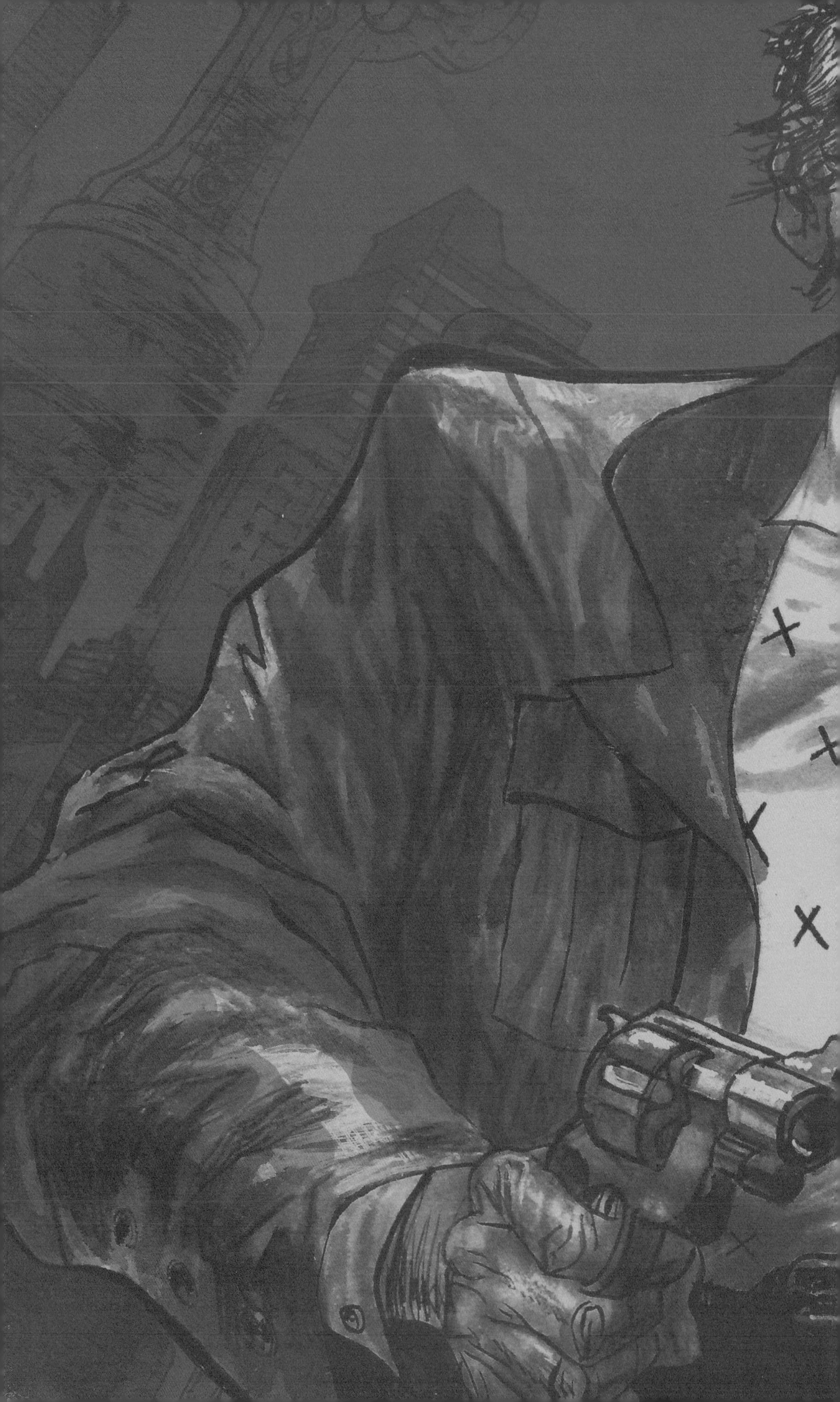

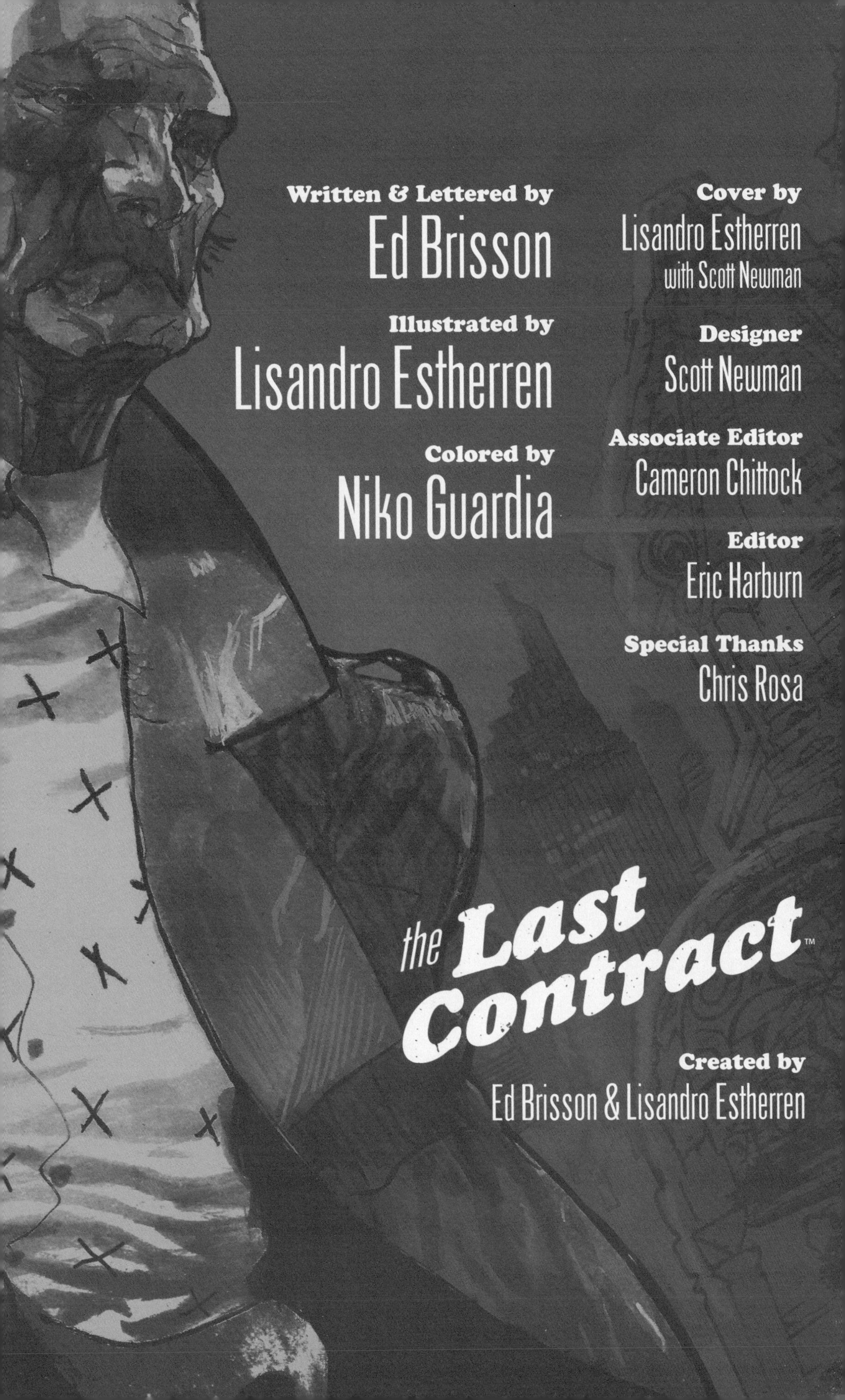

**Written & Lettered by**
Ed Brisson

**Illustrated by**
Lisandro Estherren

**Colored by**
Niko Guardia

**Cover by**
Lisandro Estherren
with Scott Newman

**Designer**
Scott Newman

**Associate Editor**
Cameron Chittock

**Editor**
Eric Harburn

**Special Thanks**
Chris Rosa

# the Last Contract™

**Created by**
Ed Brisson & Lisandro Estherren

# Chapter One

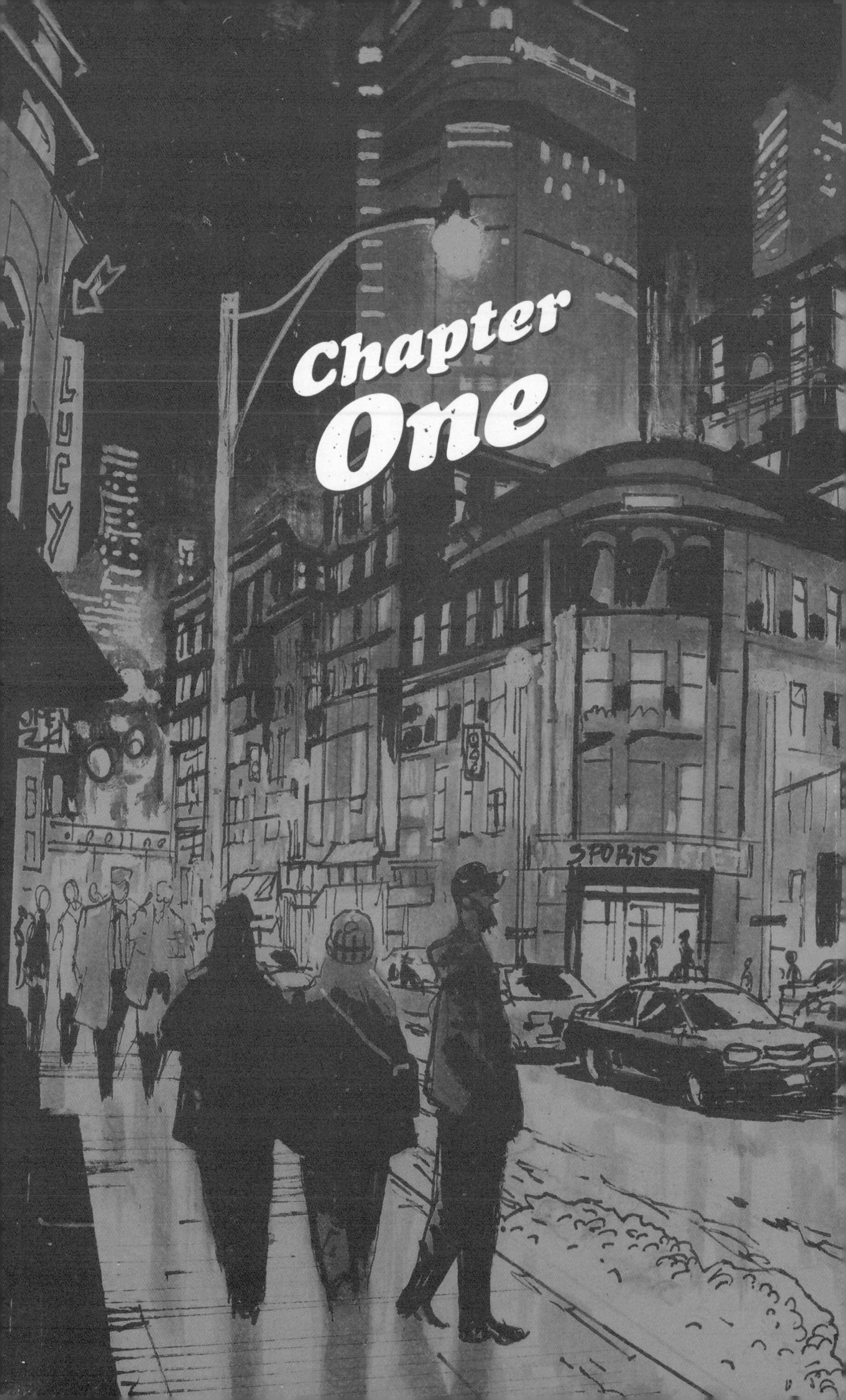
SPORTS

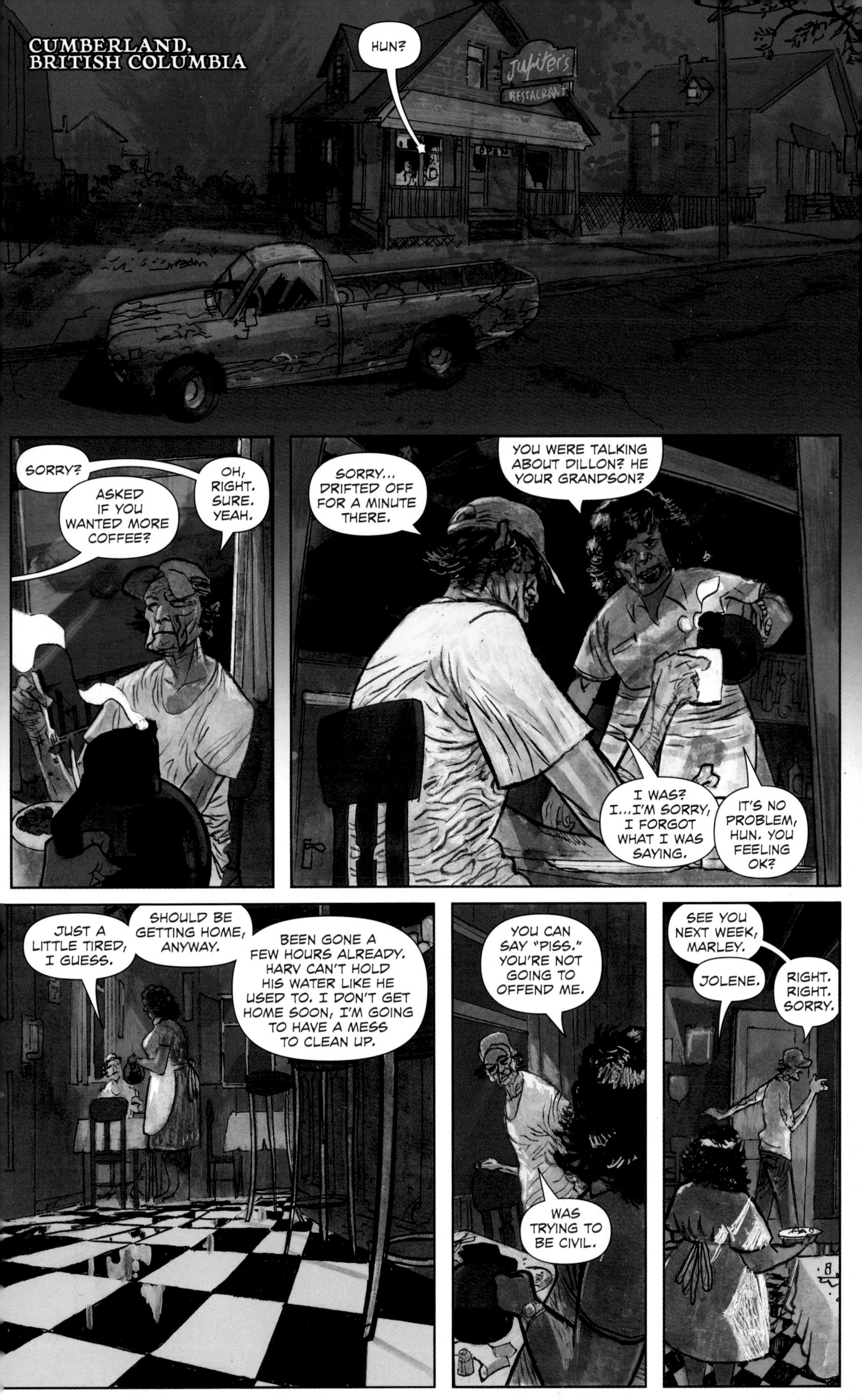

CUMBERLAND, BRITISH COLUMBIA
HUN?
Jupiter's
RESTAURANT
OPEN
SORRY?
ASKED IF YOU WANTED MORE COFFEE?
OH, RIGHT. SURE. YEAH.
SORRY... DRIFTED OFF FOR A MINUTE THERE.
YOU WERE TALKING ABOUT DILLON? HE YOUR GRANDSON?
I WAS? I...I'M SORRY, I FORGOT WHAT I WAS SAYING.
IT'S NO PROBLEM, HUN. YOU FEELING OK?
JUST A LITTLE TIRED, I GUESS.
SHOULD BE GETTING HOME, ANYWAY.
BEEN GONE A FEW HOURS ALREADY. HARV CAN'T HOLD HIS WATER LIKE HE USED TO. I DON'T GET HOME SOON, I'M GOING TO HAVE A MESS TO CLEAN UP.
YOU CAN SAY "PISS." YOU'RE NOT GOING TO OFFEND ME.
WAS TRYING TO BE CIVIL.
SEE YOU NEXT WEEK, MARLEY.
JOLENE.
RIGHT. RIGHT. SORRY.

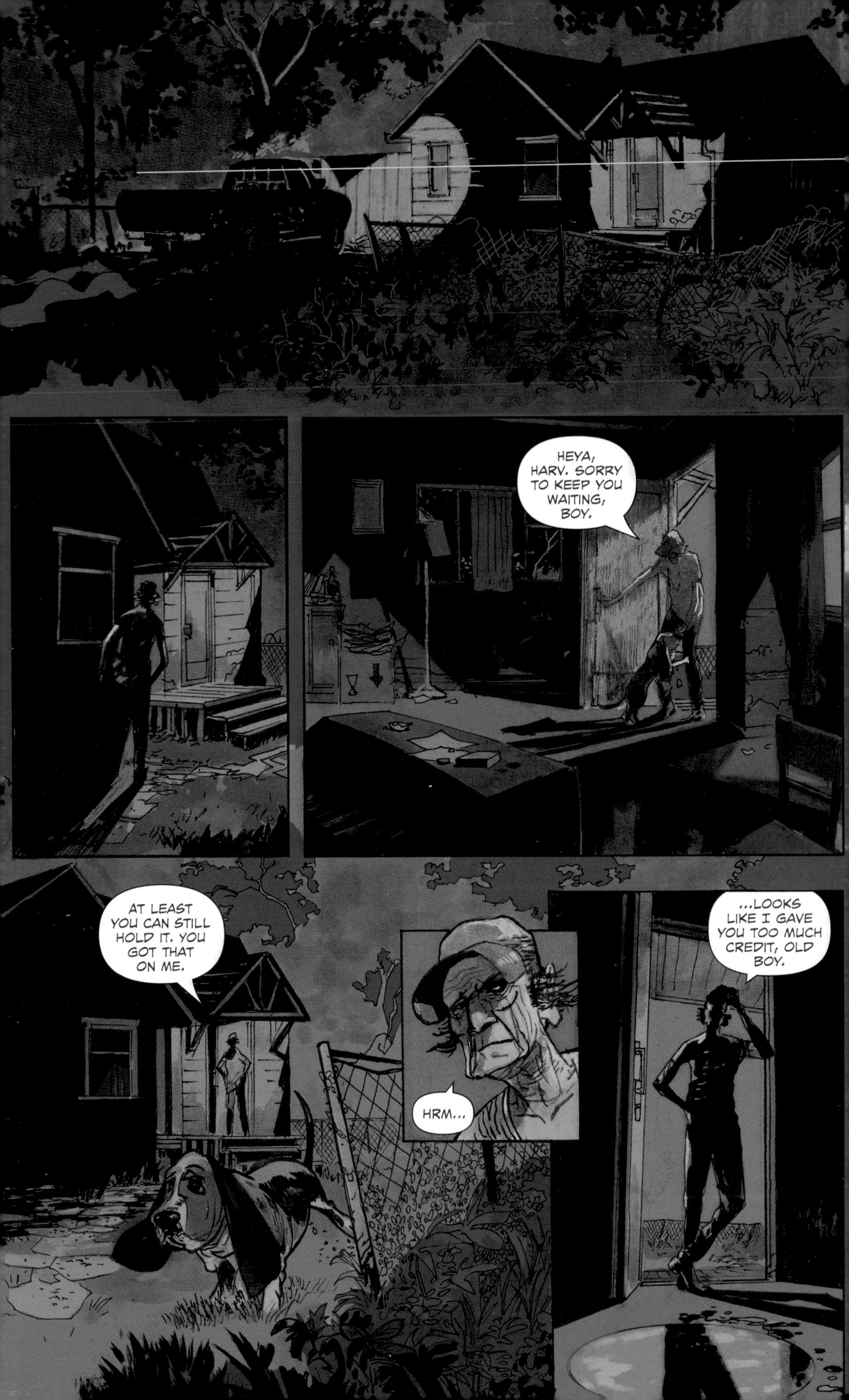
HEYA, HARV. SORRY TO KEEP YOU WAITING, BOY.
AT LEAST YOU CAN STILL HOLD IT. YOU GOT THAT ON ME.
HRM...
...LOOKS LIKE I GAVE YOU TOO MUCH CREDIT, OLD BOY.

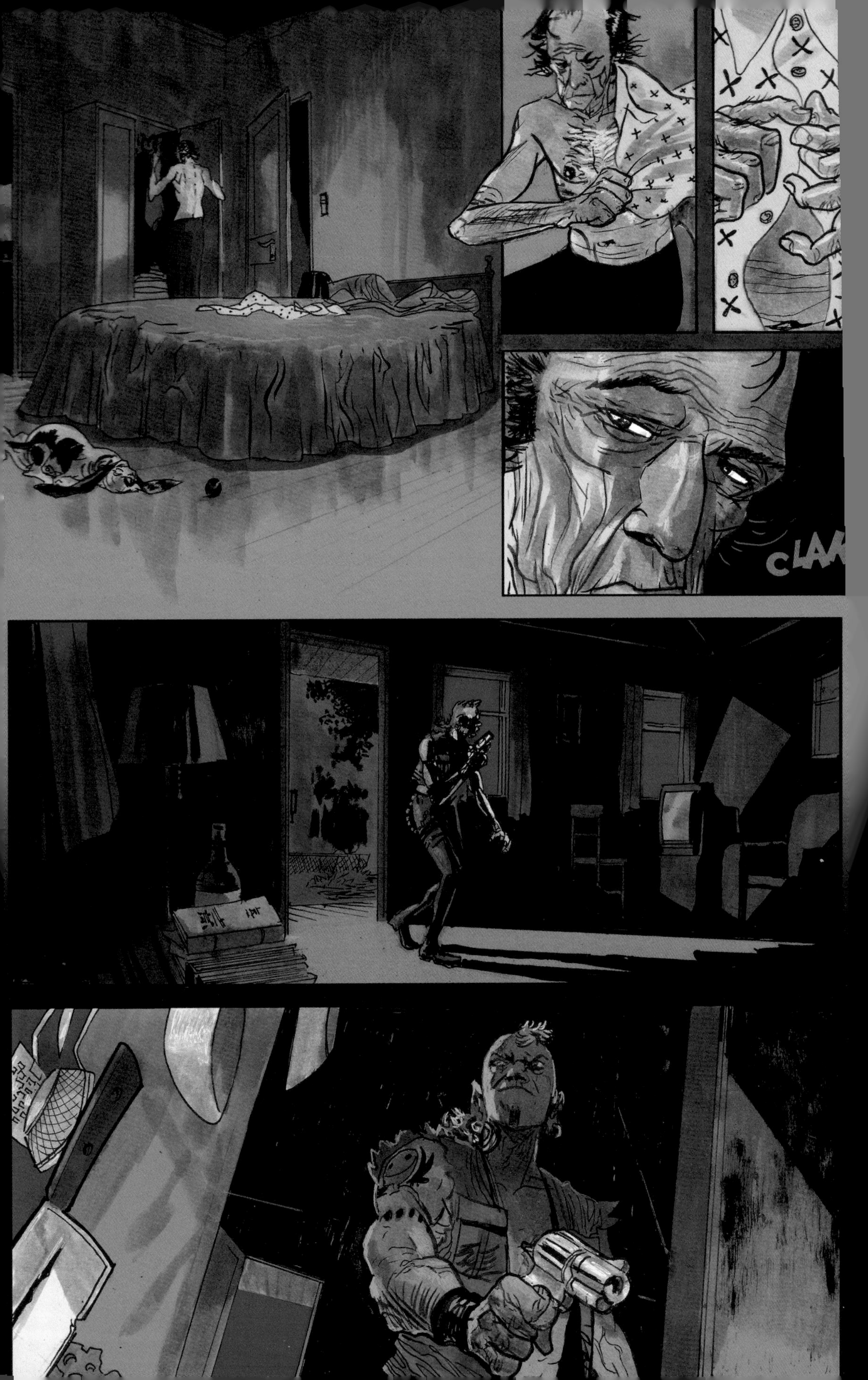
CLAK

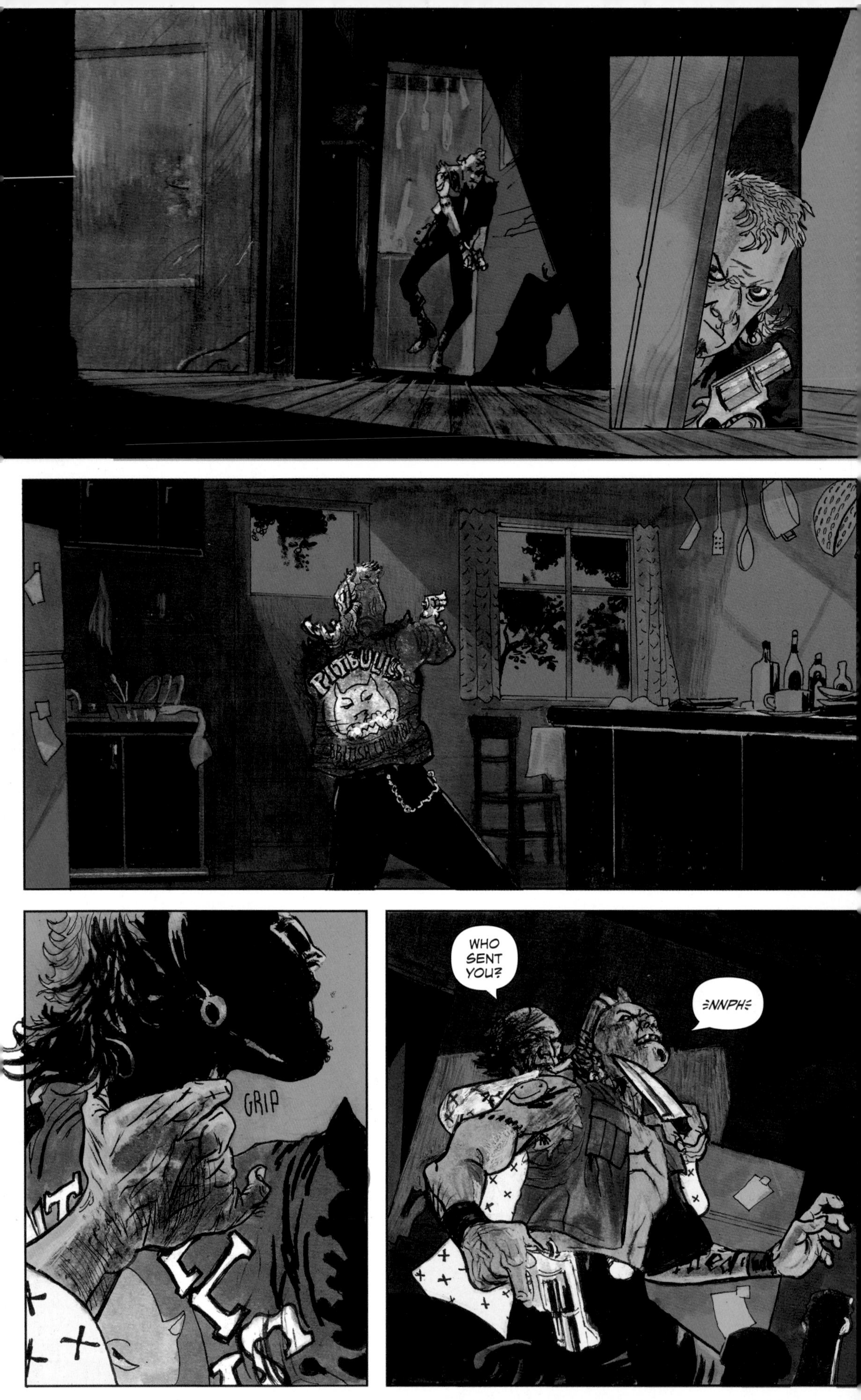
PITBULLS
BRITISH COLUMBIA
GRIP
WHO SENT YOU?
NNPH

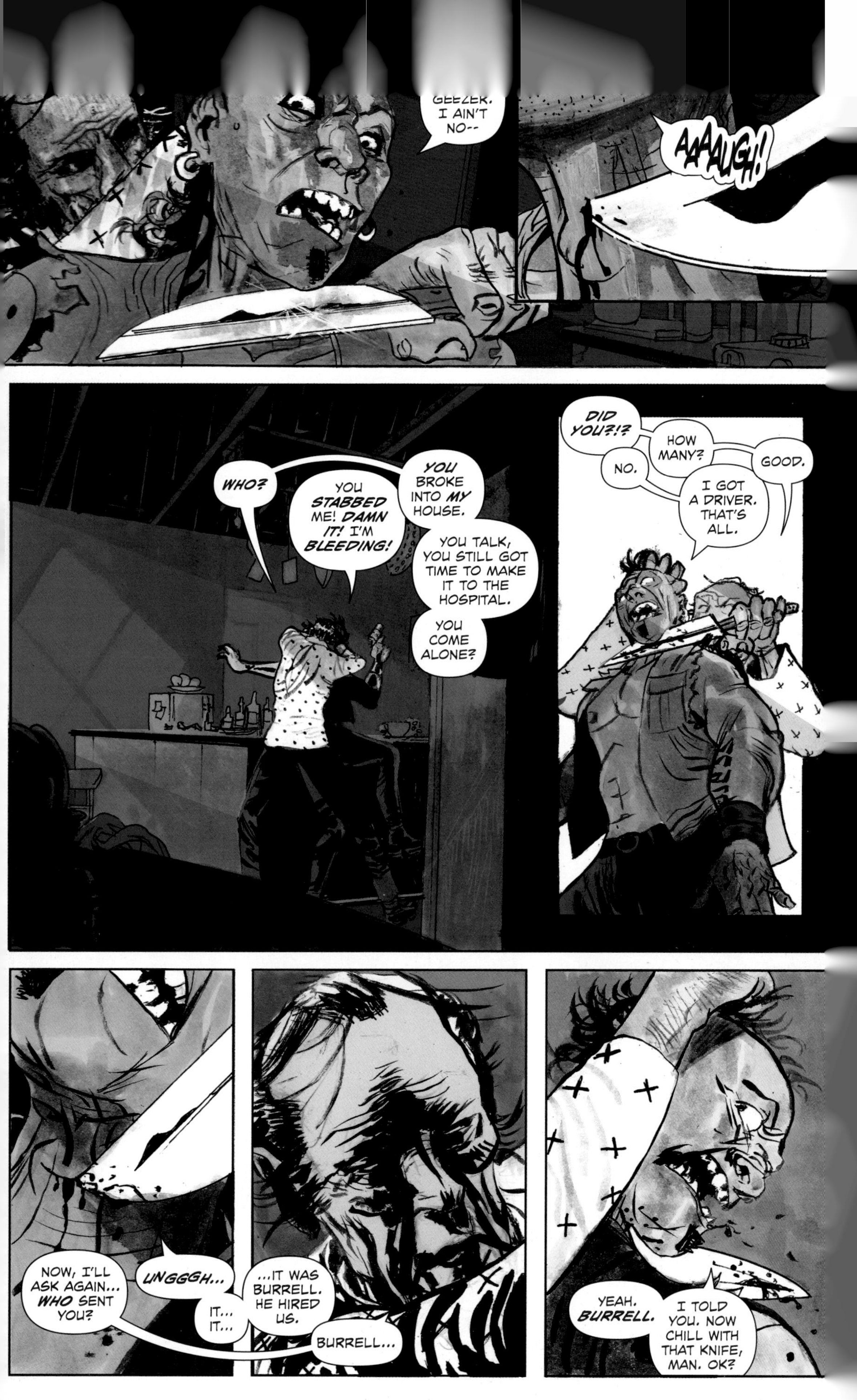
GEEZER. I AIN'T NO--
AAAAUGH!
WHO?
YOU STABBED ME! DAMN IT! I'M BLEEDING!
YOU BROKE INTO MY HOUSE.
YOU TALK, YOU STILL GOT TIME TO MAKE IT TO THE HOSPITAL.
YOU COME ALONE?
DID YOU?!?
NO.
HOW MANY?
I GOT A DRIVER. THAT'S ALL.
GOOD.
NOW, I'LL ASK AGAIN... WHO SENT YOU?
UNGGGH...
IT... IT...
...IT WAS BURRELL. HE HIRED US.
BURRELL...
YEAH. BURRELL.
I TOLD YOU. NOW CHILL WITH THAT KNIFE, MAN. OK?

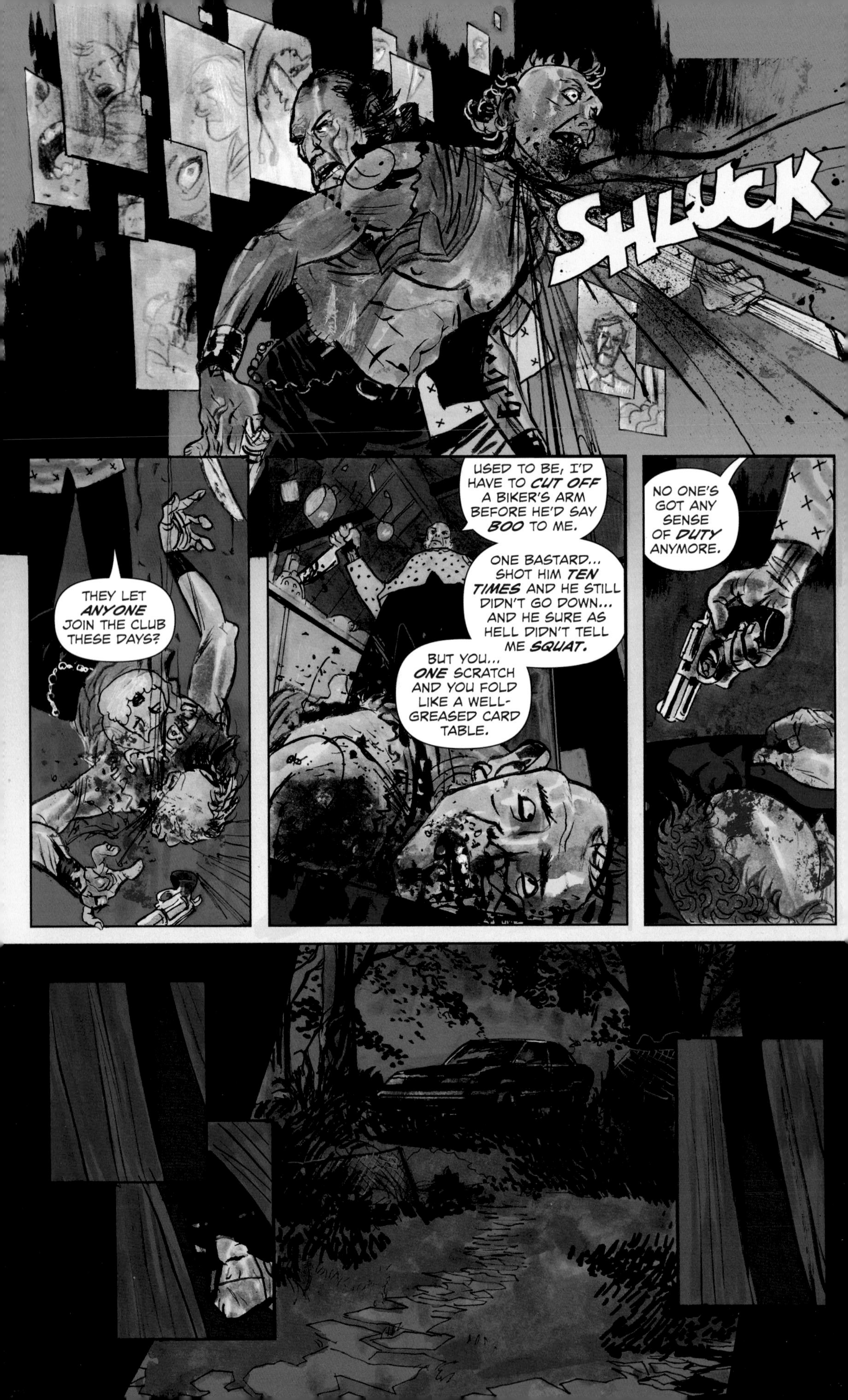

SHLUCK
THEY LET ANYONE JOIN THE CLUB THESE DAYS?
USED TO BE, I'D HAVE TO CUT OFF A BIKER'S ARM BEFORE HE'D SAY BOO TO ME.
ONE BASTARD... SHOT HIM TEN TIMES AND HE STILL DIDN'T GO DOWN... AND HE SURE AS HELL DIDN'T TELL ME SQUAT.
BUT YOU... ONE SCRATCH AND YOU FOLD LIKE A WELL-GREASED CARD TABLE.
NO ONE'S GOT ANY SENSE OF DUTY ANYMORE.

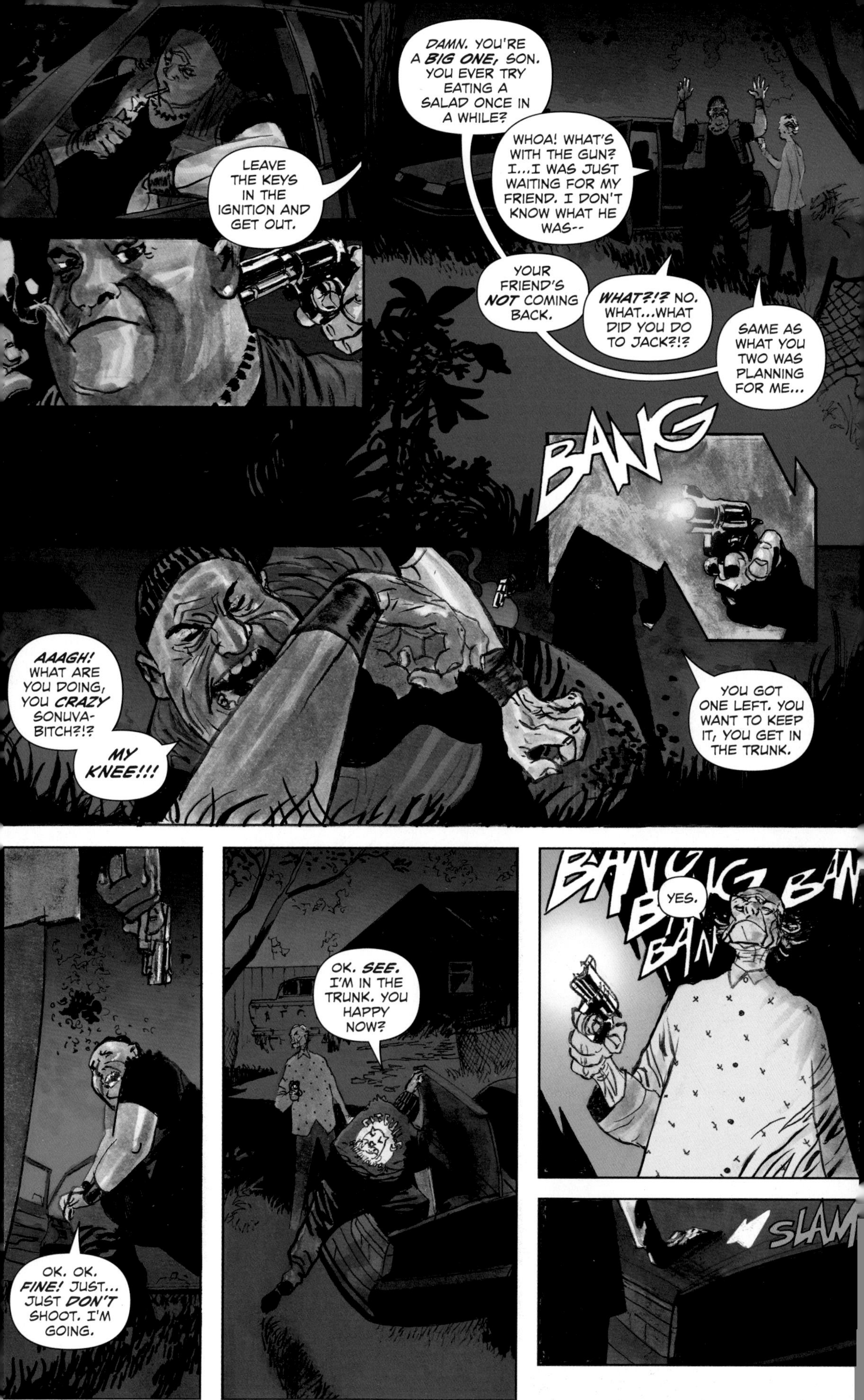
LEAVE THE KEYS IN THE IGNITION AND GET OUT.
DAMN. YOU'RE A BIG ONE, SON. YOU EVER TRY EATING A SALAD ONCE IN A WHILE?
WHOA! WHAT'S WITH THE GUN? I...I WAS JUST WAITING FOR MY FRIEND. I DON'T KNOW WHAT HE WAS--
YOUR FRIEND'S NOT COMING BACK.
WHAT?!? NO. WHAT...WHAT DID YOU DO TO JACK?!?
SAME AS WHAT YOU TWO WAS PLANNING FOR ME...
BANG
AAAGH! WHAT ARE YOU DOING, YOU CRAZY SONUVA-BITCH?!?
MY KNEE!!!
YOU GOT ONE LEFT. YOU WANT TO KEEP IT, YOU GET IN THE TRUNK.
OK. OK. FINE! JUST... JUST DON'T SHOOT. I'M GOING.
OK. SEE. I'M IN THE TRUNK. YOU HAPPY NOW?
YES.
SLAM

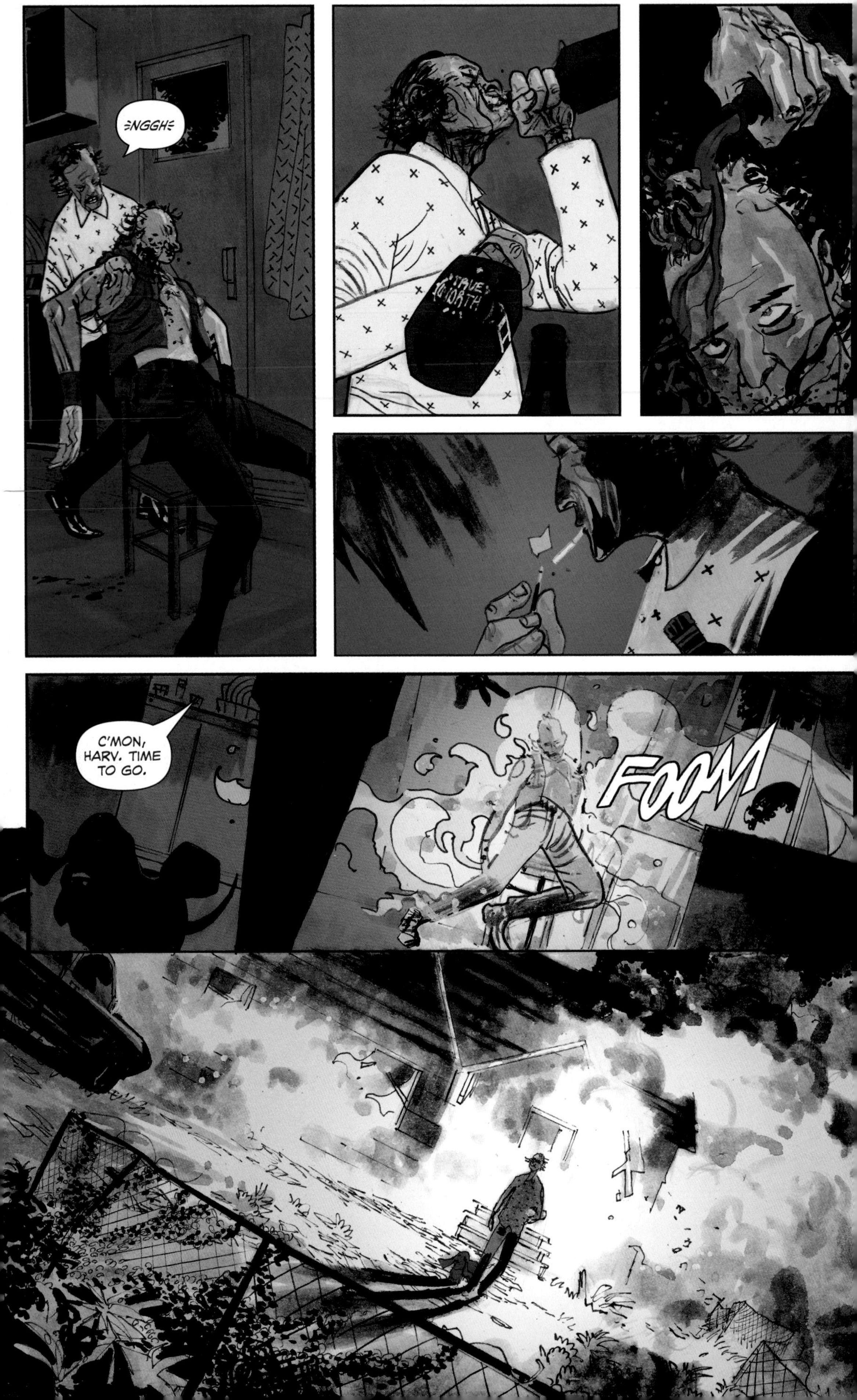
NGGH
STAVES NORTH
C'MON, HARV. TIME TO GO.
FOOM

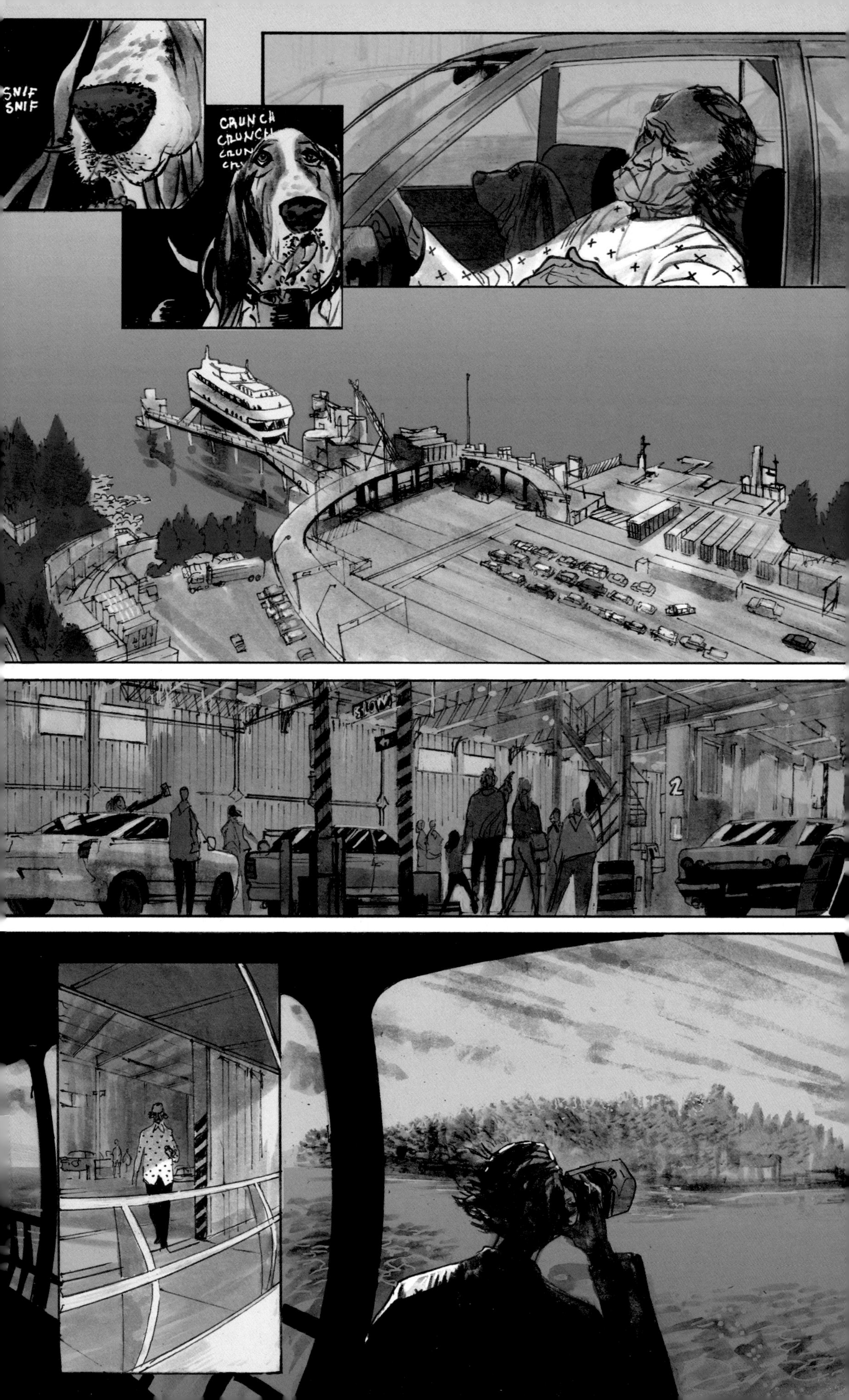
SNIF
SNIF
CRUNCH
CRUNCH
CRUN
SLOW
2

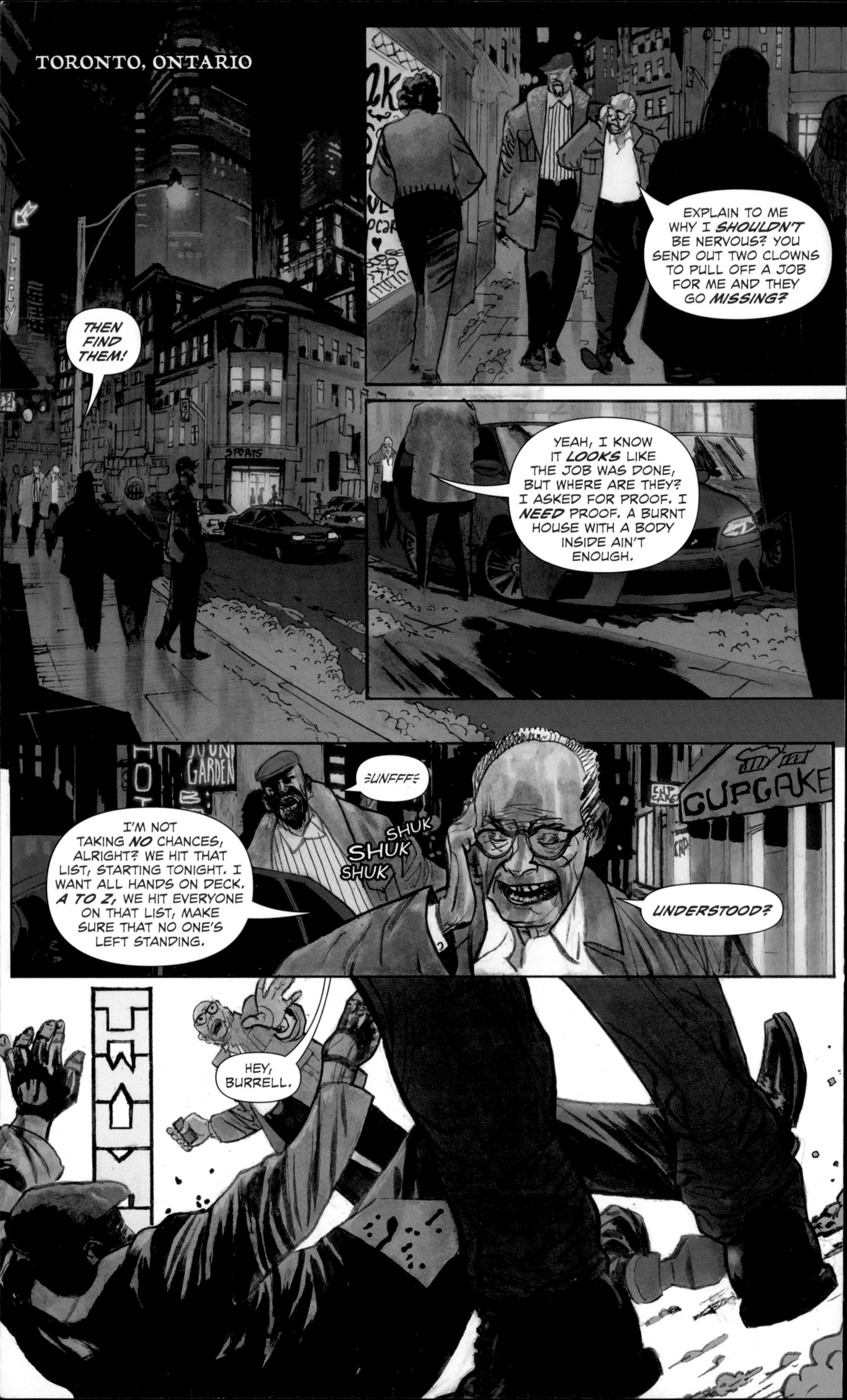
TORONTO, ONTARIO
EXPLAIN TO ME WHY I SHOULDN'T BE NERVOUS? YOU SEND OUT TWO CLOWNS TO PULL OFF A JOB FOR ME AND THEY GO MISSING?
THEN FIND THEM!
YEAH, I KNOW IT LOOKS LIKE THE JOB WAS DONE, BUT WHERE ARE THEY? I ASKED FOR PROOF. I NEED PROOF. A BURNT HOUSE WITH A BODY INSIDE AIN'T ENOUGH.
SPORTS
GARDEN
CUPCAKE
UNFFF
I'M NOT TAKING NO CHANCES, ALRIGHT? WE HIT THAT LIST, STARTING TONIGHT. I WANT ALL HANDS ON DECK. A TO Z, WE HIT EVERYONE ON THAT LIST, MAKE SURE THAT NO ONE'S LEFT STANDING.
SHUK SHUK SHUK
UNDERSTOOD?
HEY, BURRELL.

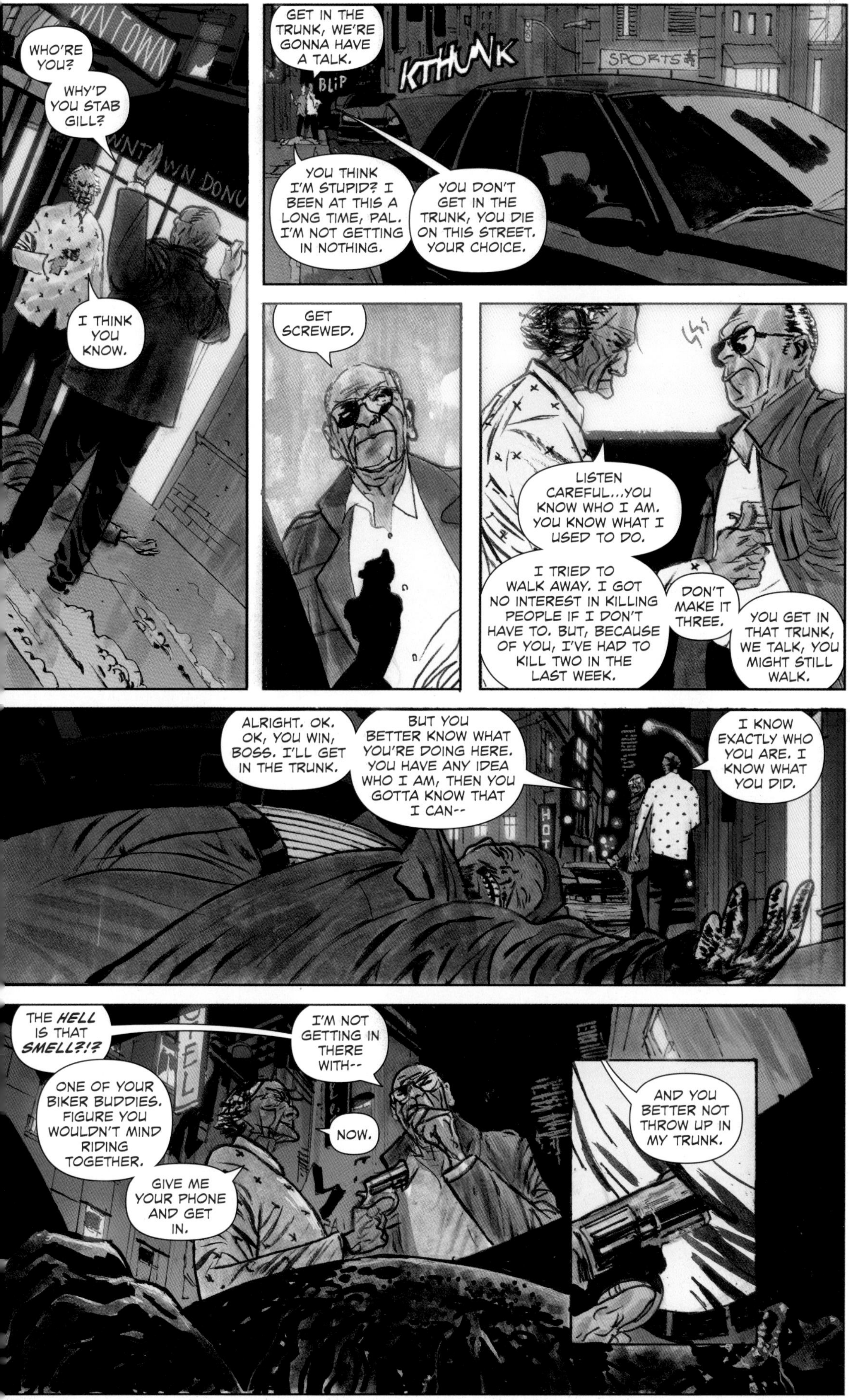
WHO'RE YOU?
WHY'D YOU STAB GILL?
I THINK YOU KNOW.
GET IN THE TRUNK, WE'RE GONNA HAVE A TALK.
BLIP
KTHUNK
YOU THINK I'M STUPID? I BEEN AT THIS A LONG TIME, PAL. I'M NOT GETTING IN NOTHING.
YOU DON'T GET IN THE TRUNK, YOU DIE ON THIS STREET. YOUR CHOICE.
SPORTS
GET SCREWED.
LISTEN CAREFUL...YOU KNOW WHO I AM. YOU KNOW WHAT I USED TO DO.
I TRIED TO WALK AWAY. I GOT NO INTEREST IN KILLING PEOPLE IF I DON'T HAVE TO. BUT, BECAUSE OF YOU, I'VE HAD TO KILL TWO IN THE LAST WEEK.
DON'T MAKE IT THREE.
YOU GET IN THAT TRUNK, WE TALK, YOU MIGHT STILL WALK.
ALRIGHT. OK. OK, YOU WIN, BOSS. I'LL GET IN THE TRUNK.
BUT YOU BETTER KNOW WHAT YOU'RE DOING HERE. YOU HAVE ANY IDEA WHO I AM, THEN YOU GOTTA KNOW THAT I CAN--
I KNOW EXACTLY WHO YOU ARE. I KNOW WHAT YOU DID.
THE *HELL* IS THAT *SMELL?!?*
I'M NOT GETTING IN THERE WITH--
ONE OF YOUR BIKER BUDDIES. FIGURE YOU WOULDN'T MIND RIDING TOGETHER.
NOW.
GIVE ME YOUR PHONE AND GET IN.
AND YOU BETTER NOT THROW UP IN MY TRUNK.

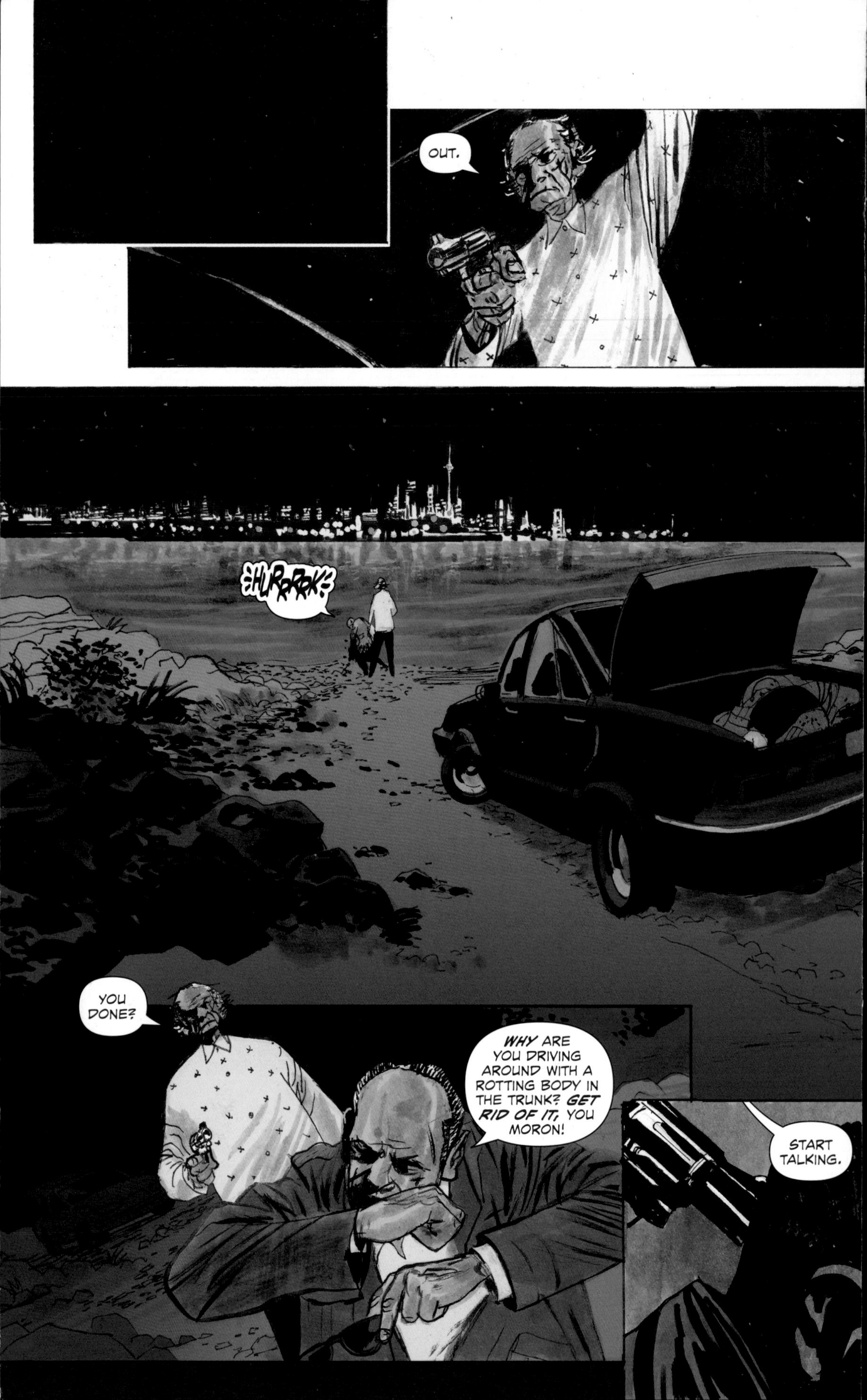
OUT.
HURRRRK
YOU DONE?
WHY ARE YOU DRIVING AROUND WITH A ROTTING BODY IN THE TRUNK? GET RID OF IT, YOU MORON!
START TALKING.

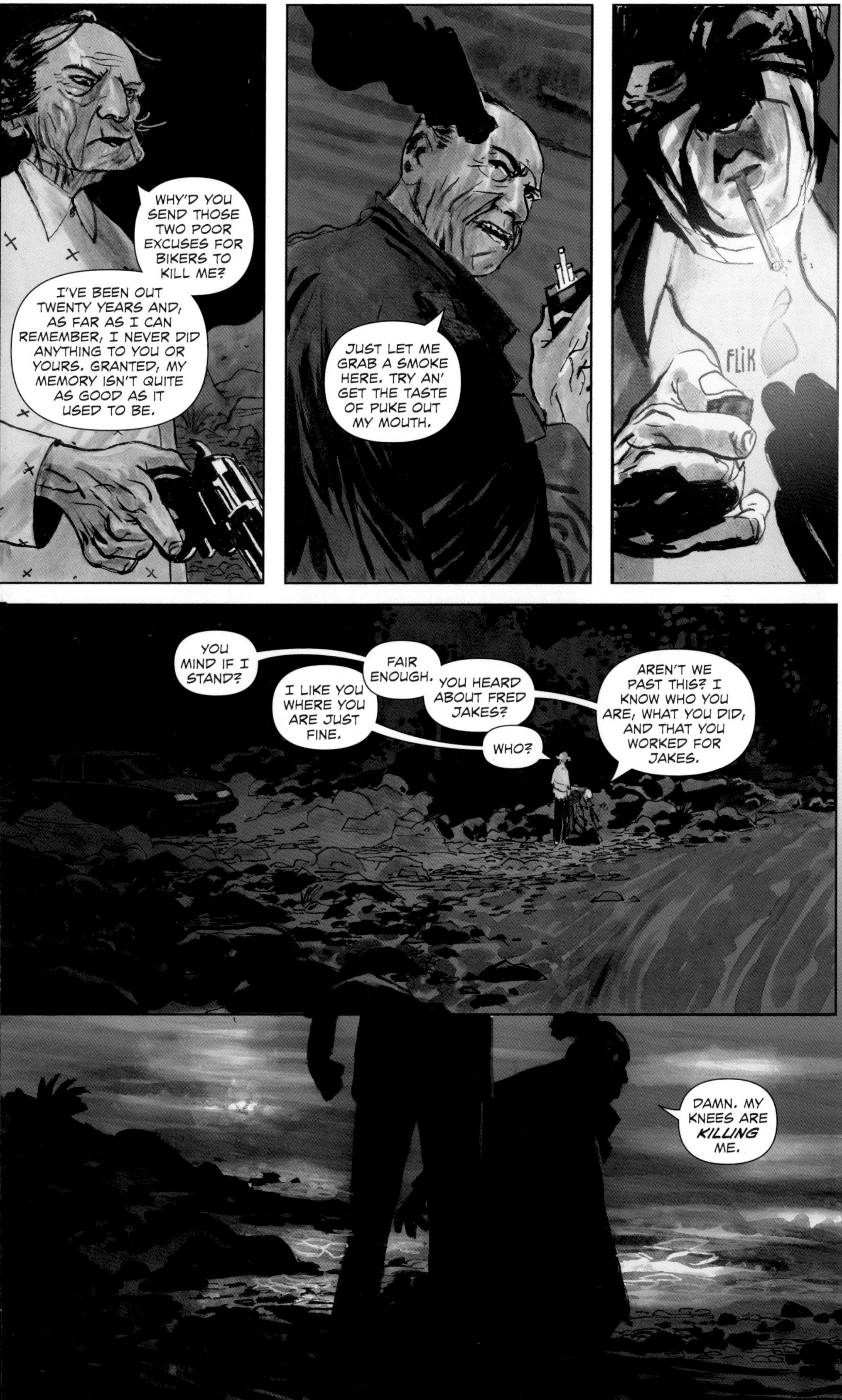
WHY'D YOU SEND THOSE TWO POOR EXCUSES FOR BIKERS TO KILL ME?
I'VE BEEN OUT TWENTY YEARS AND, AS FAR AS I CAN REMEMBER, I NEVER DID ANYTHING TO YOU OR YOURS. GRANTED, MY MEMORY ISN'T QUITE AS GOOD AS IT USED TO BE.
JUST LET ME GRAB A SMOKE HERE. TRY AN' GET THE TASTE OF PUKE OUT MY MOUTH.
FLIK
YOU MIND IF I STAND?
FAIR ENOUGH.
I LIKE YOU WHERE YOU ARE JUST FINE.
YOU HEARD ABOUT FRED JAKES?
WHO?
AREN'T WE PAST THIS? I KNOW WHO YOU ARE, WHAT YOU DID, AND THAT YOU WORKED FOR JAKES.
DAMN. MY KNEES ARE *KILLING* ME.

JAKES, YOUR BOSS, WAS MY GO-TO IF I NEEDED SOMEONE GANKED AND COULDN'T DO IT MYSELF. WHEN I NEEDED A BUFFER BETWEEN ME AND THE BODY.

I'M SURE *YOU* WERE THAT BUFFER MORE OFTEN THAN NOT.

ANYWAY.

ABOUT FIVE, SIX MONTHS AGO, HE OFFED HIMSELF. BULLET TO THE ROOF OF HIS MOUTH AND UP THROUGH THE BRAIN PAN. DEAD BEFORE HE HIT THE GROUND.

ABOUT A MONTH LATER, I GET THIS EMAIL. SOMEONE CLAIMING THAT THEY GOT JAKES'S LIST. THAT THEY KNOW EVERYTHING.

WHAT LIST?

EVERY HIT JAKES HAD ORGANIZED.

CLIENTS, TARGETS, HOW MUCH. WHERE AND WHEN. *EVERY. THING.*

SHOWED ME JUST ENOUGH TO LET ME KNOW IT'S REAL AND THAT I'M ON IT. *A LOT.*

THEY COME AT ME. TELL ME THAT I GOTTA TAKE YOU OUT OR ELSE THEY'RE GOING TO RELEASE A LIST OF ALL THE PEOPLE I HAD KILLED.

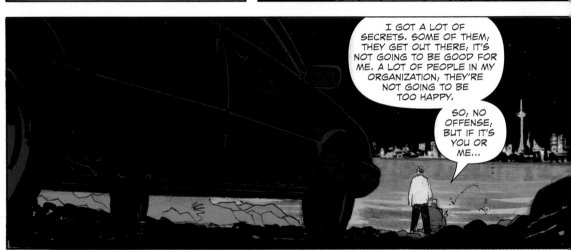

I GOT A LOT OF SECRETS. SOME OF THEM, THEY GET OUT THERE, IT'S NOT GOING TO BE GOOD FOR ME. A LOT OF PEOPLE IN MY ORGANIZATION, THEY'RE NOT GOING TO BE TOO HAPPY.

SO, NO OFFENSE, BUT IF IT'S YOU OR ME...

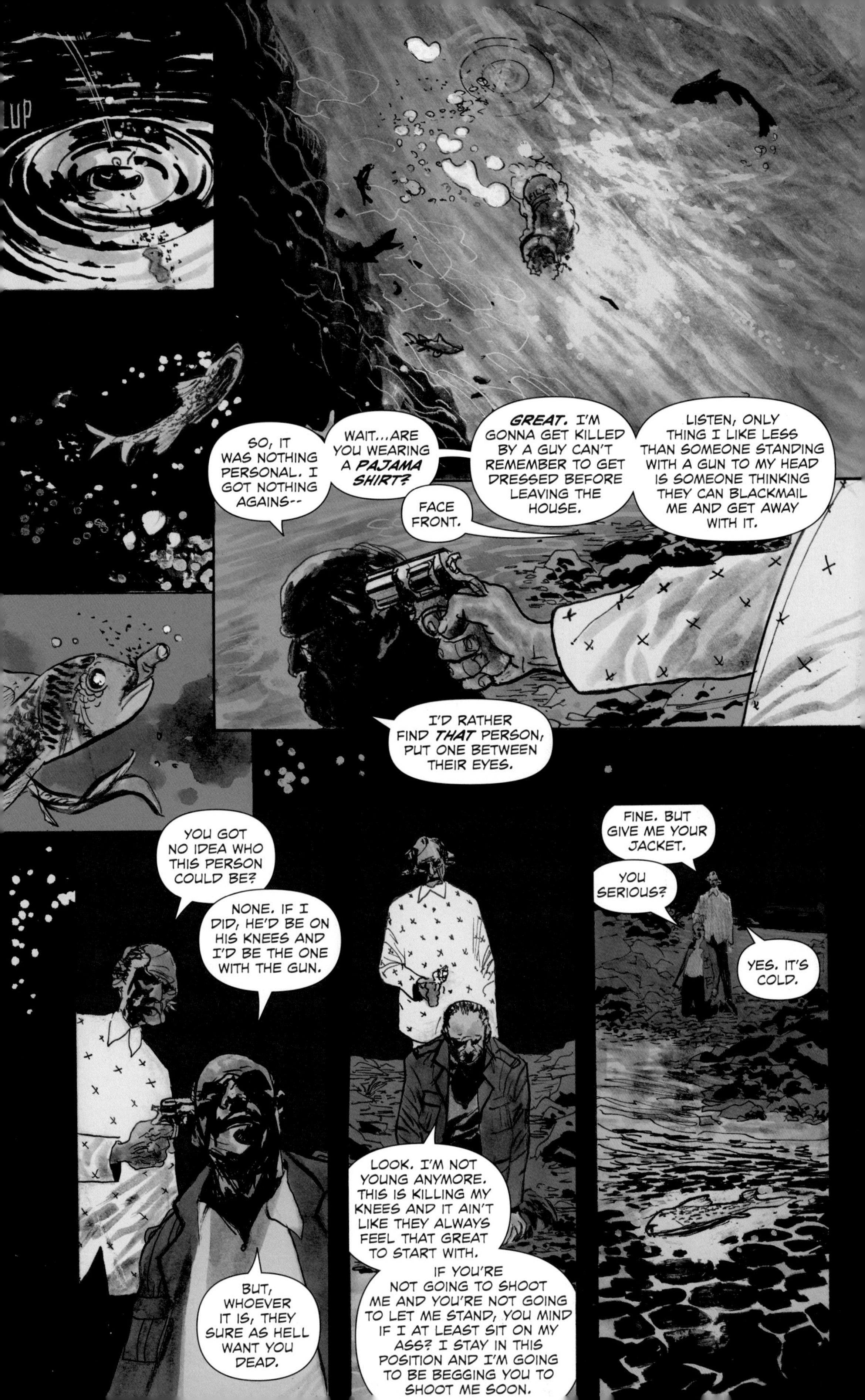

LUP
SO, IT WAS NOTHING PERSONAL. I GOT NOTHING AGAINS--
WAIT...ARE YOU WEARING A PAJAMA SHIRT?
GREAT. I'M GONNA GET KILLED BY A GUY CAN'T REMEMBER TO GET DRESSED BEFORE LEAVING THE HOUSE.
FACE FRONT.
LISTEN, ONLY THING I LIKE LESS THAN SOMEONE STANDING WITH A GUN TO MY HEAD IS SOMEONE THINKING THEY CAN BLACKMAIL ME AND GET AWAY WITH IT.
I'D RATHER FIND THAT PERSON, PUT ONE BETWEEN THEIR EYES.
YOU GOT NO IDEA WHO THIS PERSON COULD BE?
NONE. IF I DID, HE'D BE ON HIS KNEES AND I'D BE THE ONE WITH THE GUN.
BUT, WHOEVER IT IS, THEY SURE AS HELL WANT YOU DEAD.
LOOK. I'M NOT YOUNG ANYMORE. THIS IS KILLING MY KNEES AND IT AIN'T LIKE THEY ALWAYS FEEL THAT GREAT TO START WITH.
IF YOU'RE NOT GOING TO SHOOT ME AND YOU'RE NOT GOING TO LET ME STAND, YOU MIND IF I AT LEAST SIT ON MY ASS? I STAY IN THIS POSITION AND I'M GOING TO BE BEGGING YOU TO SHOOT ME SOON.
FINE. BUT GIVE ME YOUR JACKET.
YOU SERIOUS?
YES. IT'S COLD.

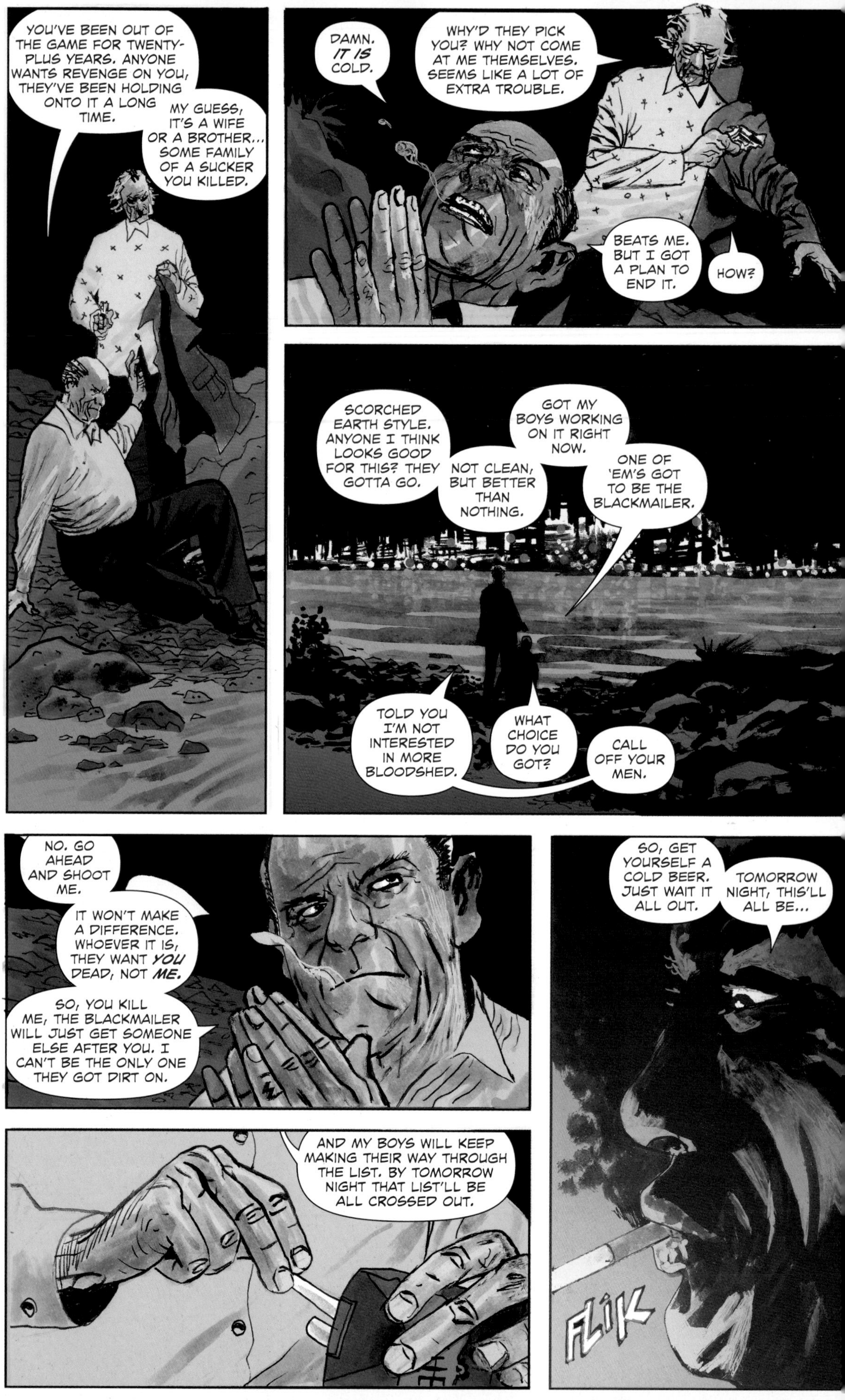

YOU'VE BEEN OUT OF THE GAME FOR TWENTY-PLUS YEARS. ANYONE WANTS REVENGE ON YOU, THEY'VE BEEN HOLDING ONTO IT A LONG TIME.
MY GUESS, IT'S A WIFE OR A BROTHER... SOME FAMILY OF A SUCKER YOU KILLED.
DAMN. *IT IS* COLD.
WHY'D THEY PICK YOU? WHY NOT COME AT ME THEMSELVES. SEEMS LIKE A LOT OF EXTRA TROUBLE.
BEATS ME. BUT I GOT A PLAN TO END IT.
HOW?
SCORCHED EARTH STYLE. ANYONE I THINK LOOKS GOOD FOR THIS? THEY GOTTA GO.
NOT CLEAN, BUT BETTER THAN NOTHING.
GOT MY BOYS WORKING ON IT RIGHT NOW.
ONE OF 'EM'S GOT TO BE THE BLACKMAILER.
TOLD YOU I'M NOT INTERESTED IN MORE BLOODSHED.
WHAT CHOICE DO YOU GOT?
CALL OFF YOUR MEN.
NO. GO AHEAD AND SHOOT ME.
IT WON'T MAKE A DIFFERENCE. WHOEVER IT IS, THEY WANT *YOU* DEAD, NOT *ME.*
SO, YOU KILL ME, THE BLACKMAILER WILL JUST GET SOMEONE ELSE AFTER YOU. I CAN'T BE THE ONLY ONE THEY GOT DIRT ON.
AND MY BOYS WILL KEEP MAKING THEIR WAY THROUGH THE LIST. BY TOMORROW NIGHT THAT LIST'LL BE ALL CROSSED OUT.
SO, GET YOURSELF A COLD BEER. JUST WAIT IT ALL OUT.
TOMORROW NIGHT, THIS'LL ALL BE...
FLIK

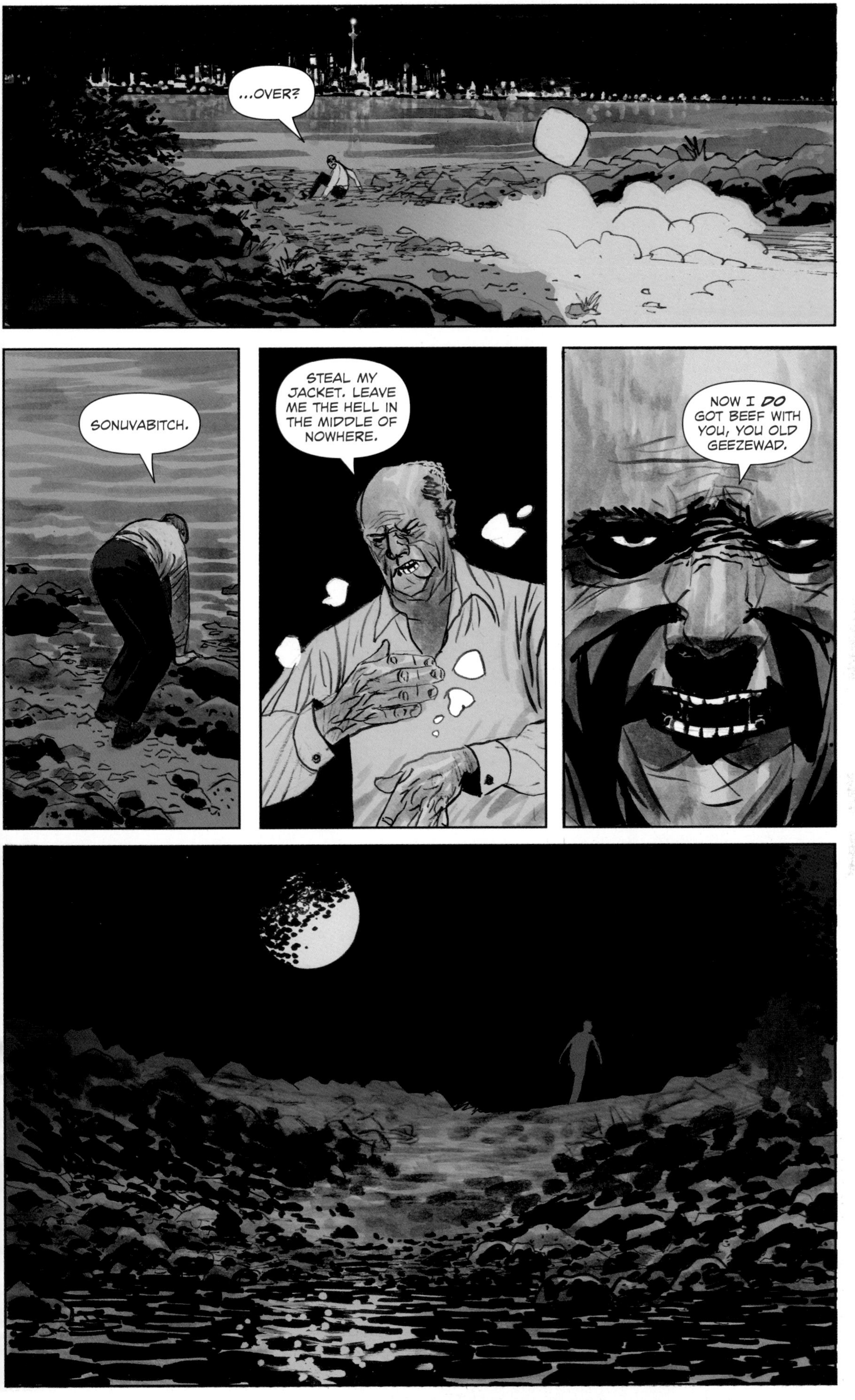
...OVER?
SONUVABITCH.
STEAL MY JACKET. LEAVE ME THE HELL IN THE MIDDLE OF NOWHERE.
NOW I *DO* GOT BEEF WITH YOU, YOU OLD GEEZEWAD.

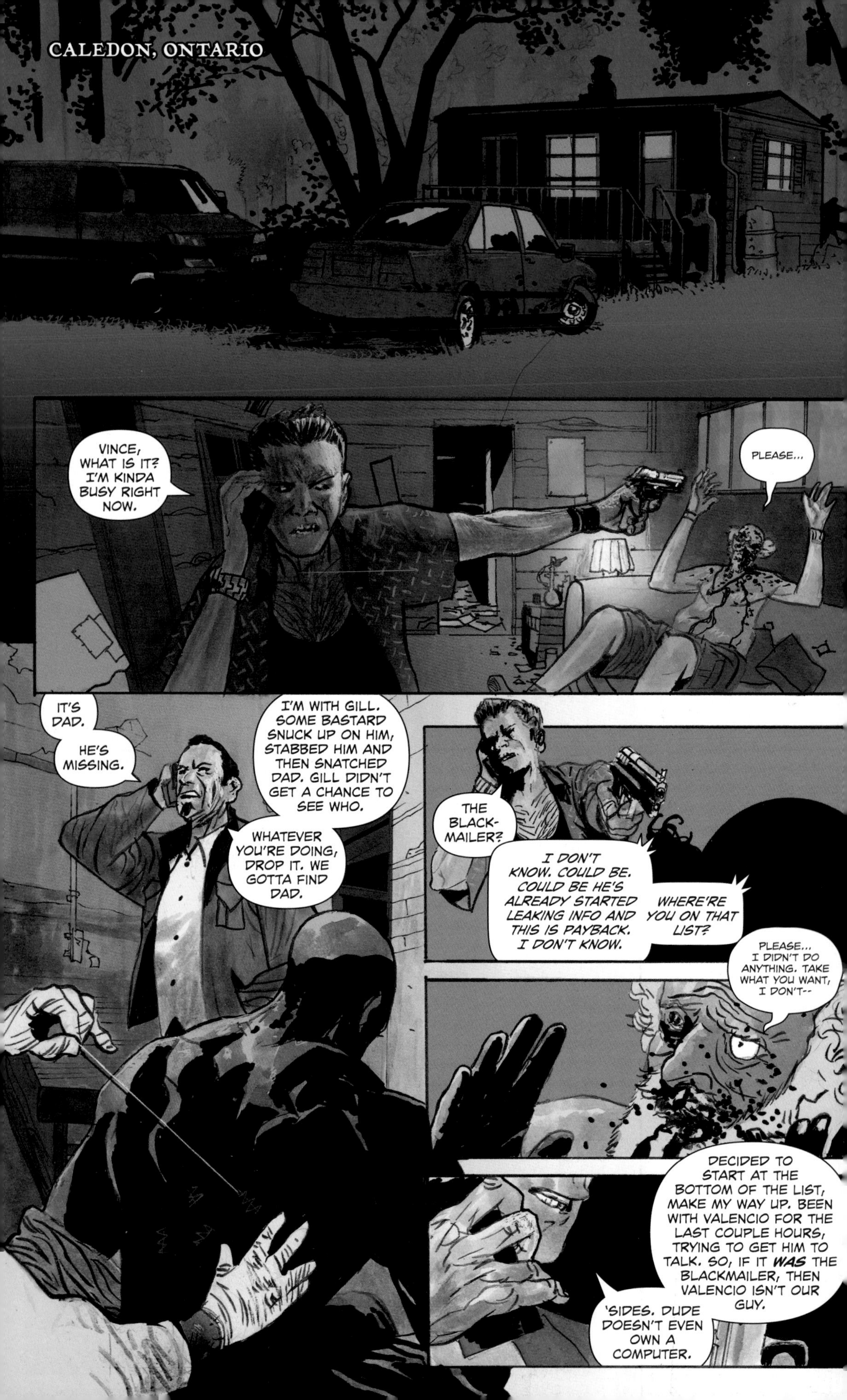
CALEDON, ONTARIO
VINCE, WHAT IS IT? I'M KINDA BUSY RIGHT NOW.
PLEASE...
IT'S DAD.
HE'S MISSING.
I'M WITH GILL. SOME BASTARD SNUCK UP ON HIM, STABBED HIM AND THEN SNATCHED DAD. GILL DIDN'T GET A CHANCE TO SEE WHO.
WHATEVER YOU'RE DOING, DROP IT. WE GOTTA FIND DAD.
THE BLACK-MAILER?
I DON'T KNOW. COULD BE. COULD BE HE'S ALREADY STARTED LEAKING INFO AND THIS IS PAYBACK. I DON'T KNOW.
WHERE'RE YOU ON THAT LIST?
PLEASE... I DIDN'T DO ANYTHING. TAKE WHAT YOU WANT, I DON'T--
DECIDED TO START AT THE BOTTOM OF THE LIST, MAKE MY WAY UP. BEEN WITH VALENCIO FOR THE LAST COUPLE HOURS, TRYING TO GET HIM TO TALK. SO, IF IT WAS THE BLACKMAILER, THEN VALENCIO ISN'T OUR GUY.
'SIDES. DUDE DOESN'T EVEN OWN A COMPUTER.

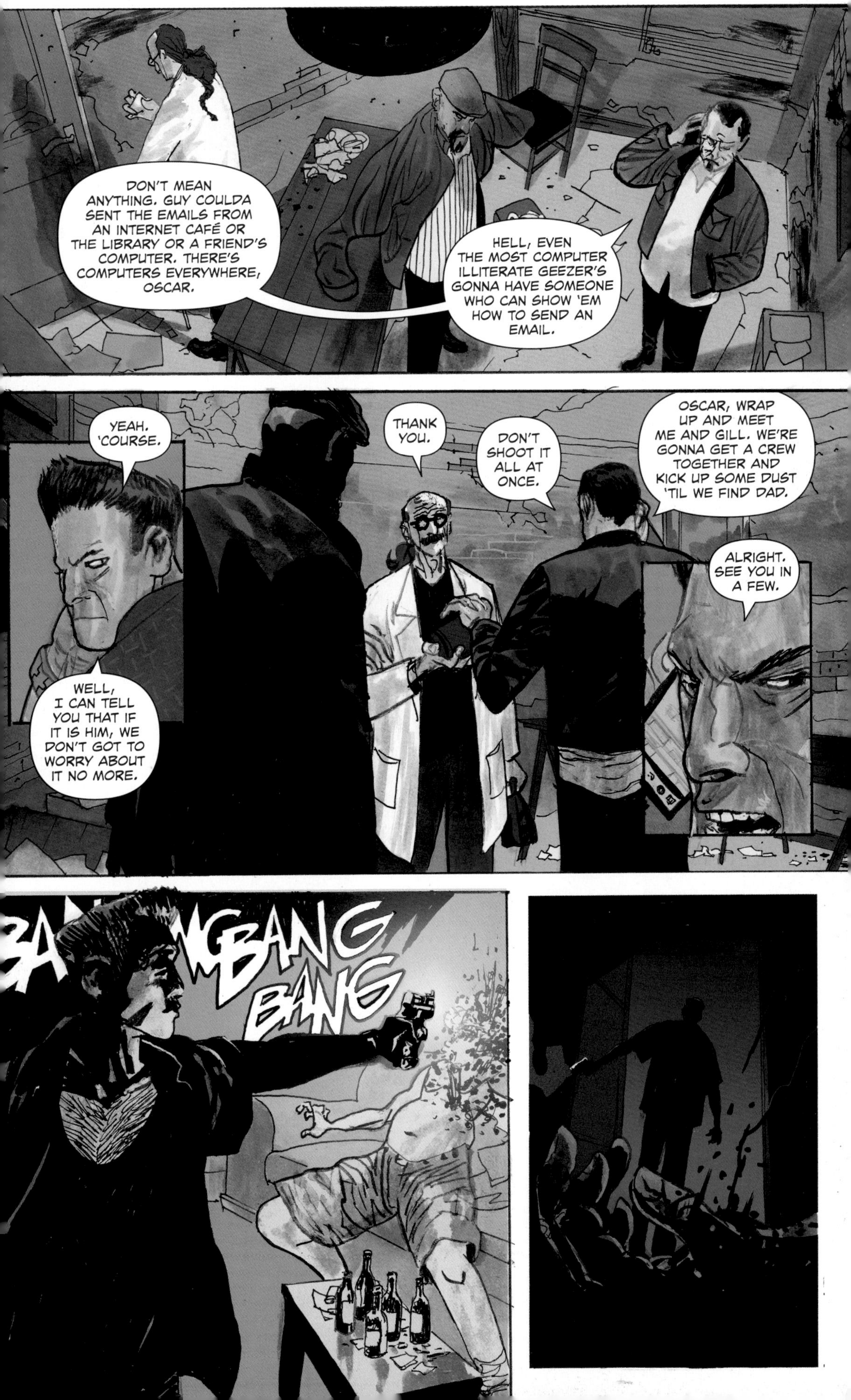
DON'T MEAN ANYTHING. GUY COULDA SENT THE EMAILS FROM AN INTERNET CAFÉ OR THE LIBRARY OR A FRIEND'S COMPUTER. THERE'S COMPUTERS EVERYWHERE, OSCAR.
HELL, EVEN THE MOST COMPUTER ILLITERATE GEEZER'S GONNA HAVE SOMEONE WHO CAN SHOW 'EM HOW TO SEND AN EMAIL.
THANK YOU.
DON'T SHOOT IT ALL AT ONCE.
OSCAR, WRAP UP AND MEET ME AND GILL. WE'RE GONNA GET A CREW TOGETHER AND KICK UP SOME DUST 'TIL WE FIND DAD.
ALRIGHT. SEE YOU IN A FEW.
WELL, I CAN TELL YOU THAT IF IT IS HIM, WE DON'T GOT TO WORRY ABOUT IT NO MORE.
YEAH. 'COURSE.
BANG
BANG

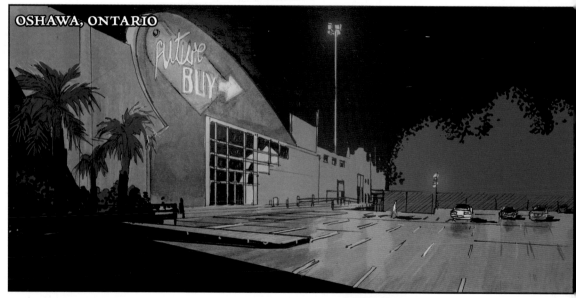

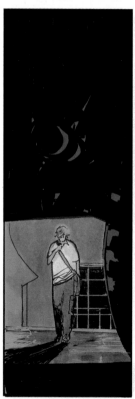

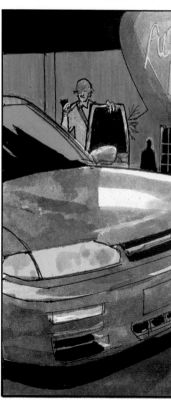

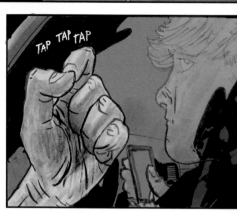

OSHAWA, ONTARIO
future BUY
TAP TAP TAP
YES?
YOU DILLON WILLIAMS?
YES. DO I--
OUT OF THE CAR.
NOW.

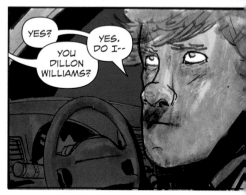

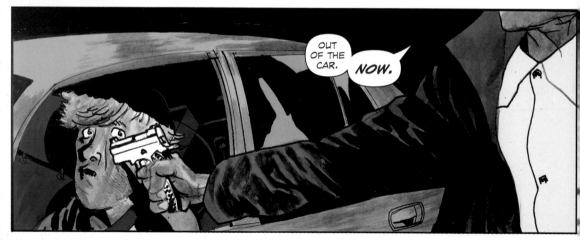

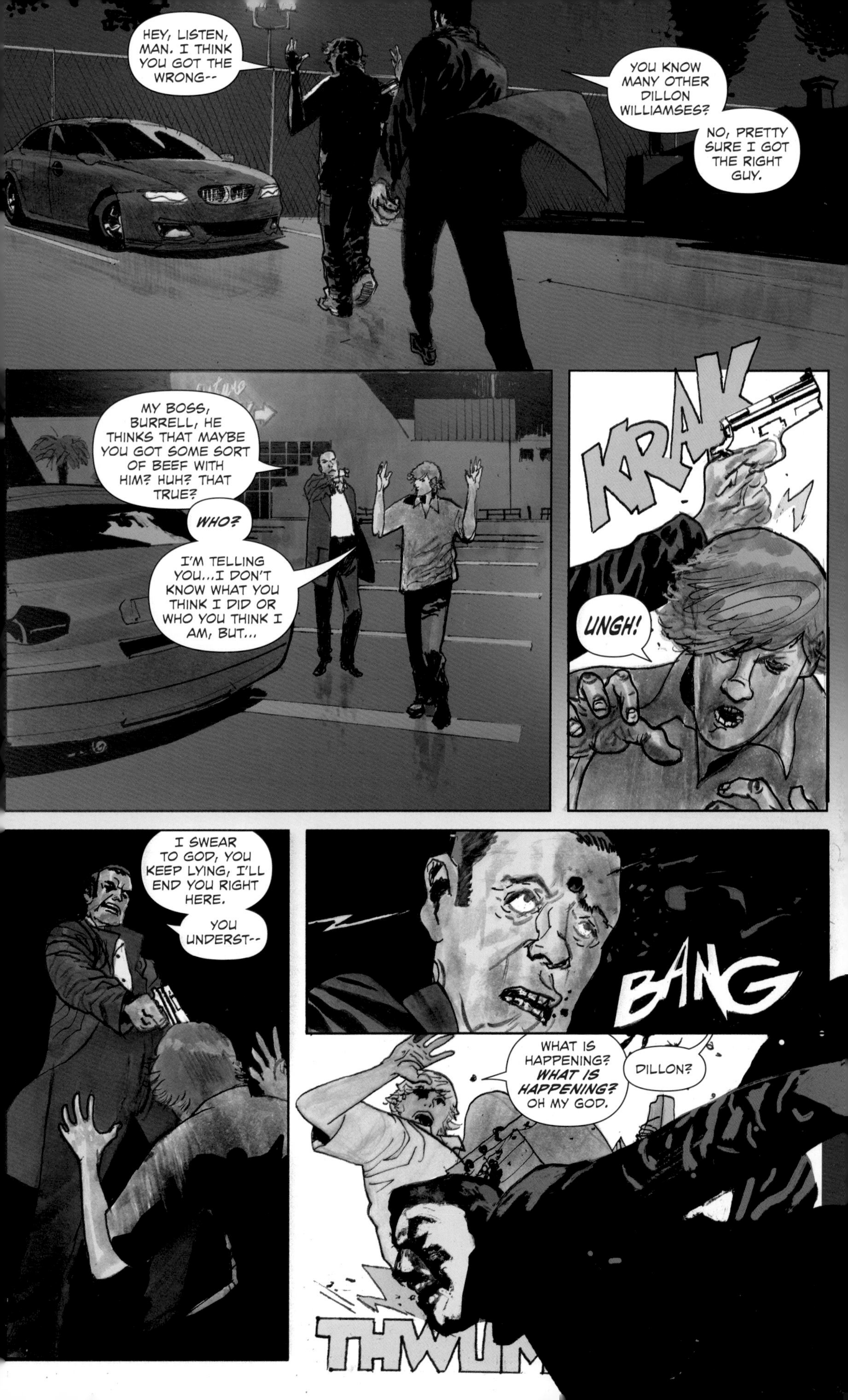
HEY, LISTEN, MAN. I THINK YOU GOT THE WRONG--
YOU KNOW MANY OTHER DILLON WILLIAMSES?
NO, PRETTY SURE I GOT THE RIGHT GUY.
MY BOSS, BURRELL, HE THINKS THAT MAYBE YOU GOT SOME SORT OF BEEF WITH HIM? HUH? THAT TRUE?
WHO?
I'M TELLING YOU...I DON'T KNOW WHAT YOU THINK I DID OR WHO YOU THINK I AM, BUT...
KRAK
UNGH!
I SWEAR TO GOD, YOU KEEP LYING, I'LL END YOU RIGHT HERE.
YOU UNDERST--
BANG
WHAT IS HAPPENING? WHAT IS HAPPENING? OH MY GOD.
DILLON?
THWUM

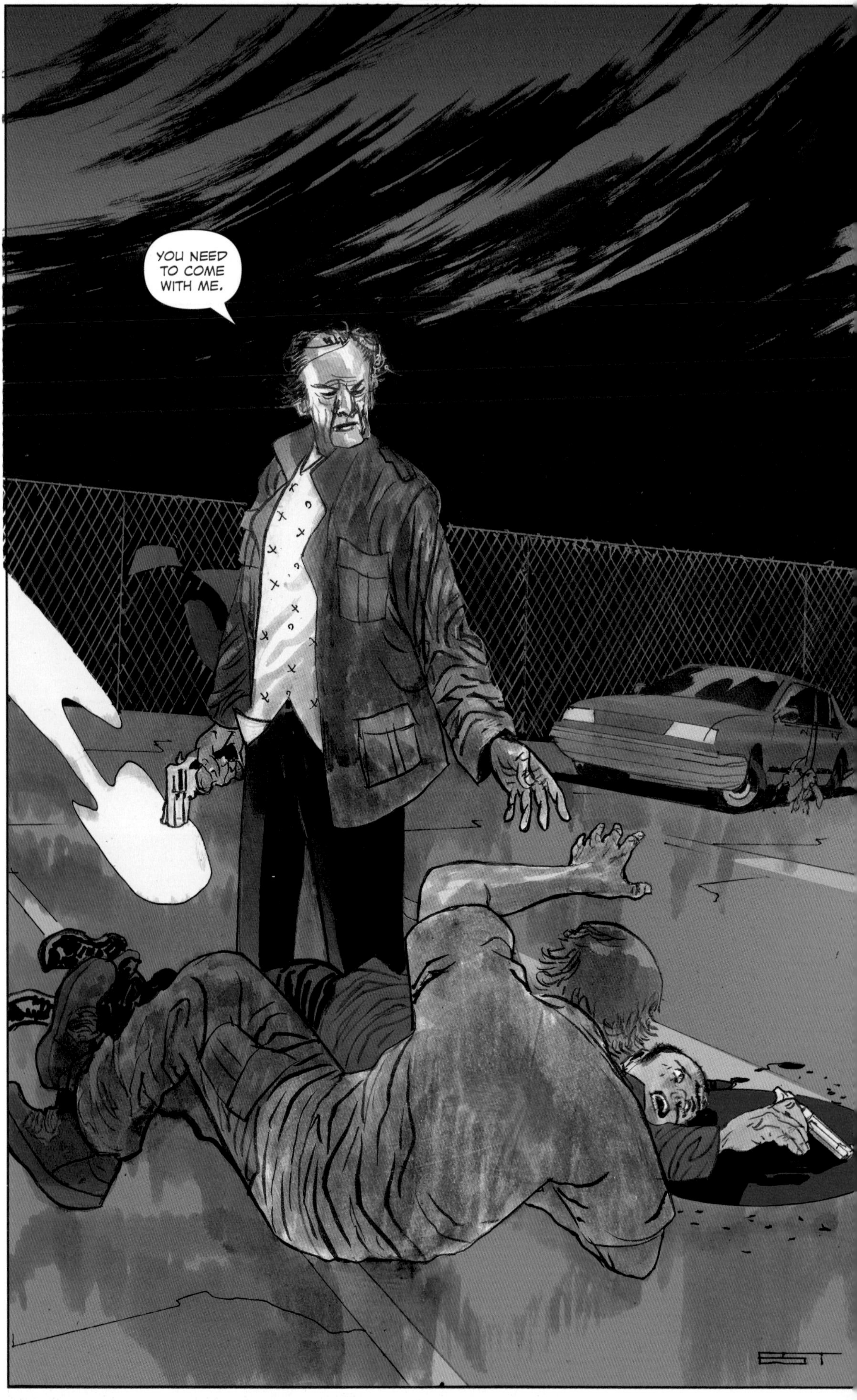
YOU NEED TO COME WITH ME.

# Chapter Two

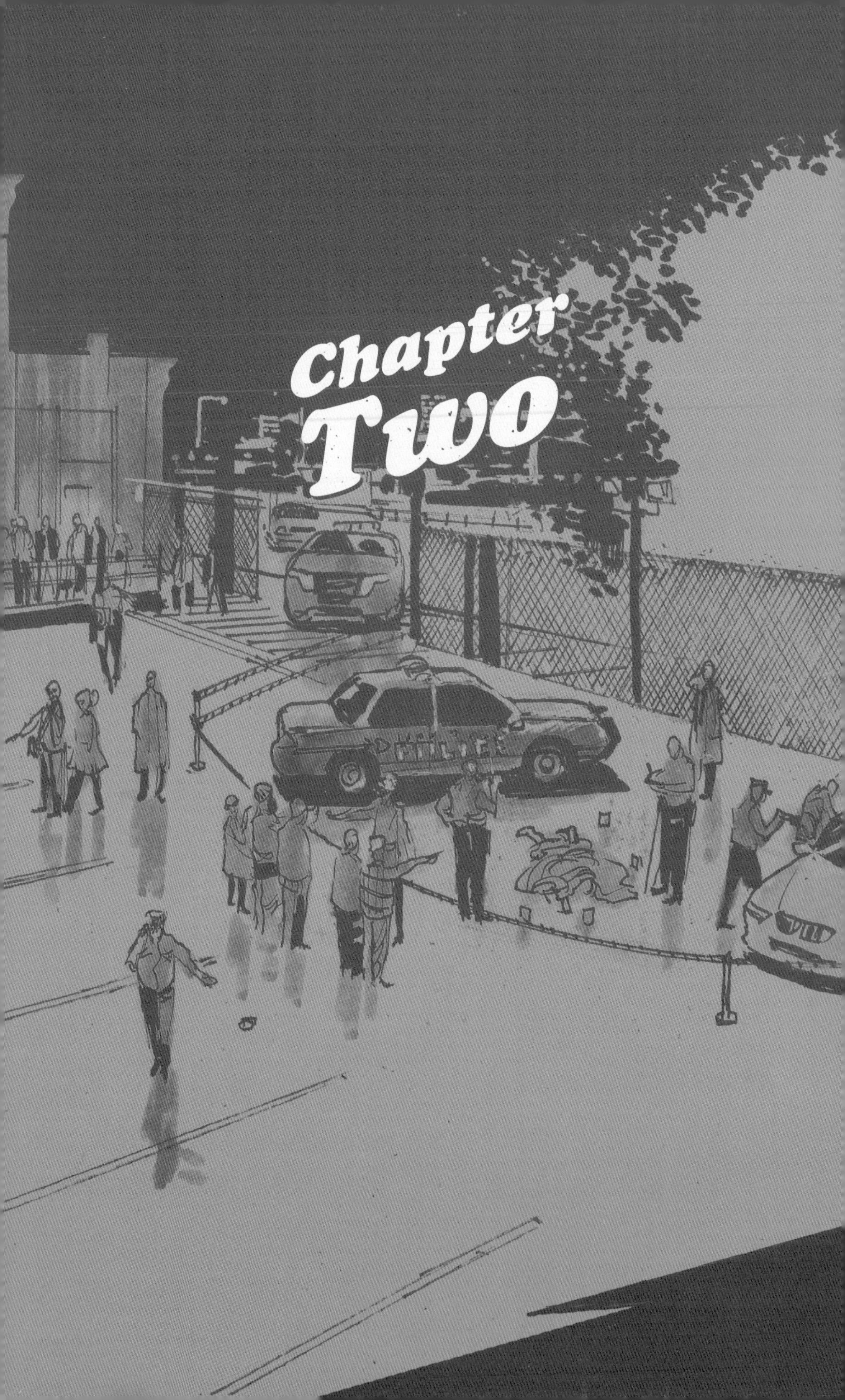

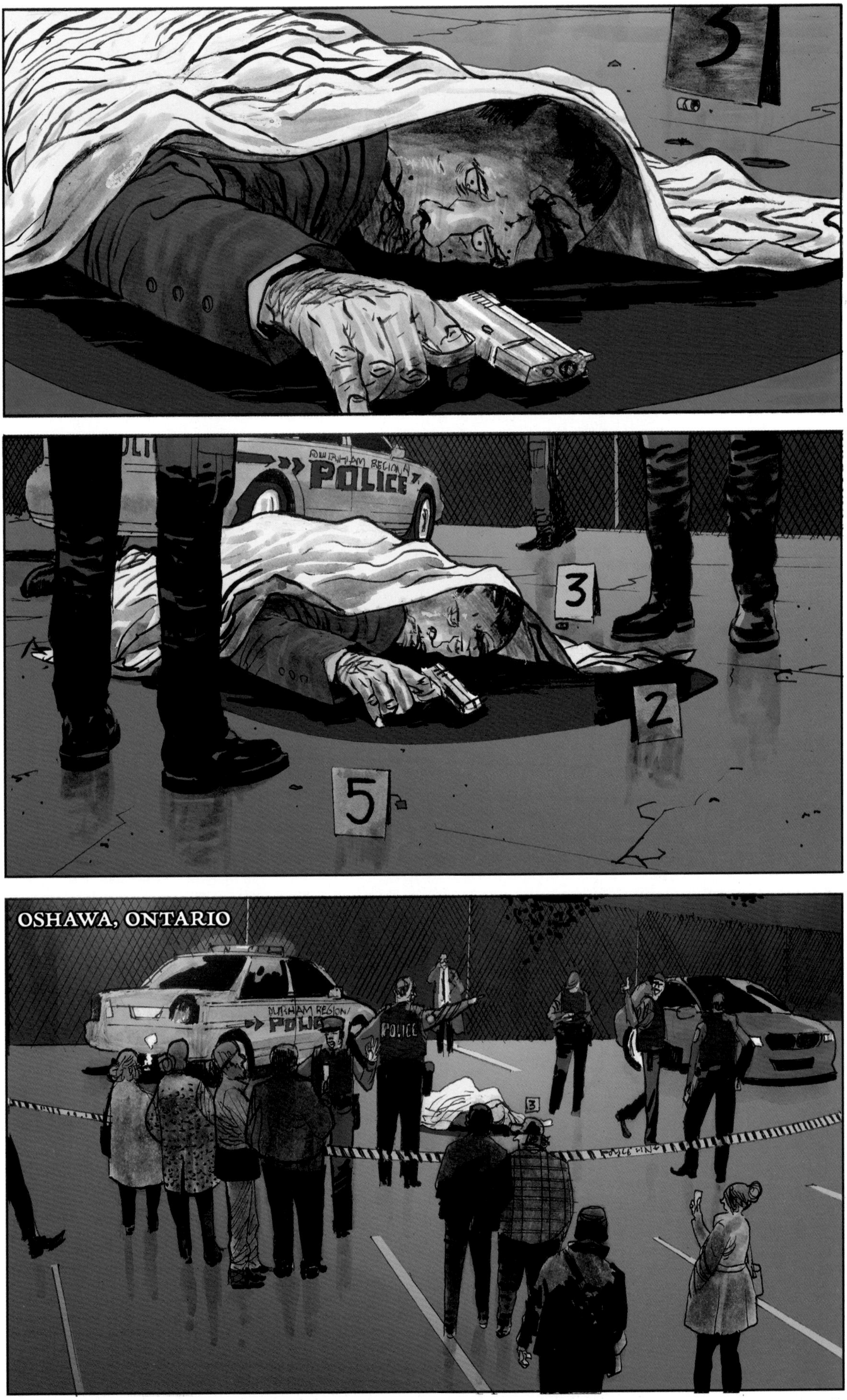
3
DURHAM REGION
POLICE
3
2
5
OSHAWA, ONTARIO
POLICE

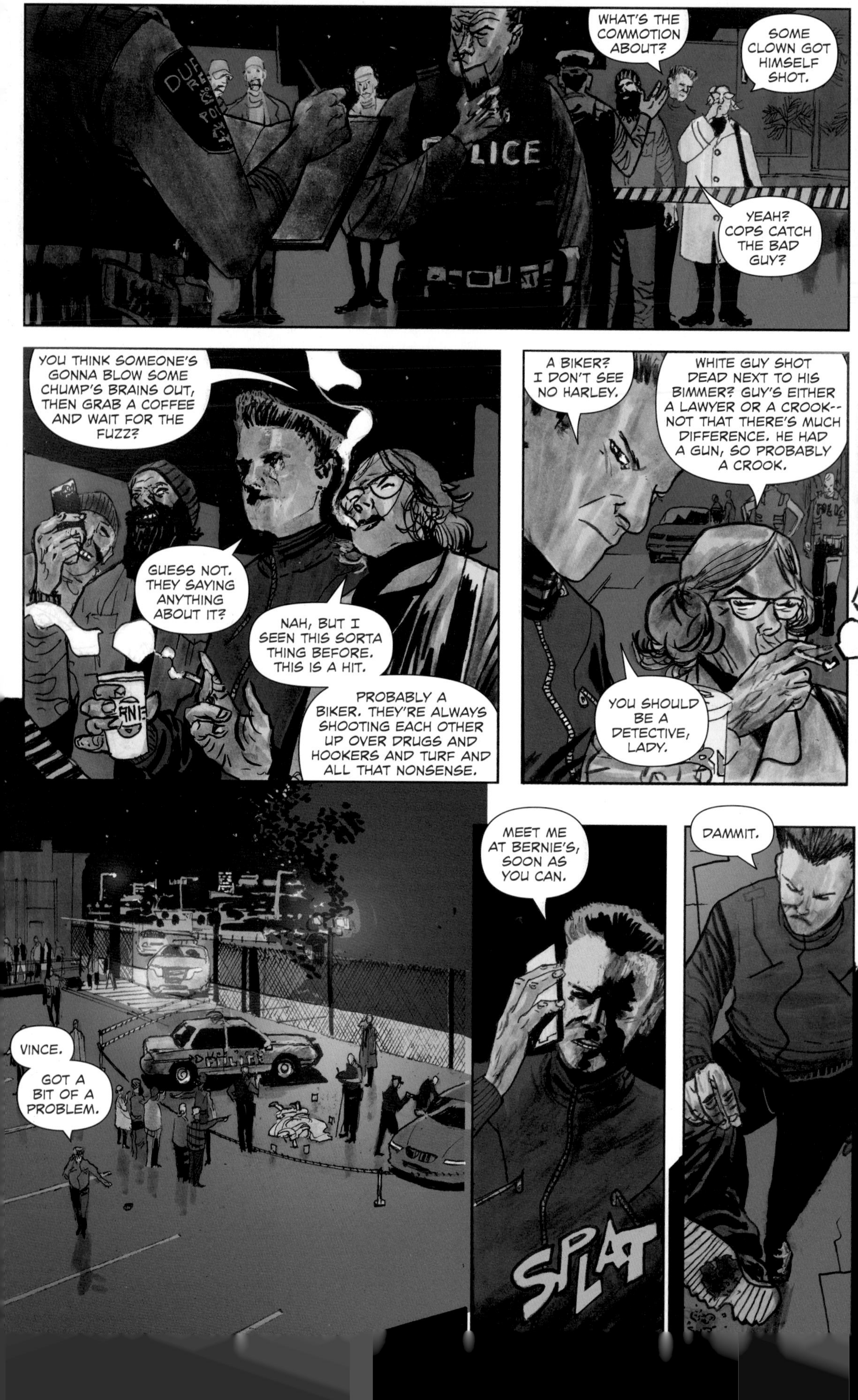
POLICE
WHAT'S THE COMMOTION ABOUT?
SOME CLOWN GOT HIMSELF SHOT.
YEAH? COPS CATCH THE BAD GUY?
YOU THINK SOMEONE'S GONNA BLOW SOME CHUMP'S BRAINS OUT, THEN GRAB A COFFEE AND WAIT FOR THE FUZZ?
GUESS NOT. THEY SAYING ANYTHING ABOUT IT?
NAH, BUT I SEEN THIS SORTA THING BEFORE. THIS IS A HIT.
PROBABLY A BIKER. THEY'RE ALWAYS SHOOTING EACH OTHER UP OVER DRUGS AND HOOKERS AND TURF AND ALL THAT NONSENSE.
A BIKER? I DON'T SEE NO HARLEY.
WHITE GUY SHOT DEAD NEXT TO HIS BIMMER? GUY'S EITHER A LAWYER OR A CROOK--NOT THAT THERE'S MUCH DIFFERENCE. HE HAD A GUN, SO PROBABLY A CROOK.
YOU SHOULD BE A DETECTIVE, LADY.
VINCE.
GOT A BIT OF A PROBLEM.
MEET ME AT BERNIE'S, SOON AS YOU CAN.
SPLAT
DAMMIT.

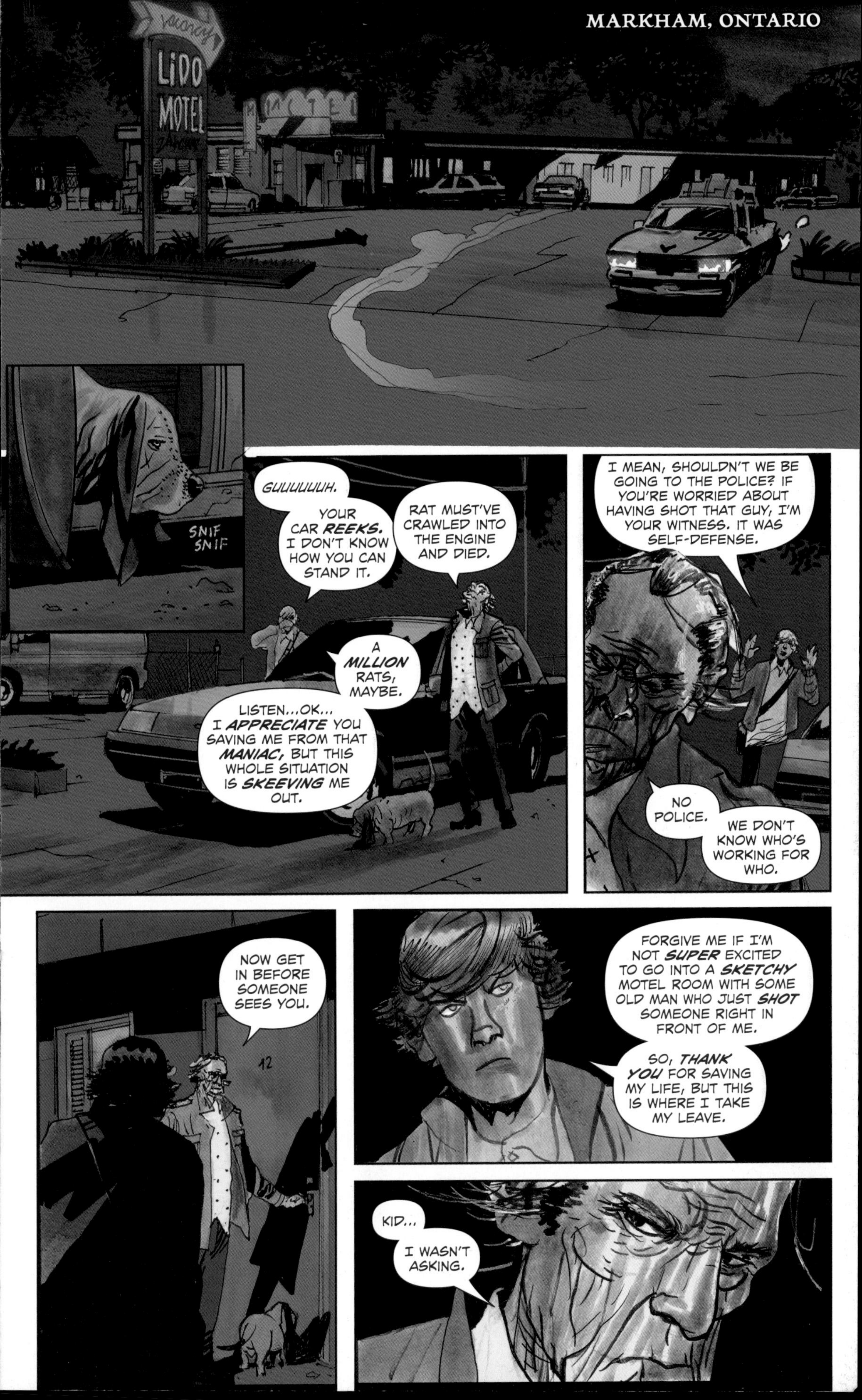
MARKHAM, ONTARIO
LIDO MOTEL
SNIF SNIF
GUUUUUUH.
YOUR CAR REEKS. I DON'T KNOW HOW YOU CAN STAND IT.
RAT MUST'VE CRAWLED INTO THE ENGINE AND DIED.
A MILLION RATS, MAYBE.
LISTEN...OK... I APPRECIATE YOU SAVING ME FROM THAT MANIAC, BUT THIS WHOLE SITUATION IS SKEEVING ME OUT.
I MEAN, SHOULDN'T WE BE GOING TO THE POLICE? IF YOU'RE WORRIED ABOUT HAVING SHOT THAT GUY, I'M YOUR WITNESS. IT WAS SELF-DEFENSE.
NO POLICE.
WE DON'T KNOW WHO'S WORKING FOR WHO.
NOW GET IN BEFORE SOMEONE SEES YOU.
12
FORGIVE ME IF I'M NOT SUPER EXCITED TO GO INTO A SKETCHY MOTEL ROOM WITH SOME OLD MAN WHO JUST SHOT SOMEONE RIGHT IN FRONT OF ME.
SO, THANK YOU FOR SAVING MY LIFE, BUT THIS IS WHERE I TAKE MY LEAVE.
KID...
I WASN'T ASKING.

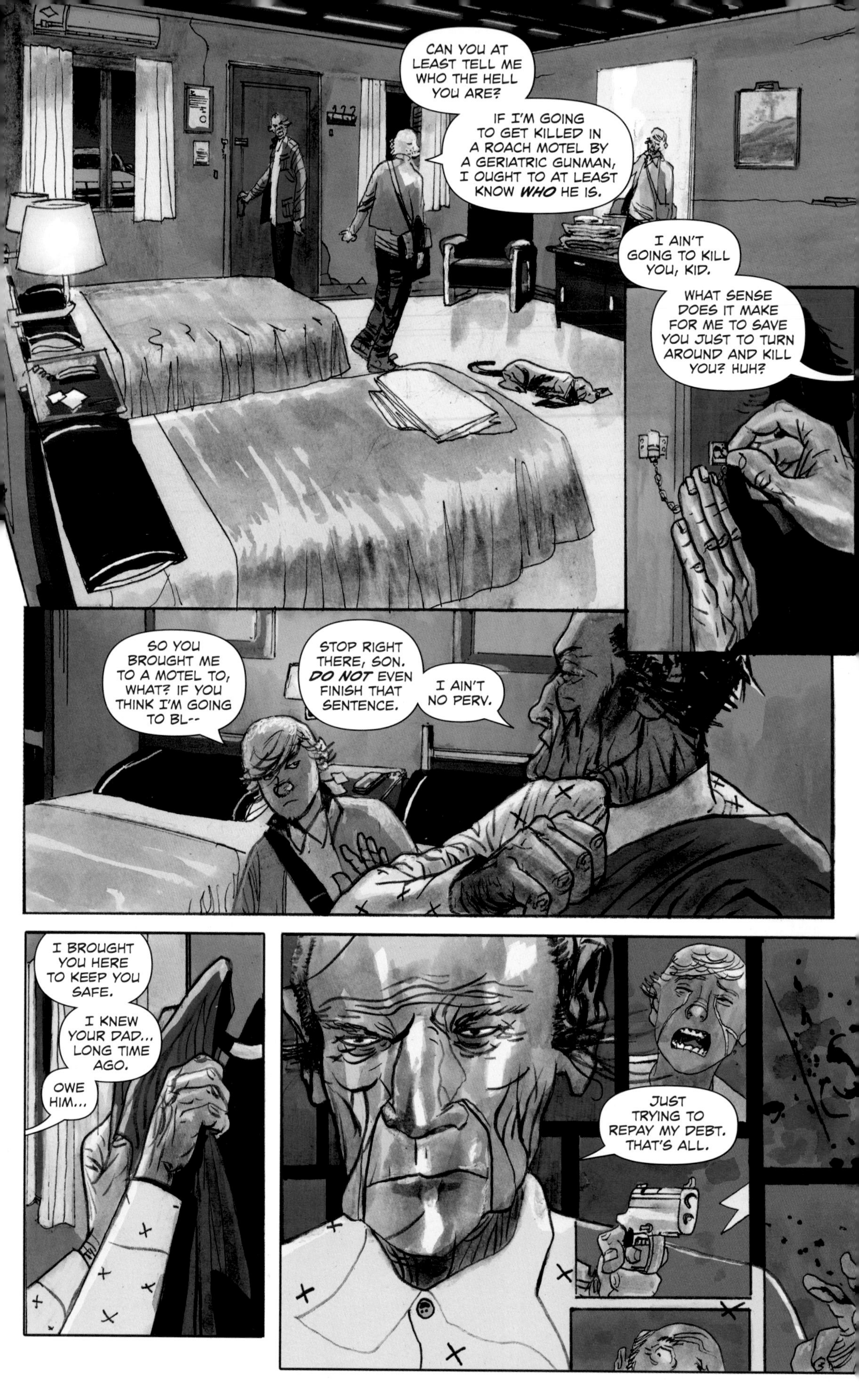
CAN YOU AT LEAST TELL ME WHO THE HELL YOU ARE?
IF I'M GOING TO GET KILLED IN A ROACH MOTEL BY A GERIATRIC GUNMAN, I OUGHT TO AT LEAST KNOW *WHO* HE IS.
I AIN'T GOING TO KILL YOU, KID.
WHAT SENSE DOES IT MAKE FOR ME TO SAVE YOU JUST TO TURN AROUND AND KILL YOU? HUH?
SO YOU BROUGHT ME TO A MOTEL TO, WHAT? IF YOU THINK I'M GOING TO BL--
STOP RIGHT THERE, SON. *DO NOT* EVEN FINISH THAT SENTENCE.
I AIN'T NO PERV.
I BROUGHT YOU HERE TO KEEP YOU SAFE.
I KNEW YOUR DAD... LONG TIME AGO.
OWE HIM...
JUST TRYING TO REPAY MY DEBT. THAT'S ALL.

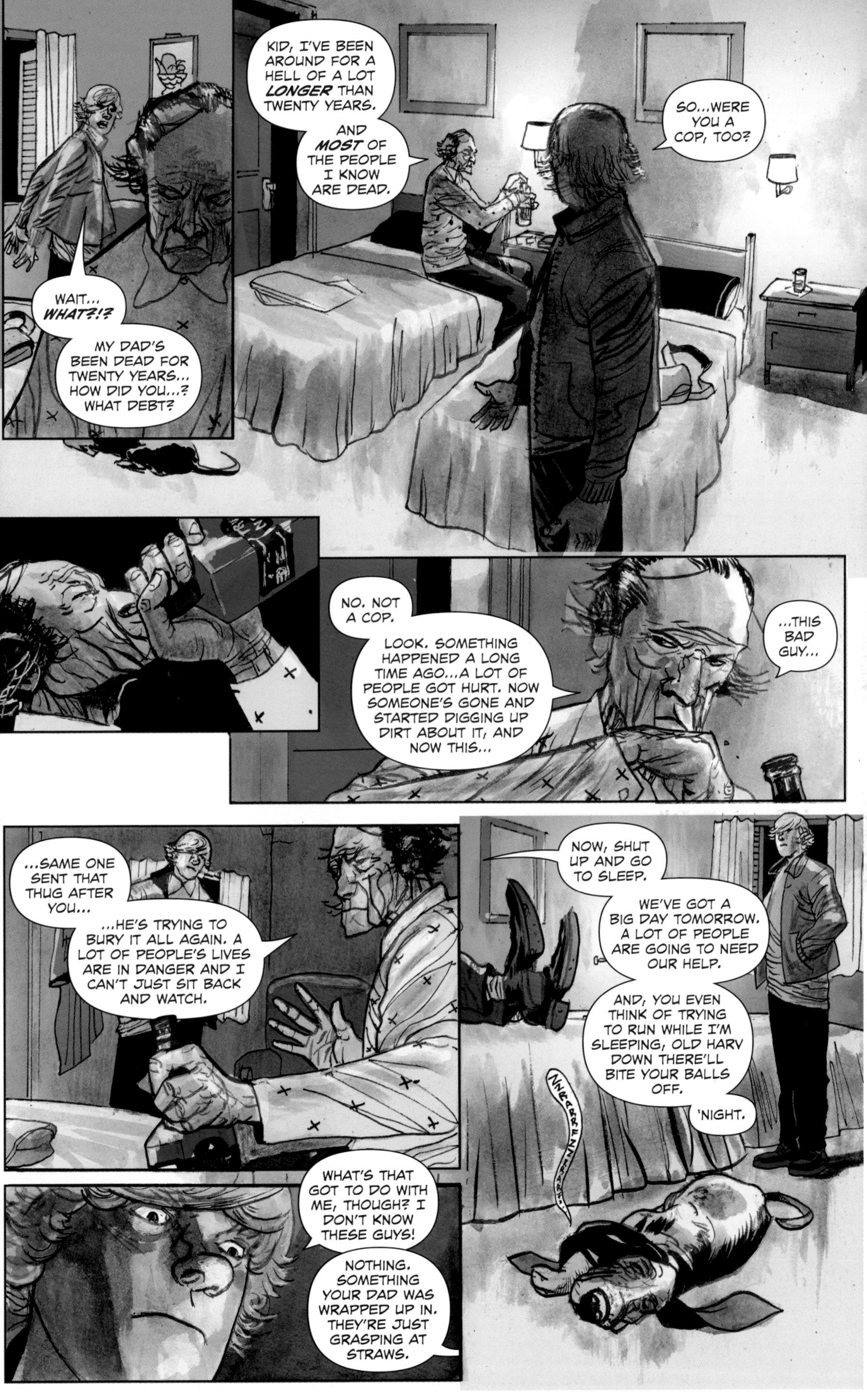
WAIT... WHAT?!?
MY DAD'S BEEN DEAD FOR TWENTY YEARS... HOW DID YOU...? WHAT DEBT?
KID, I'VE BEEN AROUND FOR A HELL OF A LOT LONGER THAN TWENTY YEARS.
AND MOST OF THE PEOPLE I KNOW ARE DEAD.
SO...WERE YOU A COP, TOO?
NO. NOT A COP.
LOOK. SOMETHING HAPPENED A LONG TIME AGO...A LOT OF PEOPLE GOT HURT. NOW SOMEONE'S GONE AND STARTED DIGGING UP DIRT ABOUT IT, AND NOW THIS...
...THIS BAD GUY...
...SAME ONE SENT THAT THUG AFTER YOU...
...HE'S TRYING TO BURY IT ALL AGAIN. A LOT OF PEOPLE'S LIVES ARE IN DANGER AND I CAN'T JUST SIT BACK AND WATCH.
WHAT'S THAT GOT TO DO WITH ME, THOUGH? I DON'T KNOW THESE GUYS!
NOTHING. SOMETHING YOUR DAD WAS WRAPPED UP IN. THEY'RE JUST GRASPING AT STRAWS.
NOW, SHUT UP AND GO TO SLEEP.
WE'VE GOT A BIG DAY TOMORROW. A LOT OF PEOPLE ARE GOING TO NEED OUR HELP.
AND, YOU EVEN THINK OF TRYING TO RUN WHILE I'M SLEEPING, OLD HARV DOWN THERE'LL BITE YOUR BALLS OFF.
'NIGHT.

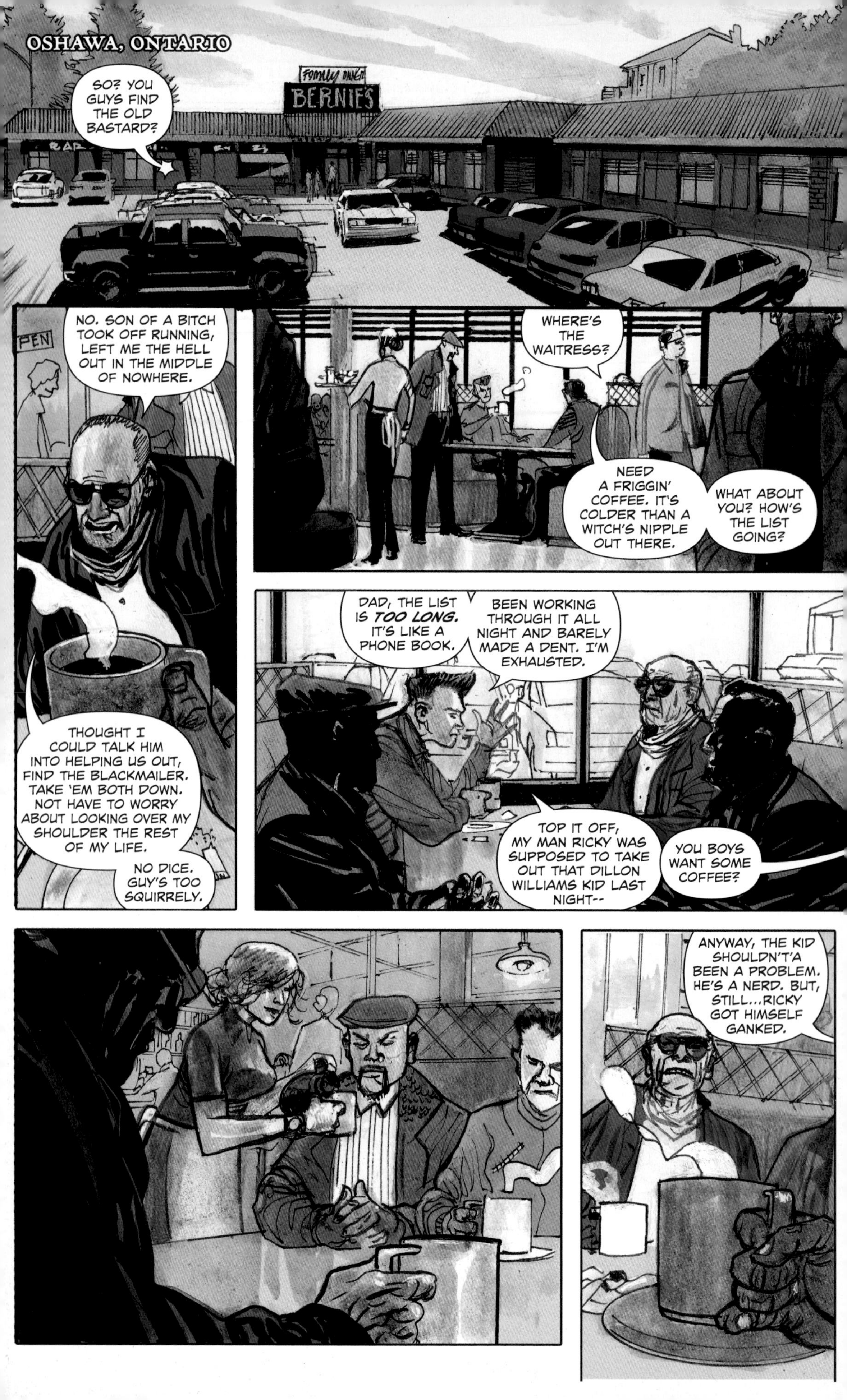
OSHAWA, ONTARIO
FAMILY DINER
BERNIE'S
SO? YOU GUYS FIND THE OLD BASTARD?
NO. SON OF A BITCH TOOK OFF RUNNING, LEFT ME THE HELL OUT IN THE MIDDLE OF NOWHERE.
THOUGHT I COULD TALK HIM INTO HELPING US OUT, FIND THE BLACKMAILER. TAKE 'EM BOTH DOWN. NOT HAVE TO WORRY ABOUT LOOKING OVER MY SHOULDER THE REST OF MY LIFE.
NO DICE. GUY'S TOO SQUIRRELY.
WHERE'S THE WAITRESS?
NEED A FRIGGIN' COFFEE. IT'S COLDER THAN A WITCH'S NIPPLE OUT THERE.
WHAT ABOUT YOU? HOW'S THE LIST GOING?
DAD, THE LIST IS ***TOO LONG.*** IT'S LIKE A PHONE BOOK.
BEEN WORKING THROUGH IT ALL NIGHT AND BARELY MADE A DENT. I'M EXHAUSTED.
TOP IT OFF, MY MAN RICKY WAS SUPPOSED TO TAKE OUT THAT DILLON WILLIAMS KID LAST NIGHT--
YOU BOYS WANT SOME COFFEE?
ANYWAY, THE KID SHOULDN'T'A BEEN A PROBLEM. HE'S A NERD. BUT, STILL...RICKY GOT HIMSELF GANKED.

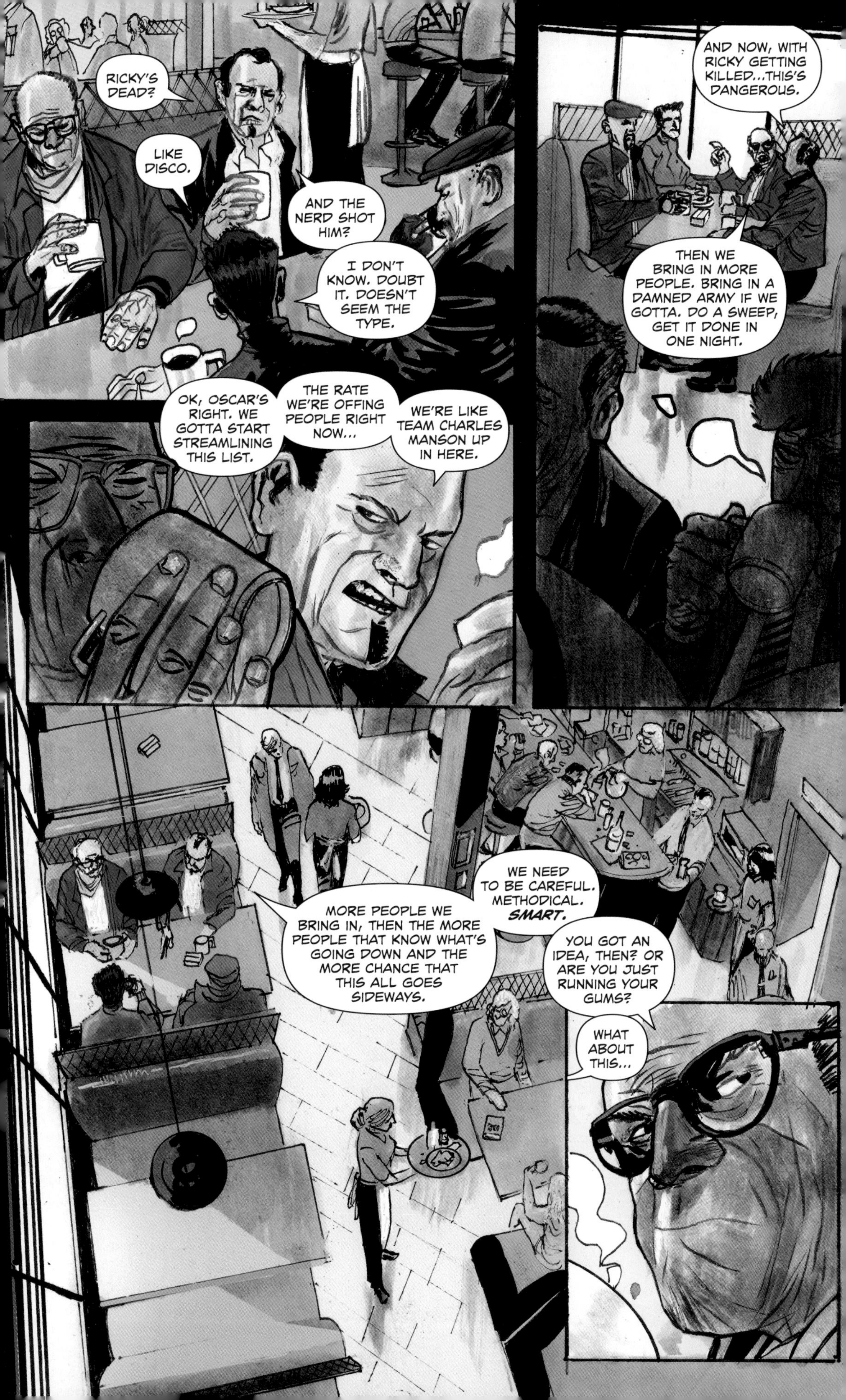
RICKY'S DEAD?
LIKE DISCO.
AND THE NERD SHOT HIM?
I DON'T KNOW. DOUBT IT. DOESN'T SEEM THE TYPE.
AND NOW, WITH RICKY GETTING KILLED...THIS'S DANGEROUS.
THEN WE BRING IN MORE PEOPLE. BRING IN A DAMNED ARMY IF WE GOTTA. DO A SWEEP, GET IT DONE IN ONE NIGHT.
OK, OSCAR'S RIGHT. WE GOTTA START STREAMLINING THIS LIST.
THE RATE WE'RE OFFING PEOPLE RIGHT NOW...
WE'RE LIKE TEAM CHARLES MANSON UP IN HERE.
WE NEED TO BE CAREFUL. METHODICAL. SMART.
MORE PEOPLE WE BRING IN, THEN THE MORE PEOPLE THAT KNOW WHAT'S GOING DOWN AND THE MORE CHANCE THAT THIS ALL GOES SIDEWAYS.
YOU GOT AN IDEA, THEN? OR ARE YOU JUST RUNNING YOUR GUMS?
WHAT ABOUT THIS...

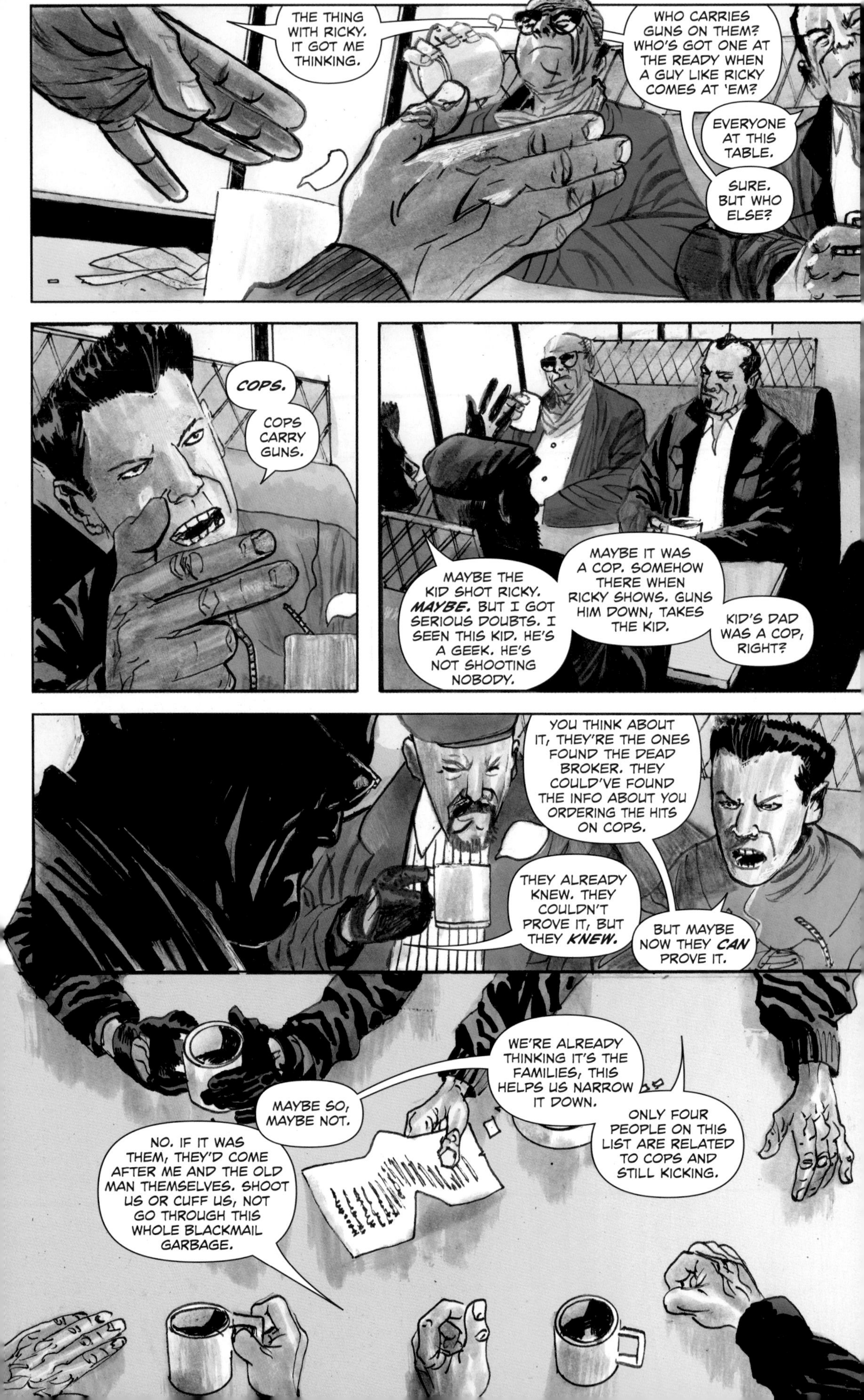
THE THING WITH RICKY. IT GOT ME THINKING.
WHO CARRIES GUNS ON THEM? WHO'S GOT ONE AT THE READY WHEN A GUY LIKE RICKY COMES AT 'EM?
EVERYONE AT THIS TABLE.
SURE. BUT WHO ELSE?
COPS.
COPS CARRY GUNS.
MAYBE THE KID SHOT RICKY. MAYBE. BUT I GOT SERIOUS DOUBTS. I SEEN THIS KID. HE'S A GEEK. HE'S NOT SHOOTING NOBODY.
MAYBE IT WAS A COP. SOMEHOW THERE WHEN RICKY SHOWS. GUNS HIM DOWN, TAKES THE KID.
KID'S DAD WAS A COP, RIGHT?
YOU THINK ABOUT IT, THEY'RE THE ONES FOUND THE DEAD BROKER. THEY COULD'VE FOUND THE INFO ABOUT YOU ORDERING THE HITS ON COPS.
THEY ALREADY KNEW. THEY COULDN'T PROVE IT, BUT THEY KNEW.
BUT MAYBE NOW THEY CAN PROVE IT.
WE'RE ALREADY THINKING IT'S THE FAMILIES, THIS HELPS US NARROW IT DOWN.
MAYBE SO, MAYBE NOT.
ONLY FOUR PEOPLE ON THIS LIST ARE RELATED TO COPS AND STILL KICKING.
NO. IF IT WAS THEM, THEY'D COME AFTER ME AND THE OLD MAN THEMSELVES. SHOOT US OR CUFF US, NOT GO THROUGH THIS WHOLE BLACKMAIL GARBAGE.

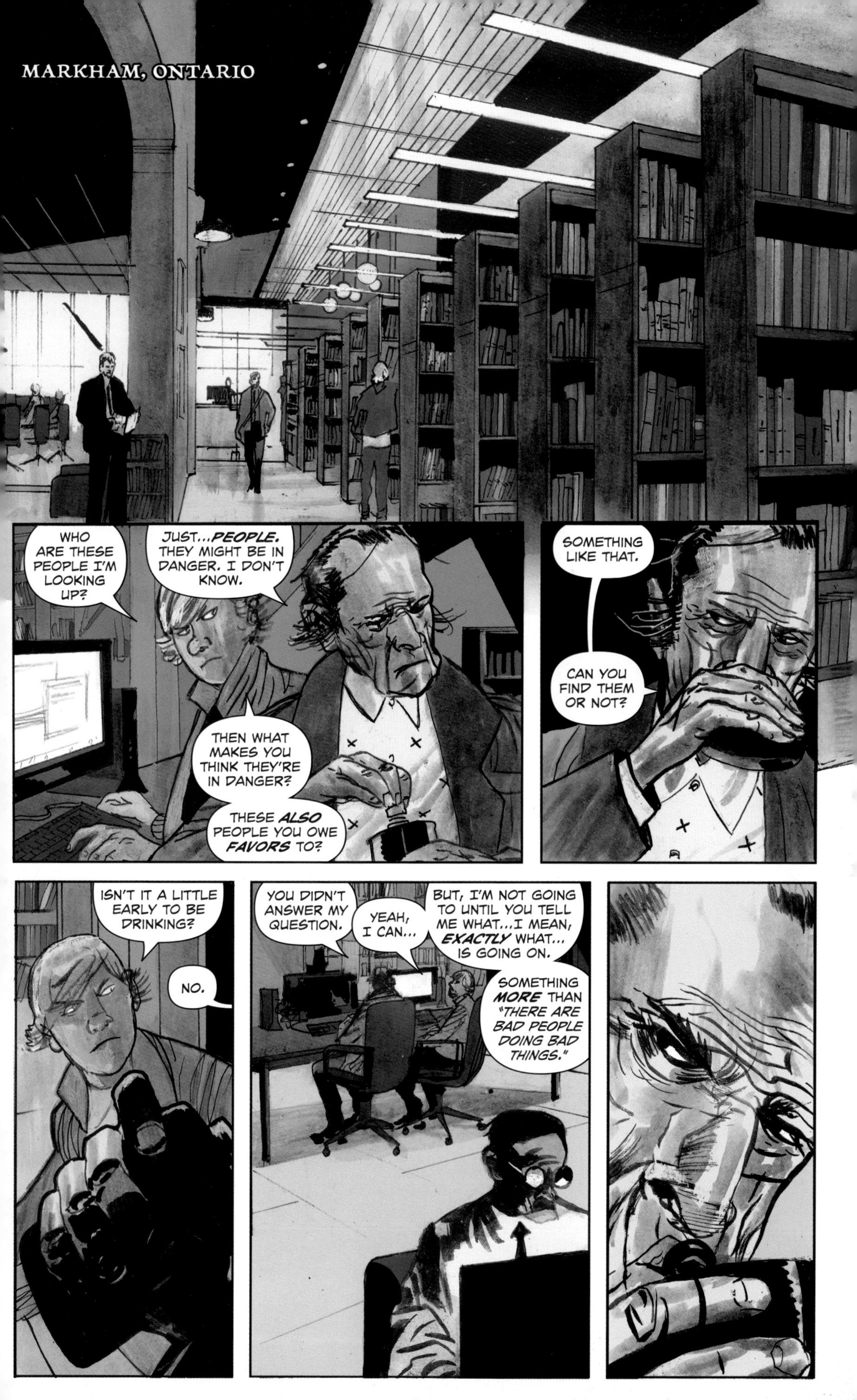
MARKHAM, ONTARIO
WHO ARE THESE PEOPLE I'M LOOKING UP?
JUST...PEOPLE. THEY MIGHT BE IN DANGER. I DON'T KNOW.
THEN WHAT MAKES YOU THINK THEY'RE IN DANGER?
THESE ALSO PEOPLE YOU OWE FAVORS TO?
SOMETHING LIKE THAT.
CAN YOU FIND THEM OR NOT?
ISN'T IT A LITTLE EARLY TO BE DRINKING?
NO.
YOU DIDN'T ANSWER MY QUESTION.
YEAH, I CAN...
BUT, I'M NOT GOING TO UNTIL YOU TELL ME WHAT...I MEAN, EXACTLY WHAT... IS GOING ON.
SOMETHING MORE THAN "THERE ARE BAD PEOPLE DOING BAD THINGS."

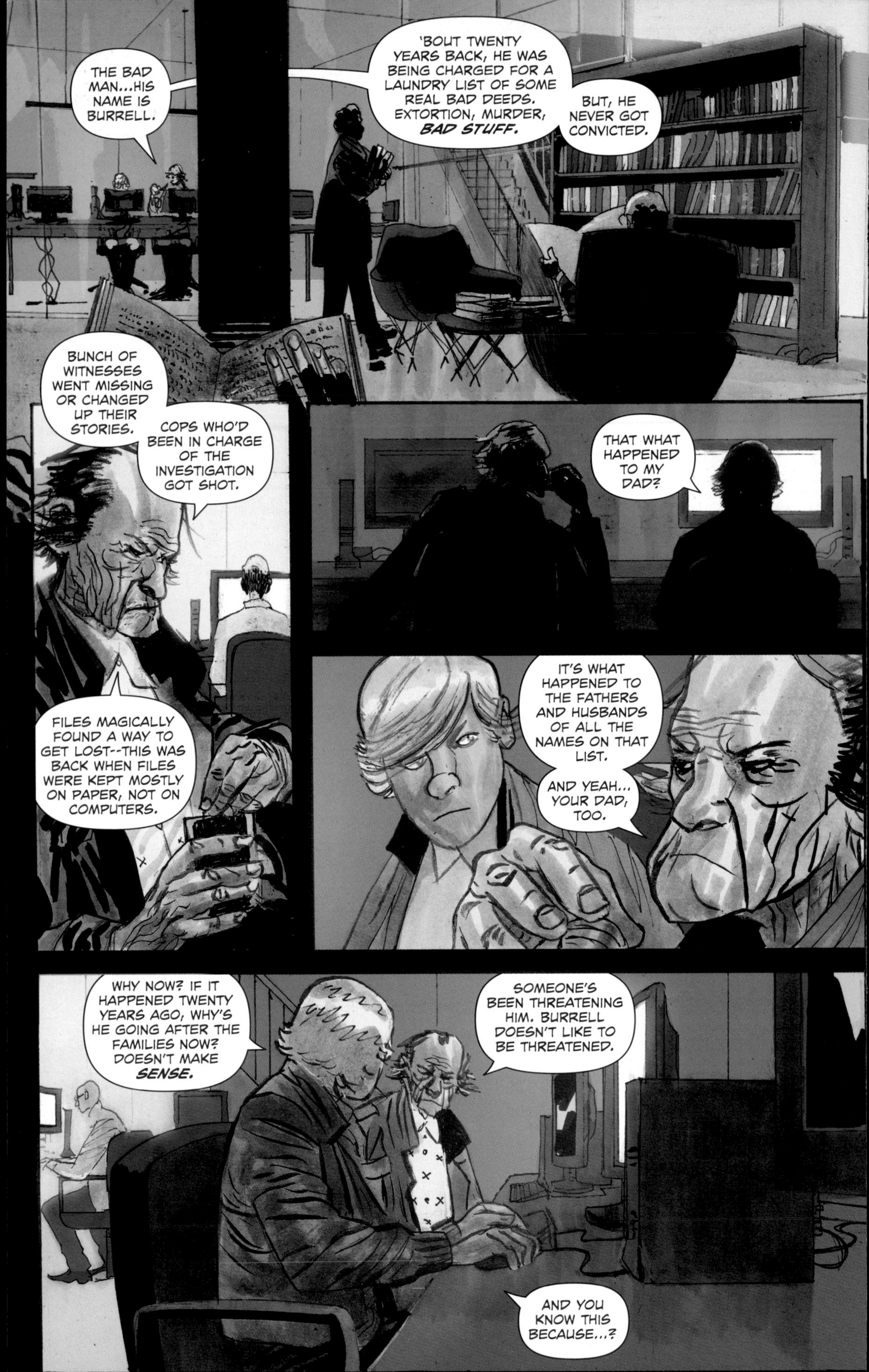
THE BAD MAN...HIS NAME IS BURRELL.
'BOUT TWENTY YEARS BACK, HE WAS BEING CHARGED FOR A LAUNDRY LIST OF SOME REAL BAD DEEDS. EXTORTION, MURDER, BAD STUFF.
BUT, HE NEVER GOT CONVICTED.
BUNCH OF WITNESSES WENT MISSING OR CHANGED UP THEIR STORIES.
COPS WHO'D BEEN IN CHARGE OF THE INVESTIGATION GOT SHOT.
FILES MAGICALLY FOUND A WAY TO GET LOST--THIS WAS BACK WHEN FILES WERE KEPT MOSTLY ON PAPER, NOT ON COMPUTERS.
THAT WHAT HAPPENED TO MY DAD?
IT'S WHAT HAPPENED TO THE FATHERS AND HUSBANDS OF ALL THE NAMES ON THAT LIST.
AND YEAH... YOUR DAD, TOO.
WHY NOW? IF IT HAPPENED TWENTY YEARS AGO, WHY'S HE GOING AFTER THE FAMILIES NOW? DOESN'T MAKE SENSE.
SOMEONE'S BEEN THREATENING HIM. BURRELL DOESN'T LIKE TO BE THREATENED.
AND YOU KNOW THIS BECAUSE...?

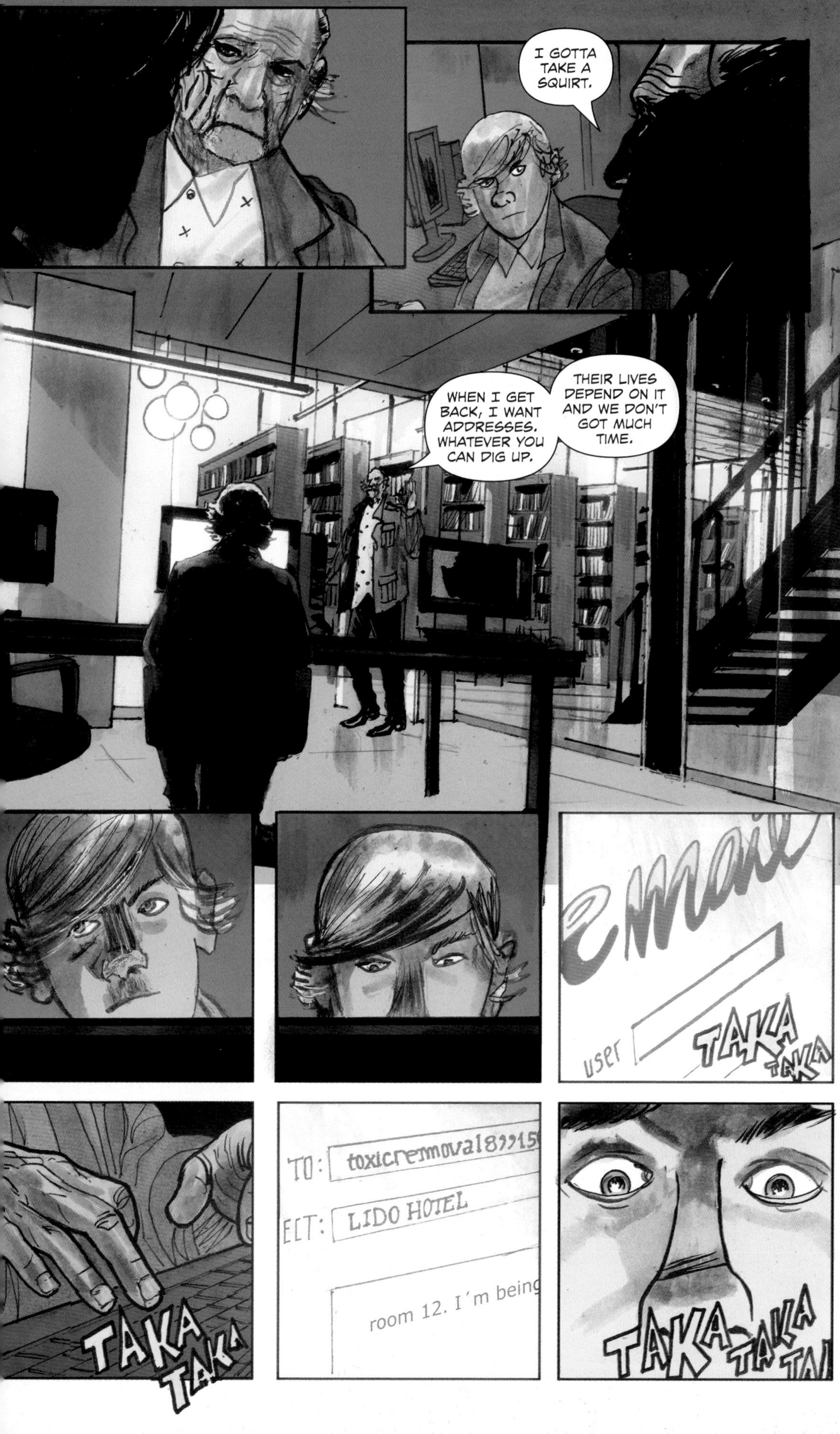
I GOTTA TAKE A SQUIRT.
WHEN I GET BACK, I WANT ADDRESSES. WHATEVER YOU CAN DIG UP.
THEIR LIVES DEPEND ON IT AND WE DON'T GOT MUCH TIME.
email
user
TAKA TAKA
TAKA TAKA
TO: toxicremoval8995
ECT: LIDO HOTEL
room 12. I´m being
TAKA TAKA TA

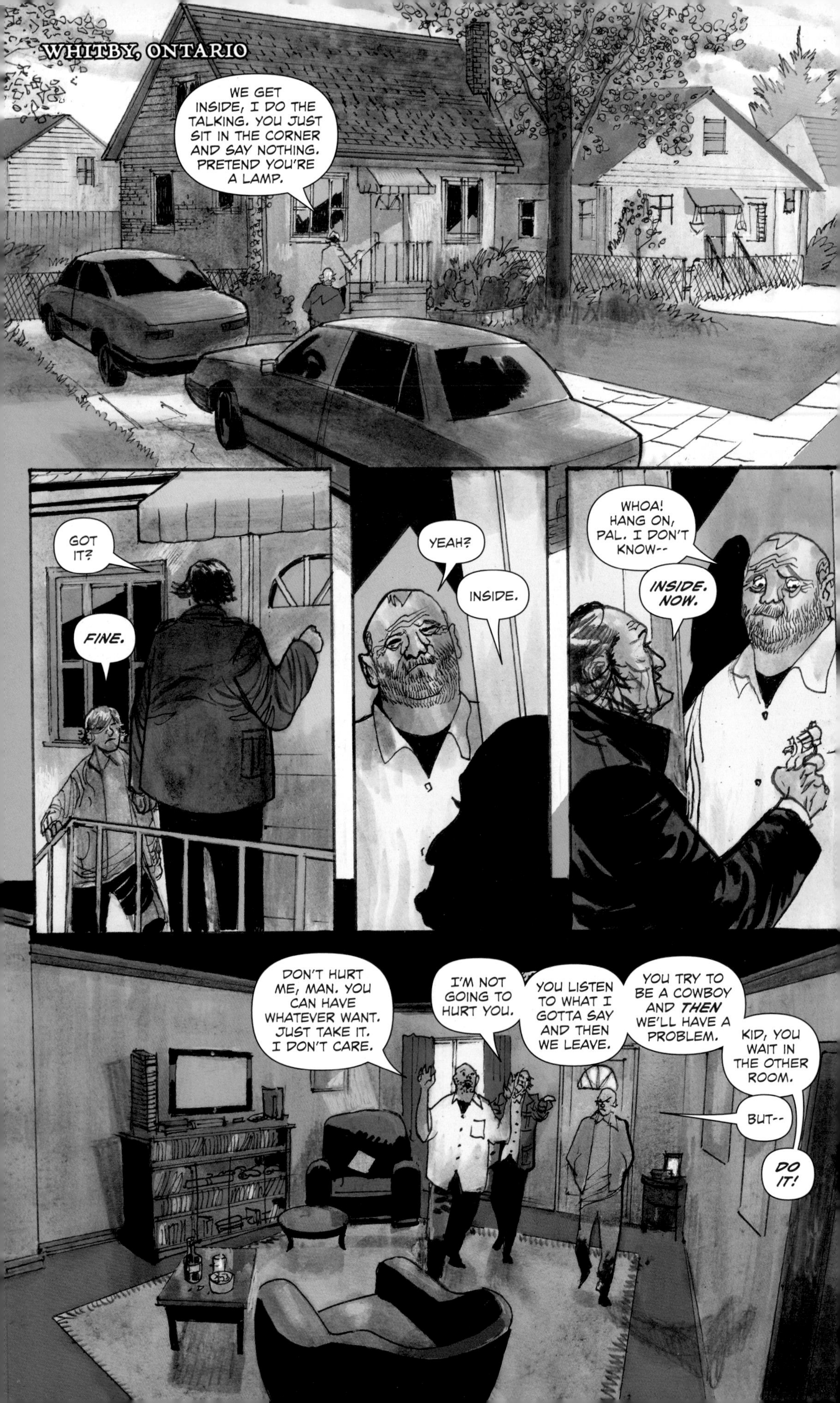
WHITBY, ONTARIO
WE GET INSIDE, I DO THE TALKING. YOU JUST SIT IN THE CORNER AND SAY NOTHING. PRETEND YOU'RE A LAMP.
GOT IT?
FINE.
YEAH?
INSIDE.
WHOA! HANG ON, PAL. I DON'T KNOW--
INSIDE. NOW.
DON'T HURT ME, MAN. YOU CAN HAVE WHATEVER WANT. JUST TAKE IT. I DON'T CARE.
I'M NOT GOING TO HURT YOU.
YOU LISTEN TO WHAT I GOTTA SAY AND THEN WE LEAVE.
YOU TRY TO BE A COWBOY AND THEN WE'LL HAVE A PROBLEM.
KID, YOU WAIT IN THE OTHER ROOM.
BUT--
DO IT!

BURRELL.

WHAT?

BURRELL. YOU KNOW THE NAME? YES OR NO?

YOU MEAN... LIKE THE GANGSTER?

IS HE EVEN STILL AROUND?

I...I DON'T UNDERSTAND... WHAT'S HE GOT TO DO WITH ME?

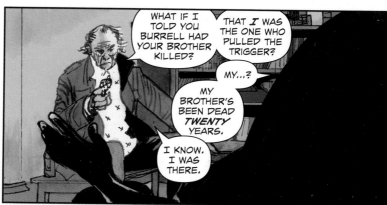

WHAT IF I TOLD YOU BURRELL HAD YOUR BROTHER KILLED?

THAT *I* WAS THE ONE WHO PULLED THE TRIGGER?

MY...?

MY BROTHER'S BEEN DEAD *TWENTY* YEARS.

I KNOW. I WAS THERE.

YOUR BROTHER WAS ONE OF THE COPS SET TO PUT BURRELL AWAY. THEY SILENCED HIM BECAUSE OF THAT.

BURRELL...

GOD. I MEAN...

YEAH...I THINK ABOUT IT NOW, THAT MAKES SENSE...I JUST NEVER THOUGHT...

HERE'S THE DEAL.

YOU WANT ME DEAD, THERE'S THE GUN. IT'S LOADED. SAFETY'S OFF.

YOU DON'T GOT TO DO IT THROUGH THIS BLACKMAILING NONSENSE.

THIS IS YOUR SHOT.

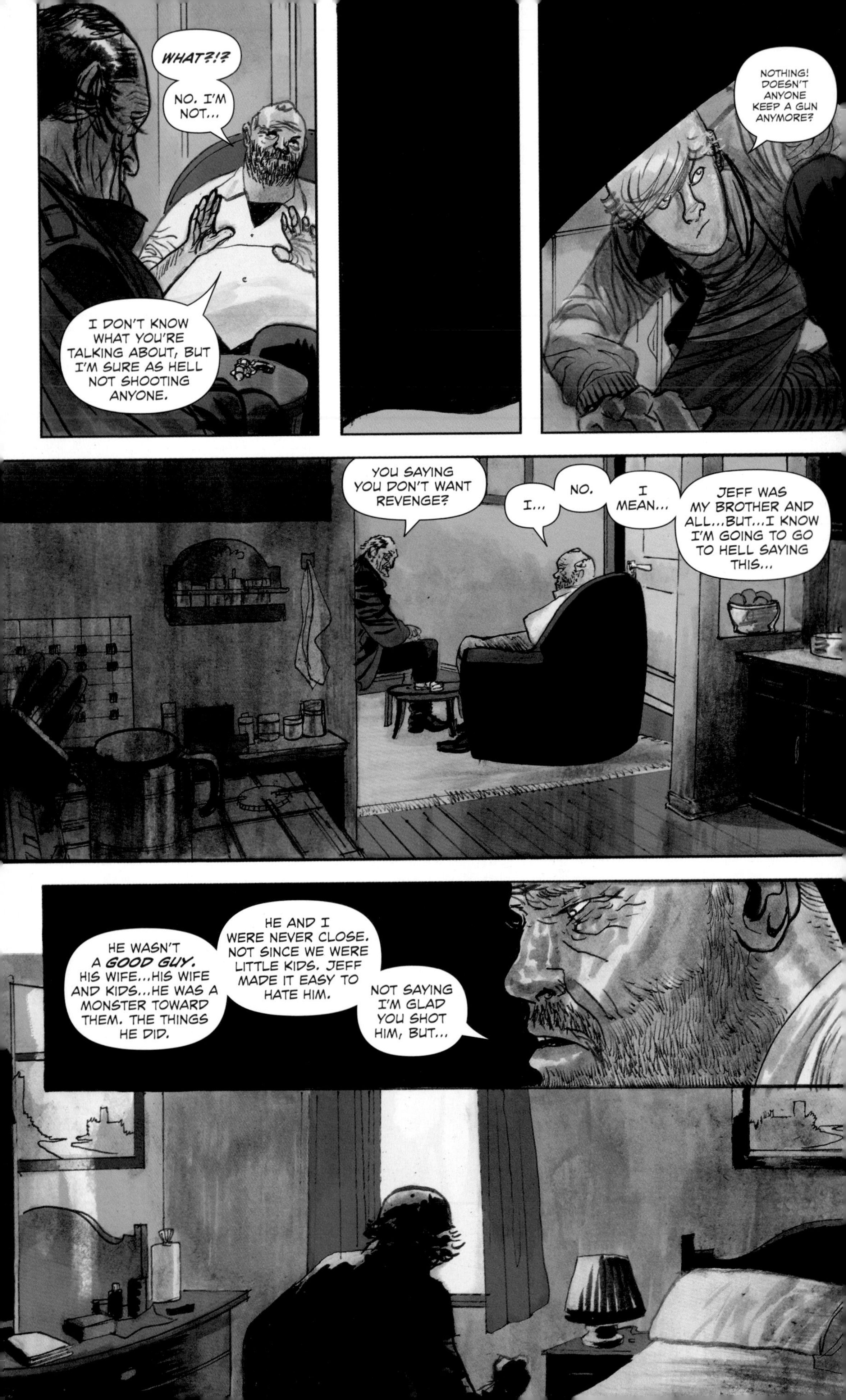
WHAT?!?
NO. I'M NOT...
I DON'T KNOW WHAT YOU'RE TALKING ABOUT, BUT I'M SURE AS HELL NOT SHOOTING ANYONE.
NOTHING! DOESN'T ANYONE KEEP A GUN ANYMORE?
YOU SAYING YOU DON'T WANT REVENGE?
I...
NO.
I MEAN...
JEFF WAS MY BROTHER AND ALL...BUT...I KNOW I'M GOING TO GO TO HELL SAYING THIS...
HE WASN'T A GOOD GUY. HIS WIFE...HIS WIFE AND KIDS...HE WAS A MONSTER TOWARD THEM. THE THINGS HE DID.
HE AND I WERE NEVER CLOSE. NOT SINCE WE WERE LITTLE KIDS. JEFF MADE IT EASY TO HATE HIM.
NOT SAYING I'M GLAD YOU SHOT HIM, BUT...

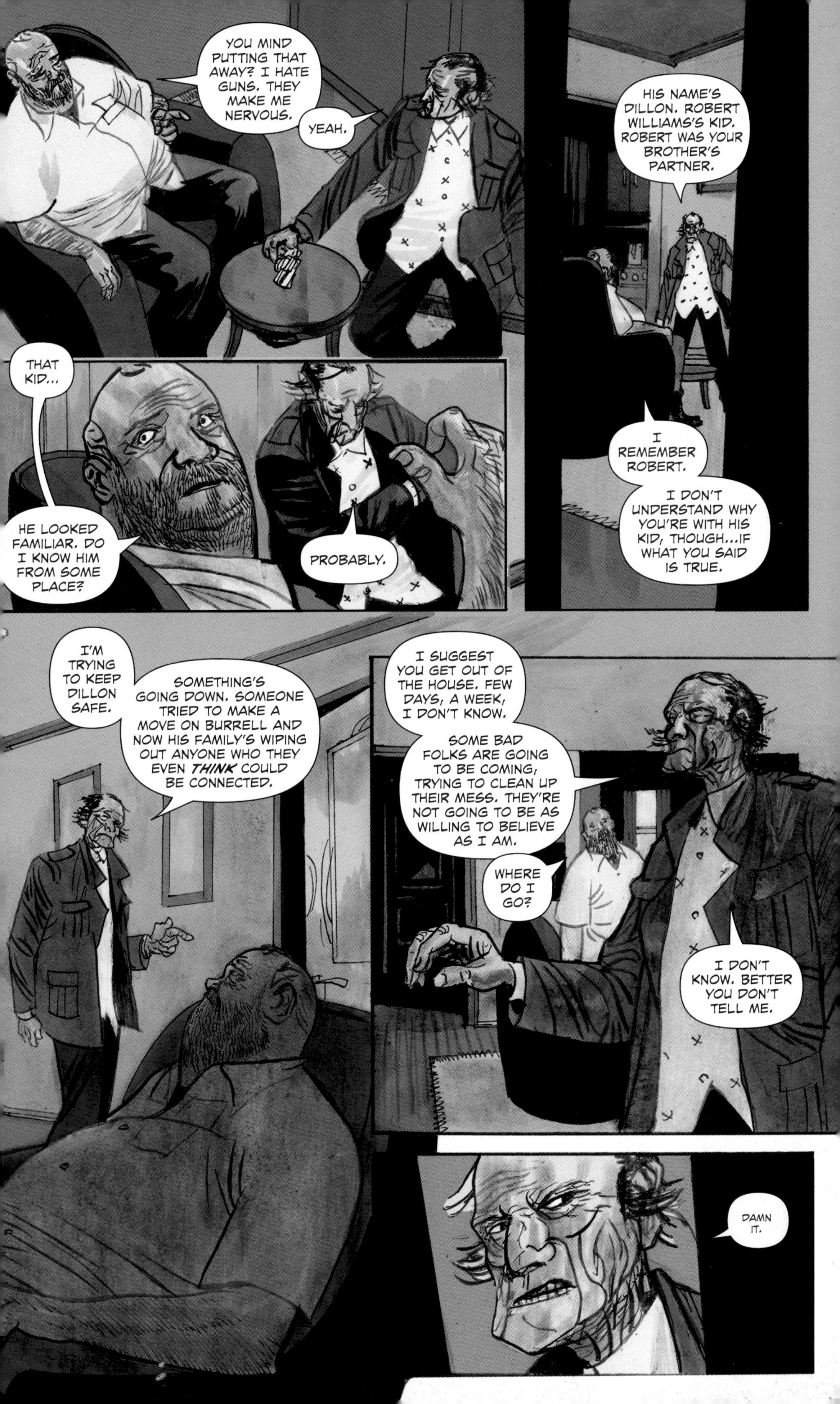
YOU MIND PUTTING THAT AWAY? I HATE GUNS. THEY MAKE ME NERVOUS.
YEAH.
HIS NAME'S DILLON. ROBERT WILLIAMS'S KID. ROBERT WAS YOUR BROTHER'S PARTNER.
THAT KID...
HE LOOKED FAMILIAR. DO I KNOW HIM FROM SOME PLACE?
PROBABLY.
I REMEMBER ROBERT.
I DON'T UNDERSTAND WHY YOU'RE WITH HIS KID, THOUGH...IF WHAT YOU SAID IS TRUE.
I'M TRYING TO KEEP DILLON SAFE.
SOMETHING'S GOING DOWN. SOMEONE TRIED TO MAKE A MOVE ON BURRELL AND NOW HIS FAMILY'S WIPING OUT ANYONE WHO THEY EVEN *THINK* COULD BE CONNECTED.
I SUGGEST YOU GET OUT OF THE HOUSE. FEW DAYS, A WEEK, I DON'T KNOW.
SOME BAD FOLKS ARE GOING TO BE COMING, TRYING TO CLEAN UP THEIR MESS. THEY'RE NOT GOING TO BE AS WILLING TO BELIEVE AS I AM.
WHERE DO I GO?
I DON'T KNOW. BETTER YOU DON'T TELL ME.
DAMN IT.

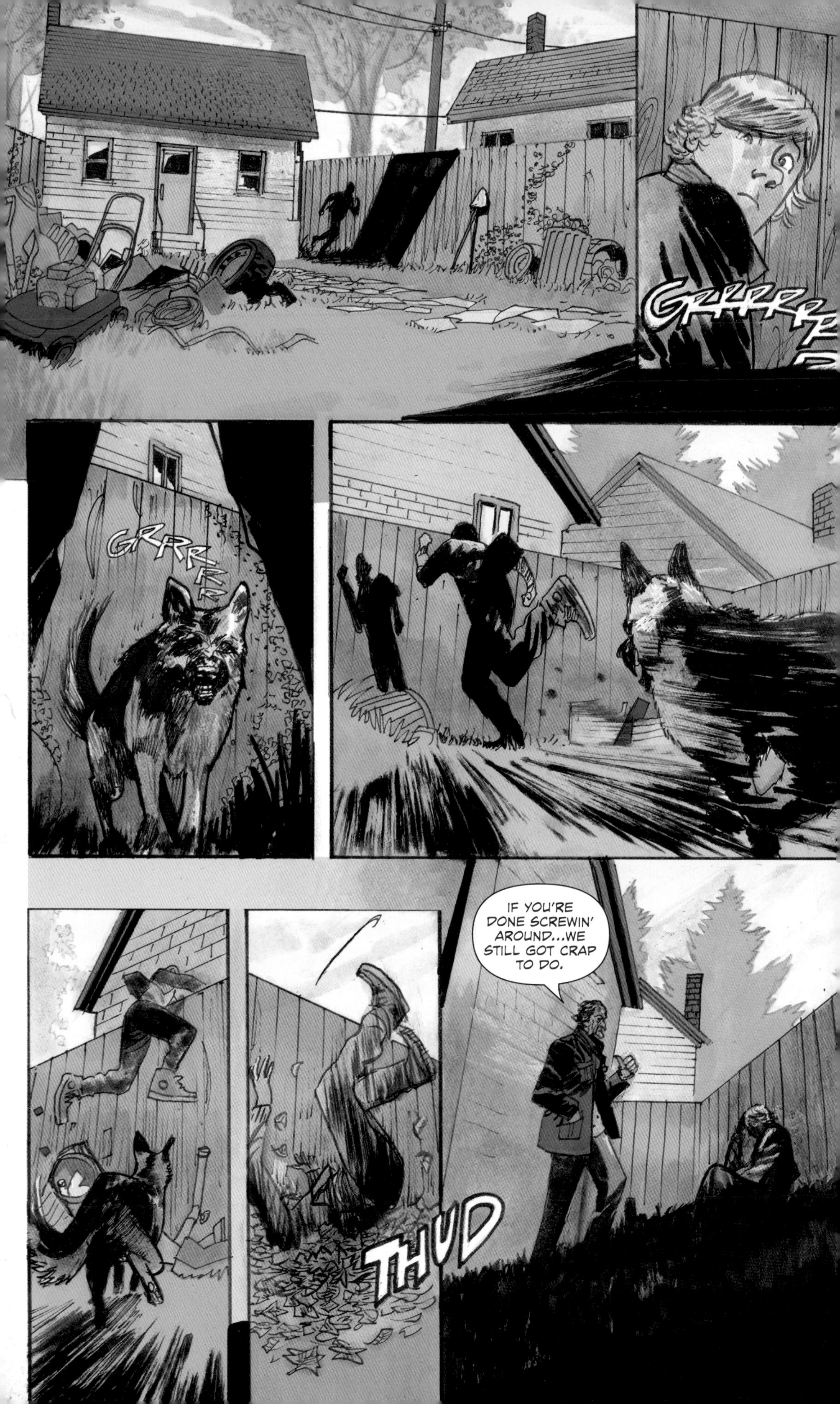
GRRRRRR
GRRRRR
IF YOU'RE DONE SCREWIN' AROUND...WE STILL GOT CRAP TO DO.
THUD

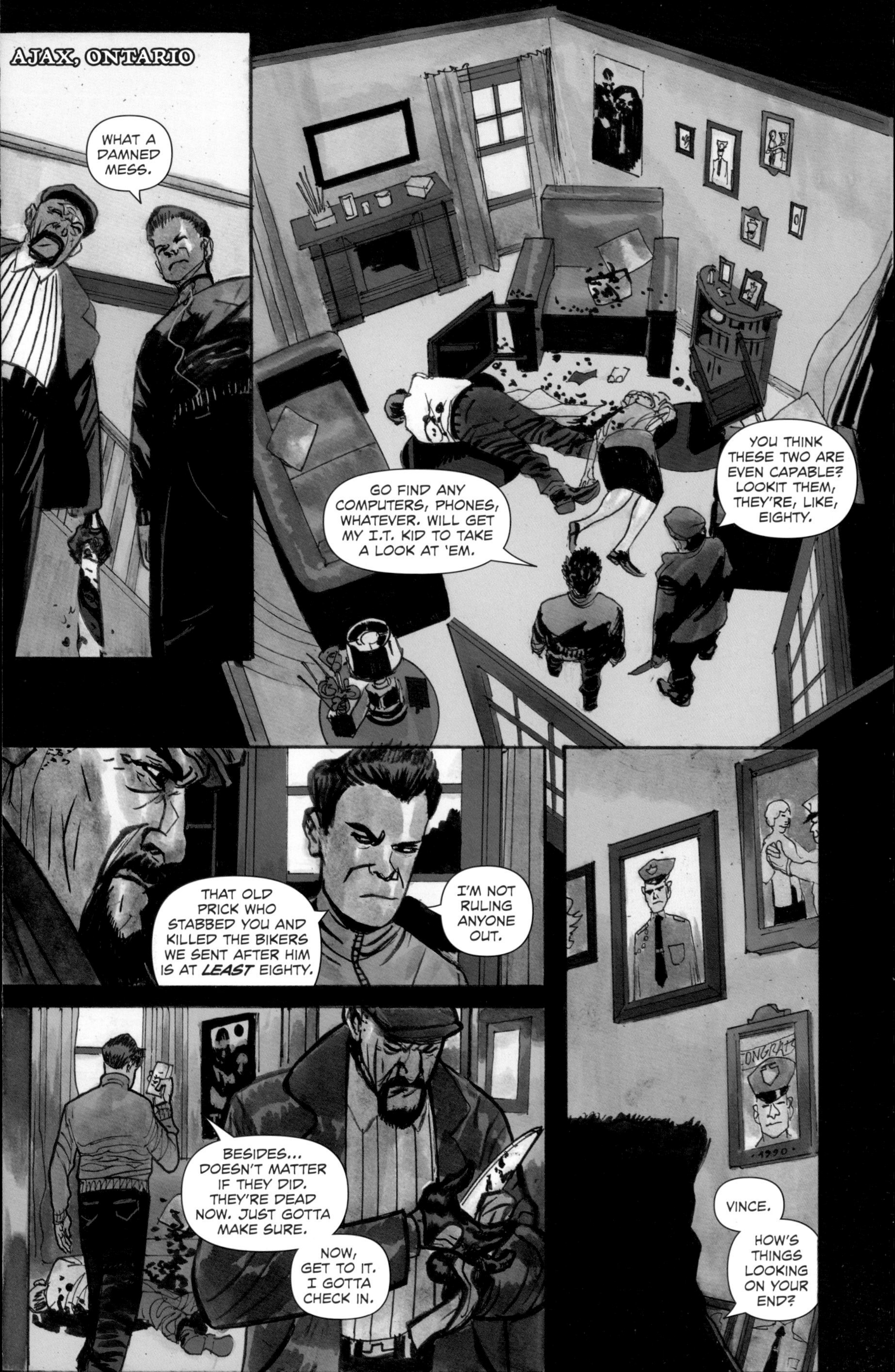

AJAX, ONTARIO
WHAT A DAMNED MESS.
GO FIND ANY COMPUTERS, PHONES, WHATEVER. WILL GET MY I.T. KID TO TAKE A LOOK AT 'EM.
YOU THINK THESE TWO ARE EVEN CAPABLE? LOOKIT THEM, THEY'RE, LIKE, EIGHTY.
THAT OLD PRICK WHO STABBED YOU AND KILLED THE BIKERS WE SENT AFTER HIM IS AT LEAST EIGHTY.
I'M NOT RULING ANYONE OUT.
BESIDES... DOESN'T MATTER IF THEY DID. THEY'RE DEAD NOW. JUST GOTTA MAKE SURE.
NOW, GET TO IT. I GOTTA CHECK IN.
CONGRATS
1990
VINCE.
HOW'S THINGS LOOKING ON YOUR END?

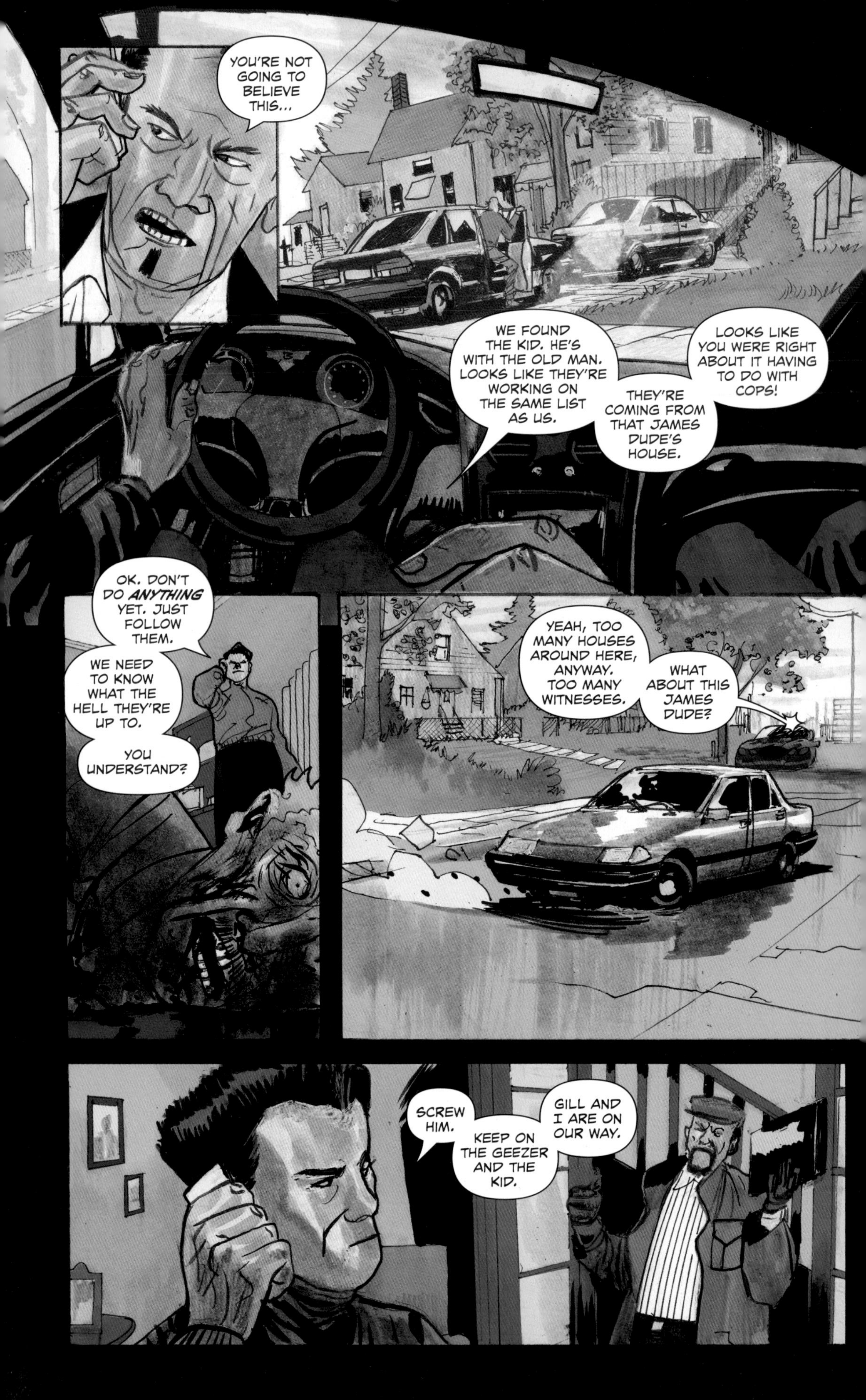
YOU'RE NOT GOING TO BELIEVE THIS...
WE FOUND THE KID. HE'S WITH THE OLD MAN. LOOKS LIKE THEY'RE WORKING ON THE SAME LIST AS US.
THEY'RE COMING FROM THAT JAMES DUDE'S HOUSE.
LOOKS LIKE YOU WERE RIGHT ABOUT IT HAVING TO DO WITH COPS!
OK. DON'T DO ANYTHING YET. JUST FOLLOW THEM.
WE NEED TO KNOW WHAT THE HELL THEY'RE UP TO.
YOU UNDERSTAND?
YEAH, TOO MANY HOUSES AROUND HERE, ANYWAY. TOO MANY WITNESSES.
WHAT ABOUT THIS JAMES DUDE?
SCREW HIM.
KEEP ON THE GEEZER AND THE KID.
GILL AND I ARE ON OUR WAY.

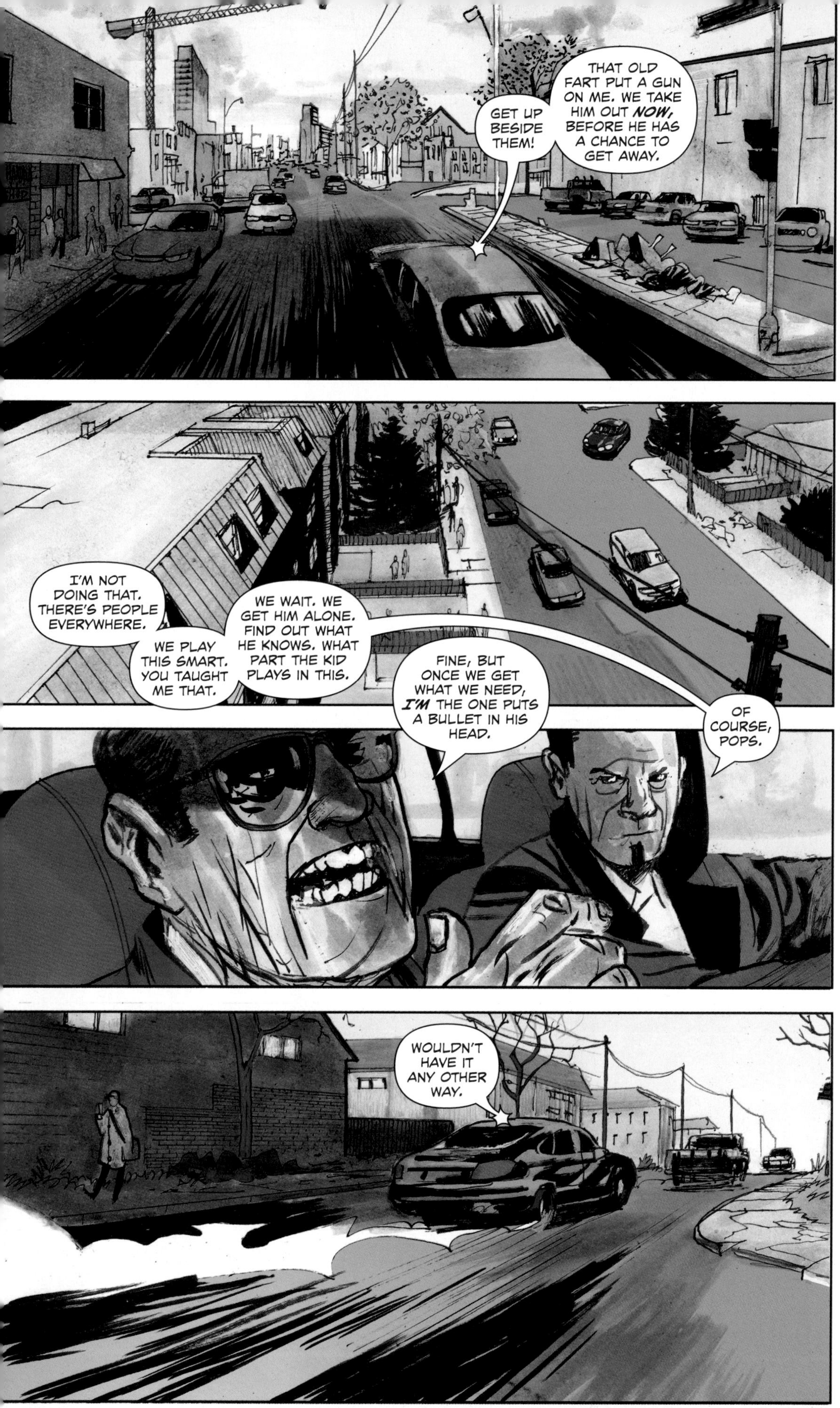
GET UP BESIDE THEM!
THAT OLD FART PUT A GUN ON ME. WE TAKE HIM OUT NOW, BEFORE HE HAS A CHANCE TO GET AWAY.
I'M NOT DOING THAT. THERE'S PEOPLE EVERYWHERE.
WE PLAY THIS SMART. YOU TAUGHT ME THAT.
WE WAIT. WE GET HIM ALONE. FIND OUT WHAT HE KNOWS. WHAT PART THE KID PLAYS IN THIS.
FINE, BUT ONCE WE GET WHAT WE NEED, I'M THE ONE PUTS A BULLET IN HIS HEAD.
OF COURSE, POPS.
WOULDN'T HAVE IT ANY OTHER WAY.

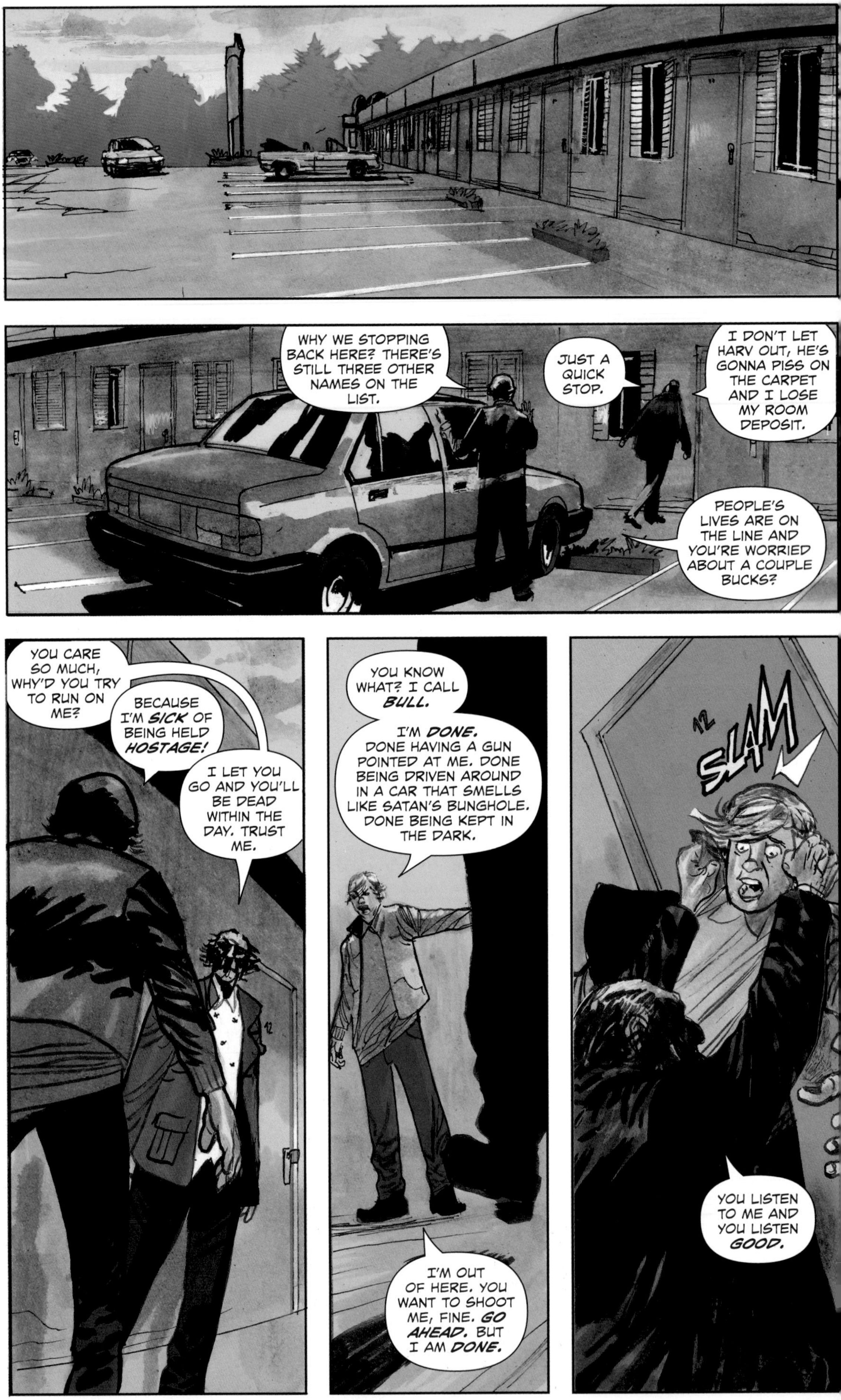
WHY WE STOPPING BACK HERE? THERE'S STILL THREE OTHER NAMES ON THE LIST.
JUST A QUICK STOP.
I DON'T LET HARV OUT, HE'S GONNA PISS ON THE CARPET AND I LOSE MY ROOM DEPOSIT.
PEOPLE'S LIVES ARE ON THE LINE AND YOU'RE WORRIED ABOUT A COUPLE BUCKS?
YOU CARE SO MUCH, WHY'D YOU TRY TO RUN ON ME?
BECAUSE I'M SICK OF BEING HELD HOSTAGE!
I LET YOU GO AND YOU'LL BE DEAD WITHIN THE DAY. TRUST ME.
YOU KNOW WHAT? I CALL BULL.
I'M DONE. DONE HAVING A GUN POINTED AT ME. DONE BEING DRIVEN AROUND IN A CAR THAT SMELLS LIKE SATAN'S BUNGHOLE. DONE BEING KEPT IN THE DARK.
I'M OUT OF HERE. YOU WANT TO SHOOT ME, FINE. GO AHEAD. BUT I AM DONE.
SLAM
YOU LISTEN TO ME AND YOU LISTEN GOOD.

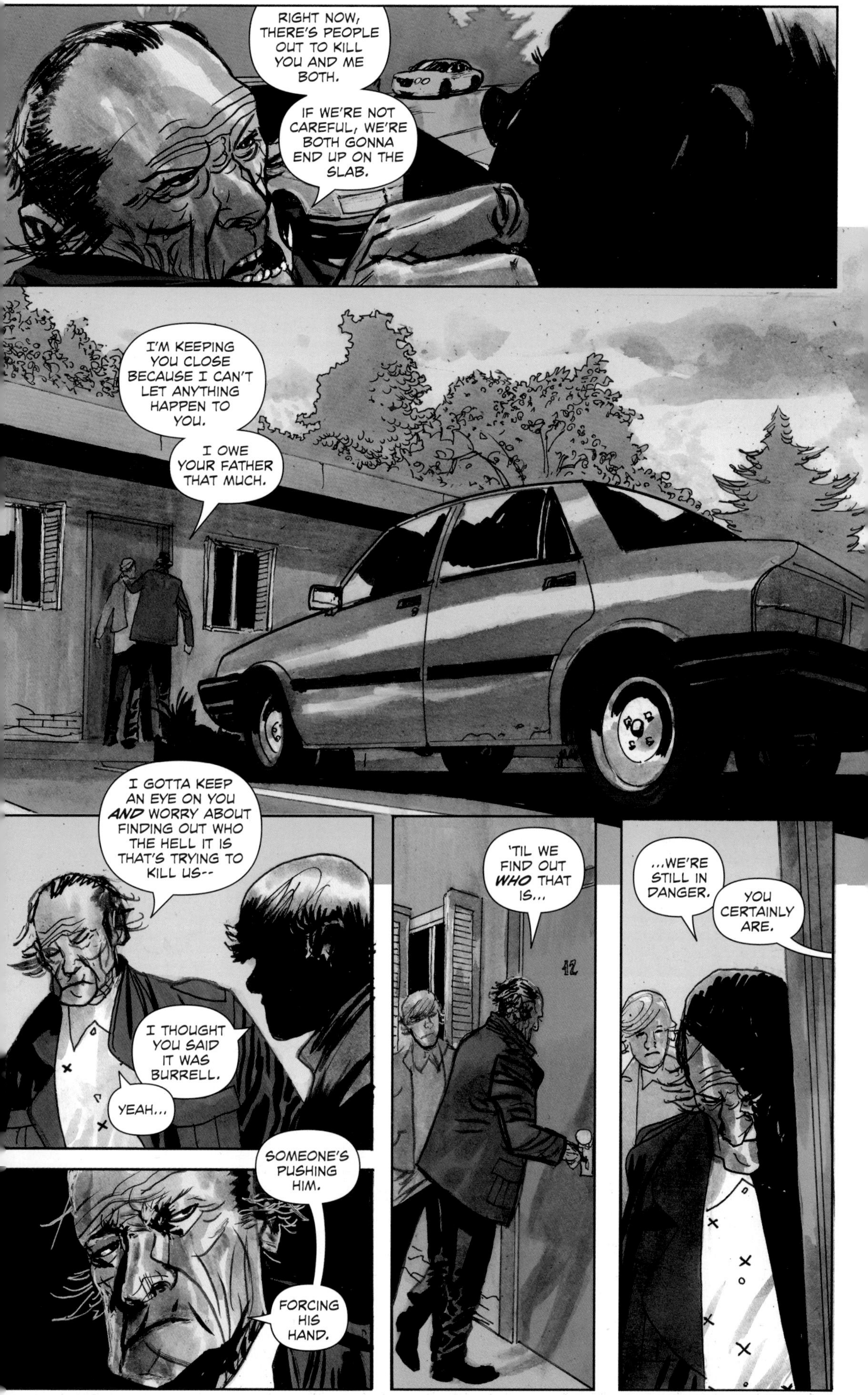

RIGHT NOW, THERE'S PEOPLE OUT TO KILL YOU AND ME BOTH.
IF WE'RE NOT CAREFUL, WE'RE BOTH GONNA END UP ON THE SLAB.
I'M KEEPING YOU CLOSE BECAUSE I CAN'T LET ANYTHING HAPPEN TO YOU.
I OWE YOUR FATHER THAT MUCH.
I GOTTA KEEP AN EYE ON YOU AND WORRY ABOUT FINDING OUT WHO THE HELL IT IS THAT'S TRYING TO KILL US--
I THOUGHT YOU SAID IT WAS BURRELL.
YEAH...
SOMEONE'S PUSHING HIM.
FORCING HIS HAND.
'TIL WE FIND OUT WHO THAT IS...
12
...WE'RE STILL IN DANGER.
YOU CERTAINLY ARE.

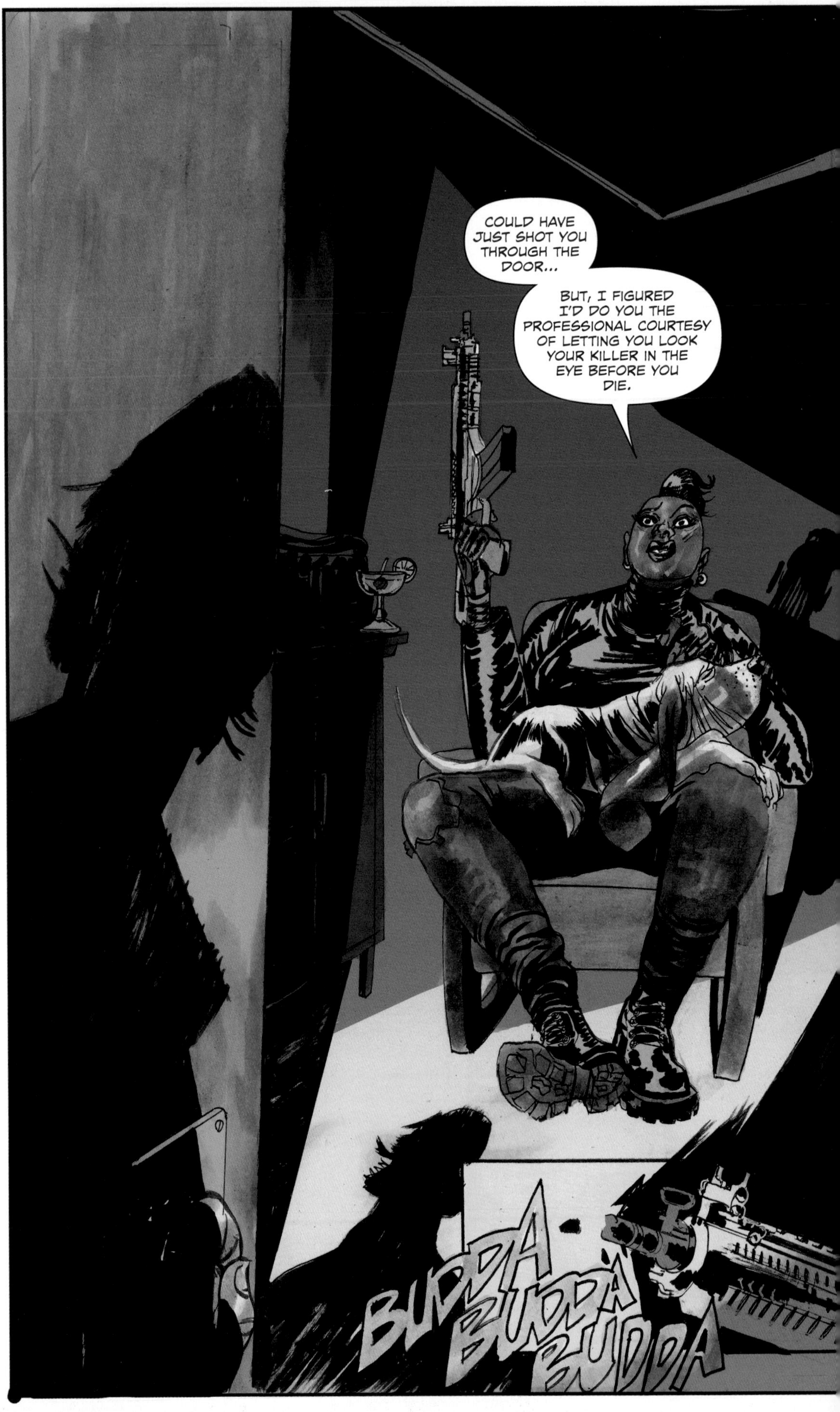
COULD HAVE JUST SHOT YOU THROUGH THE DOOR...
BUT, I FIGURED I'D DO YOU THE PROFESSIONAL COURTESY OF LETTING YOU LOOK YOUR KILLER IN THE EYE BEFORE YOU DIE.
BUDDA-BUDDA BUDDA

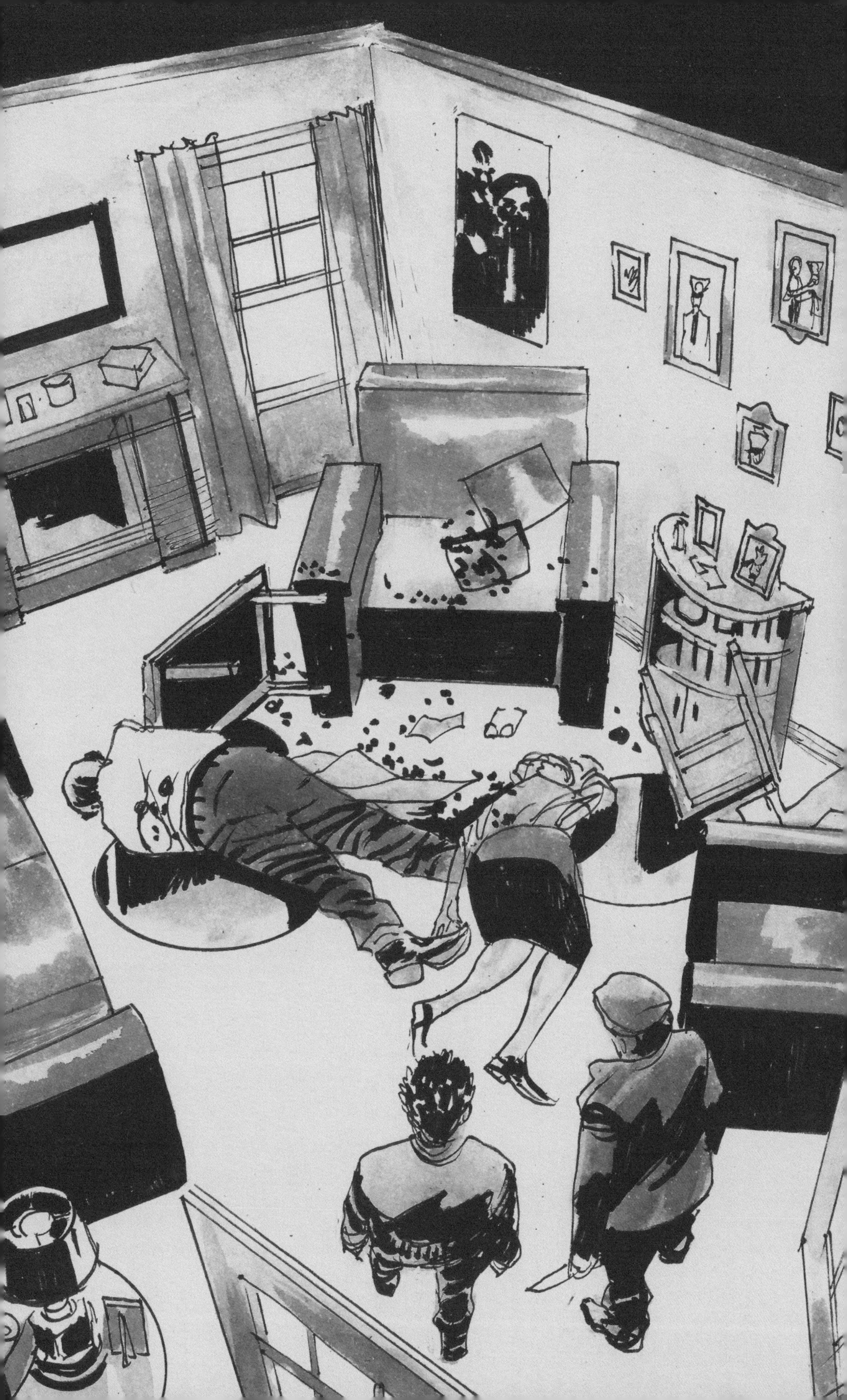

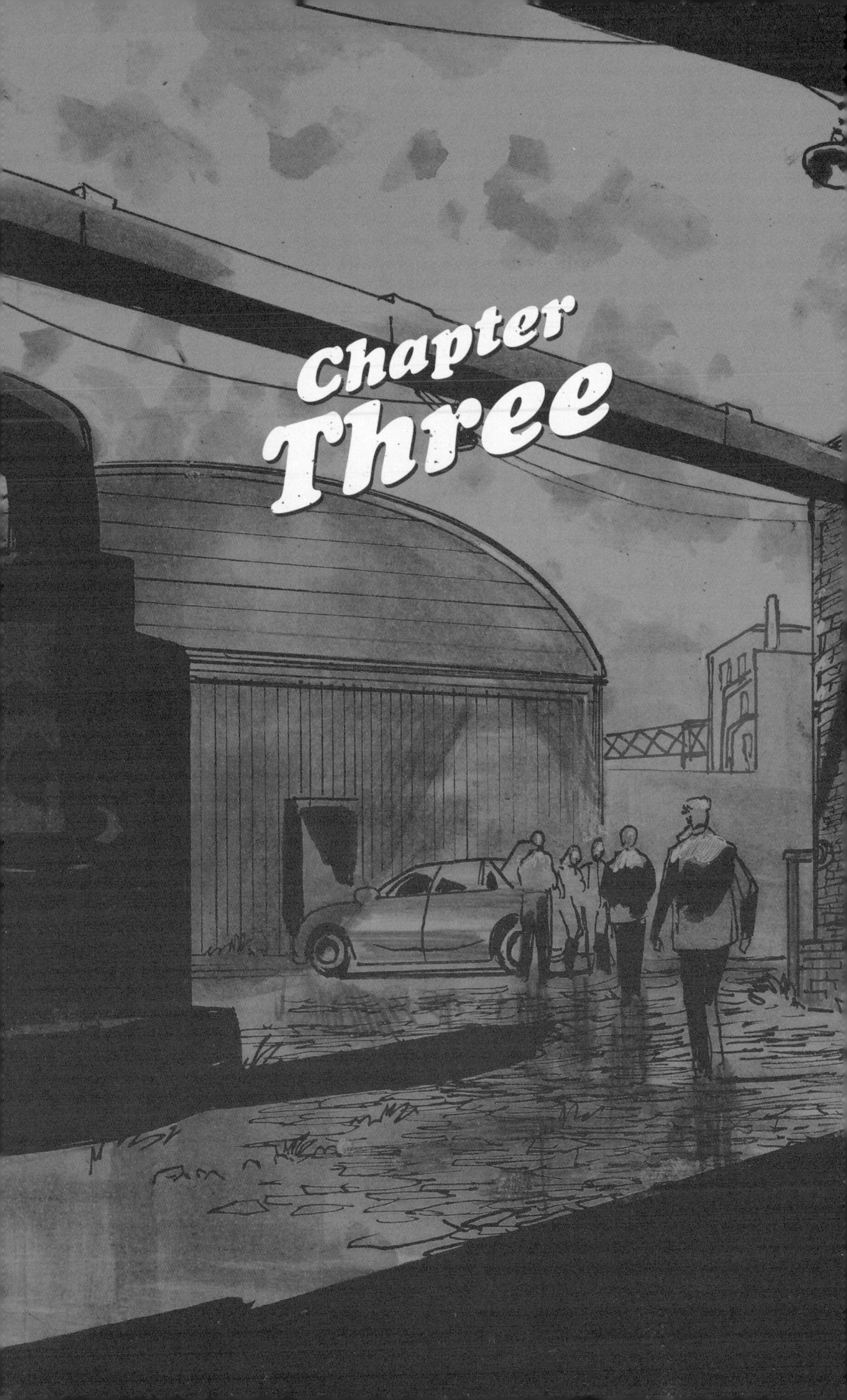
Chapter
Three

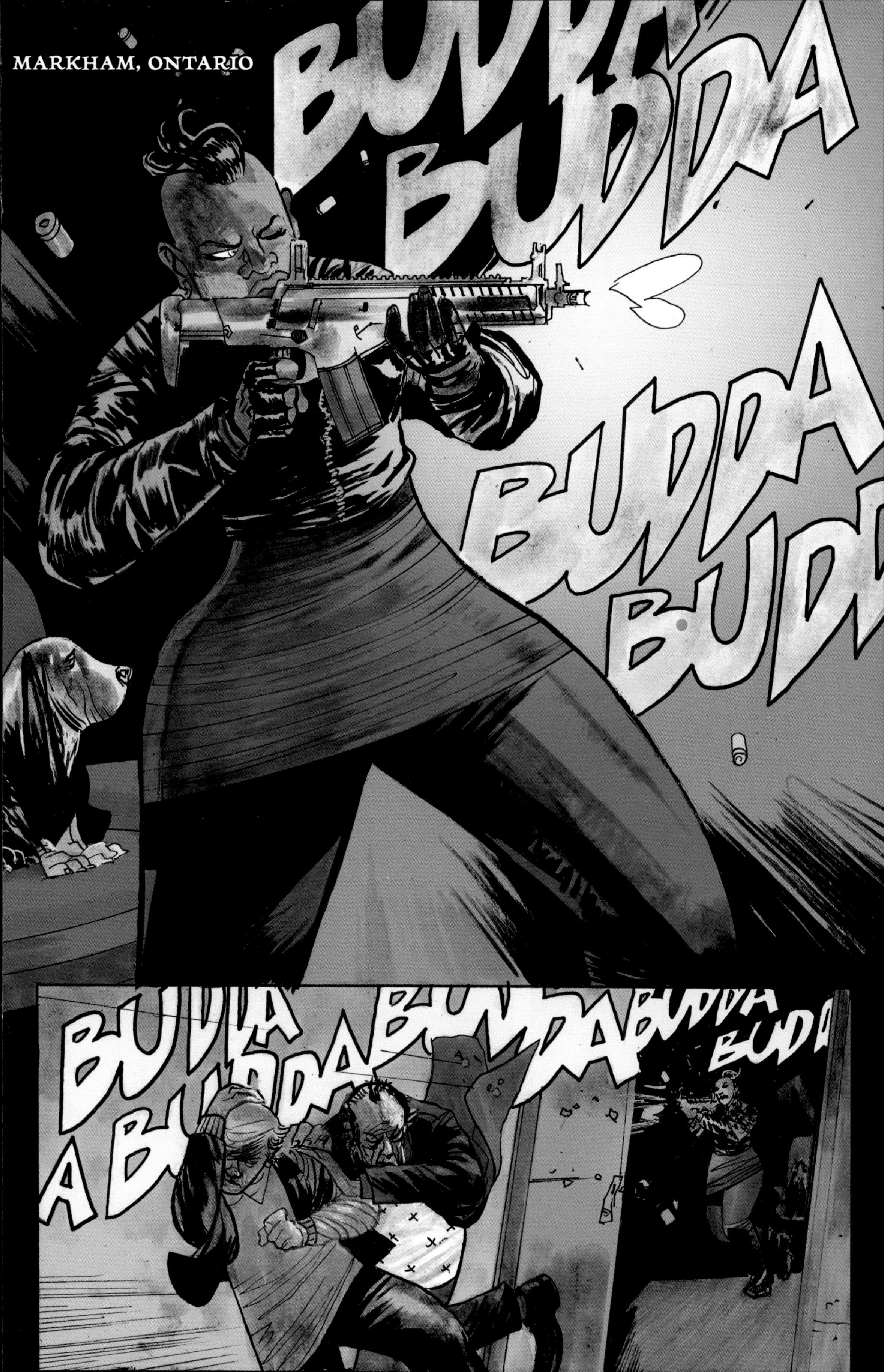
MARKHAM, ONTARIO
BUDDA
BUDDA
BUDDA

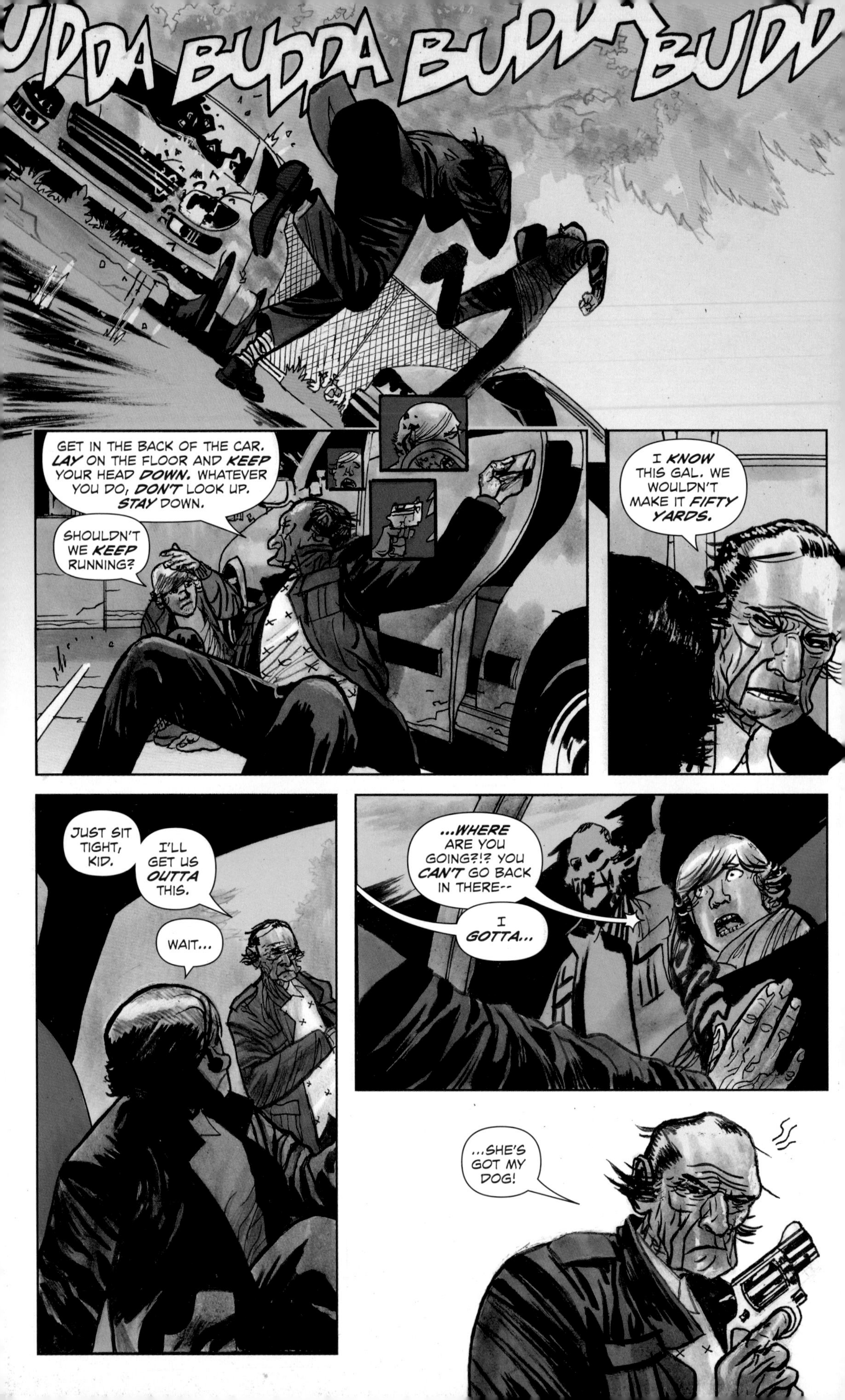
UDDA BUDDA BUDDA BUDD
GET IN THE BACK OF THE CAR. LAY ON THE FLOOR AND KEEP YOUR HEAD DOWN. WHATEVER YOU DO, DON'T LOOK UP. STAY DOWN.
SHOULDN'T WE KEEP RUNNING?
I KNOW THIS GAL. WE WOULDN'T MAKE IT FIFTY YARDS.
JUST SIT TIGHT, KID.
I'LL GET US OUTTA THIS.
WAIT...
...WHERE ARE YOU GOING?!? YOU CAN'T GO BACK IN THERE--
I GOTTA...
...SHE'S GOT MY DOG!

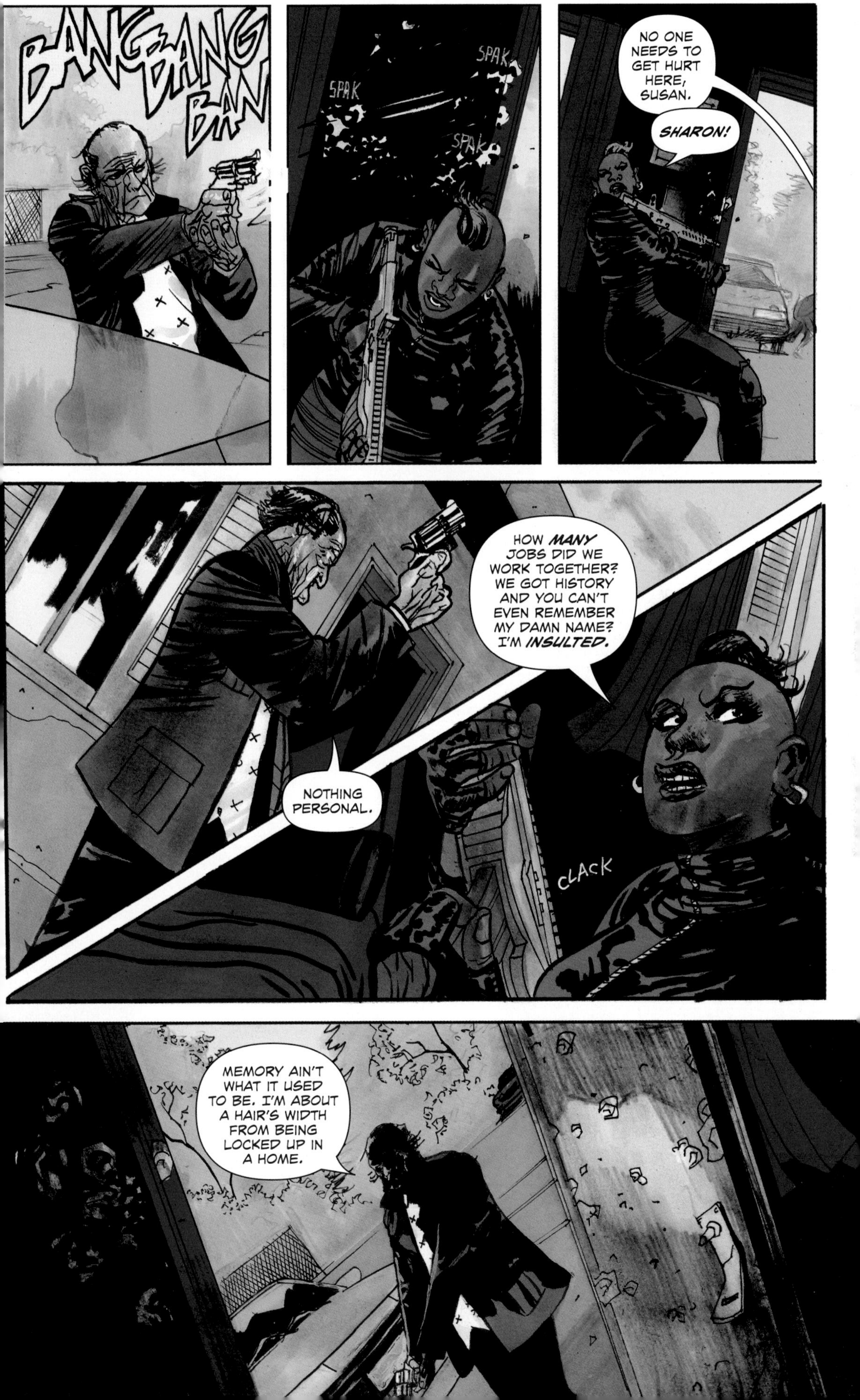
BANG BANG BAN
SPAK
SPAK
SPAK
NO ONE NEEDS TO GET HURT HERE, SUSAN.
SHARON!
HOW MANY JOBS DID WE WORK TOGETHER? WE GOT HISTORY AND YOU CAN'T EVEN REMEMBER MY DAMN NAME? I'M INSULTED.
NOTHING PERSONAL.
CLACK
MEMORY AIN'T WHAT IT USED TO BE. I'M ABOUT A HAIR'S WIDTH FROM BEING LOCKED UP IN A HOME.

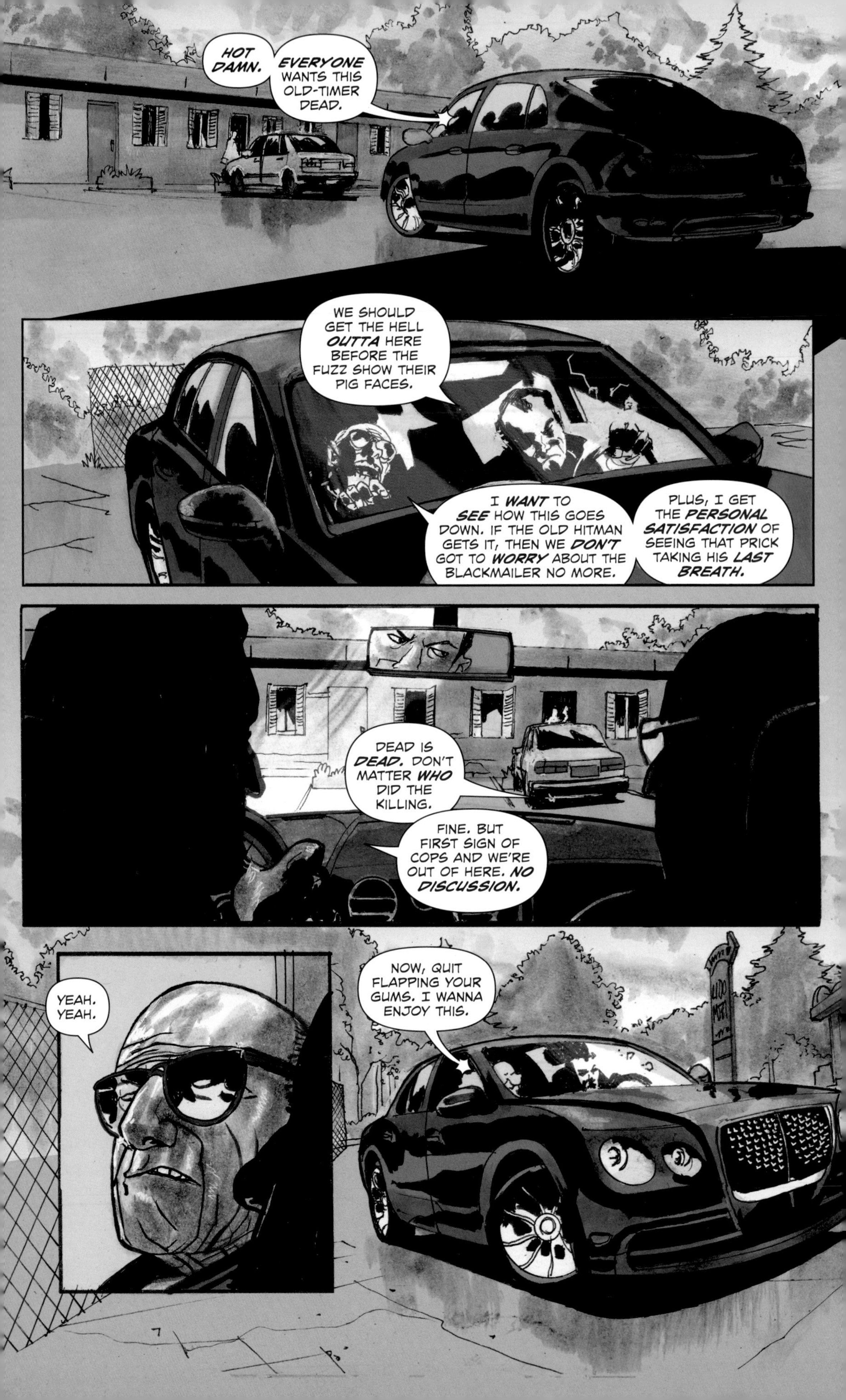
HOT DAMN.
EVERYONE WANTS THIS OLD-TIMER DEAD.
WE SHOULD GET THE HELL OUTTA HERE BEFORE THE FUZZ SHOW THEIR PIG FACES.
I WANT TO SEE HOW THIS GOES DOWN. IF THE OLD HITMAN GETS IT, THEN WE DON'T GOT TO WORRY ABOUT THE BLACKMAILER NO MORE.
PLUS, I GET THE PERSONAL SATISFACTION OF SEEING THAT PRICK TAKING HIS LAST BREATH.
DEAD IS DEAD. DON'T MATTER WHO DID THE KILLING.
FINE. BUT FIRST SIGN OF COPS AND WE'RE OUT OF HERE. NO DISCUSSION.
YEAH. YEAH.
NOW, QUIT FLAPPING YOUR GUMS. I WANNA ENJOY THIS.

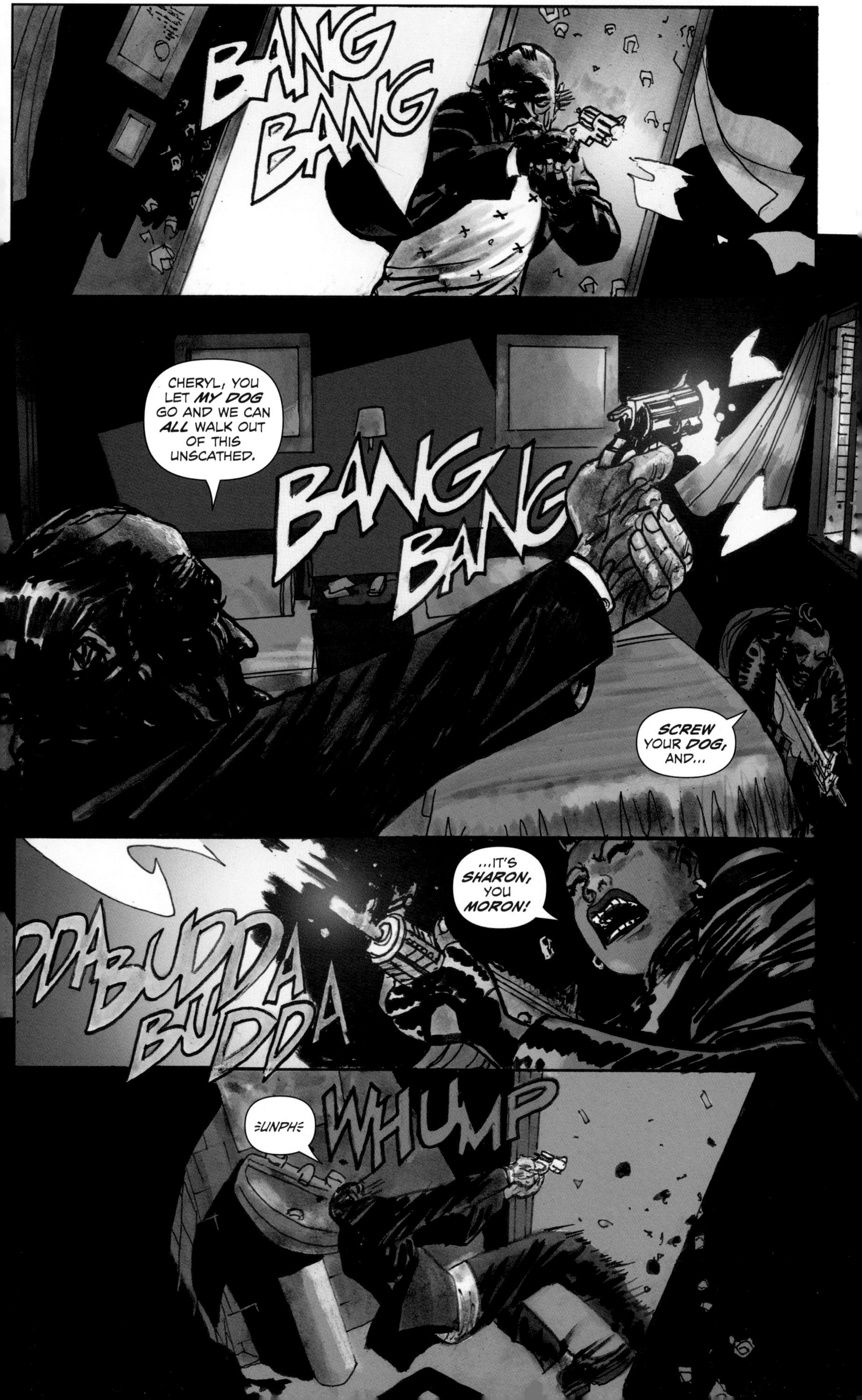
BANG BANG
CHERYL, YOU LET MY DOG GO AND WE CAN ALL WALK OUT OF THIS UNSCATHED.
BANG BANG
SCREW YOUR DOG, AND...
...IT'S SHARON, YOU MORON!
DDABUDDA BUDDA
UNPH
WHUMP

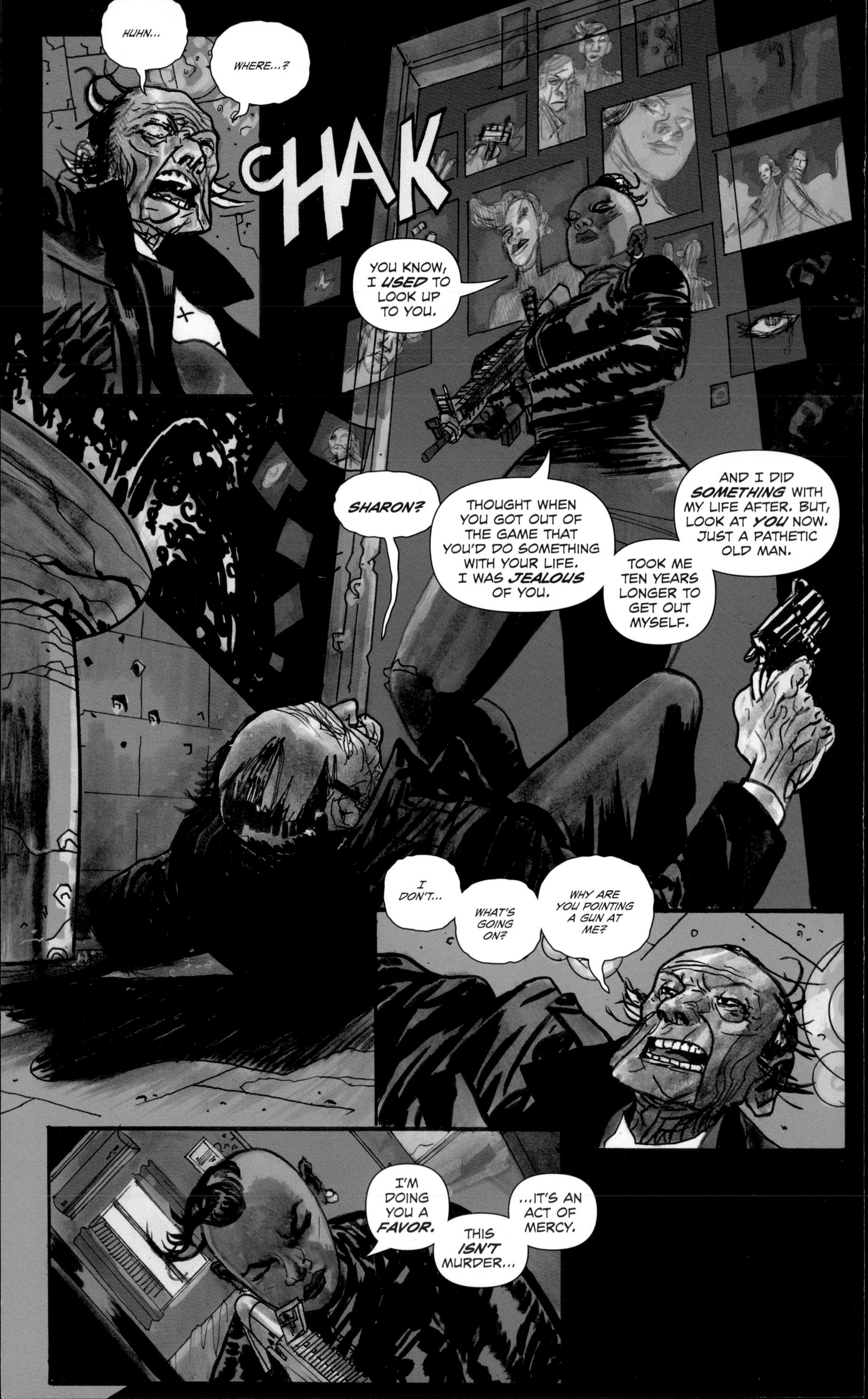
HUHN...
WHERE...?
CHAK
YOU KNOW, I USED TO LOOK UP TO YOU.
SHARON?
THOUGHT WHEN YOU GOT OUT OF THE GAME THAT YOU'D DO SOMETHING WITH YOUR LIFE. I WAS JEALOUS OF YOU.
TOOK ME TEN YEARS LONGER TO GET OUT MYSELF.
AND I DID SOMETHING WITH MY LIFE AFTER. BUT, LOOK AT YOU NOW. JUST A PATHETIC OLD MAN.
I DON'T...
WHAT'S GOING ON?
WHY ARE YOU POINTING A GUN AT ME?
I'M DOING YOU A FAVOR.
THIS ISN'T MURDER...
...IT'S AN ACT OF MERCY.

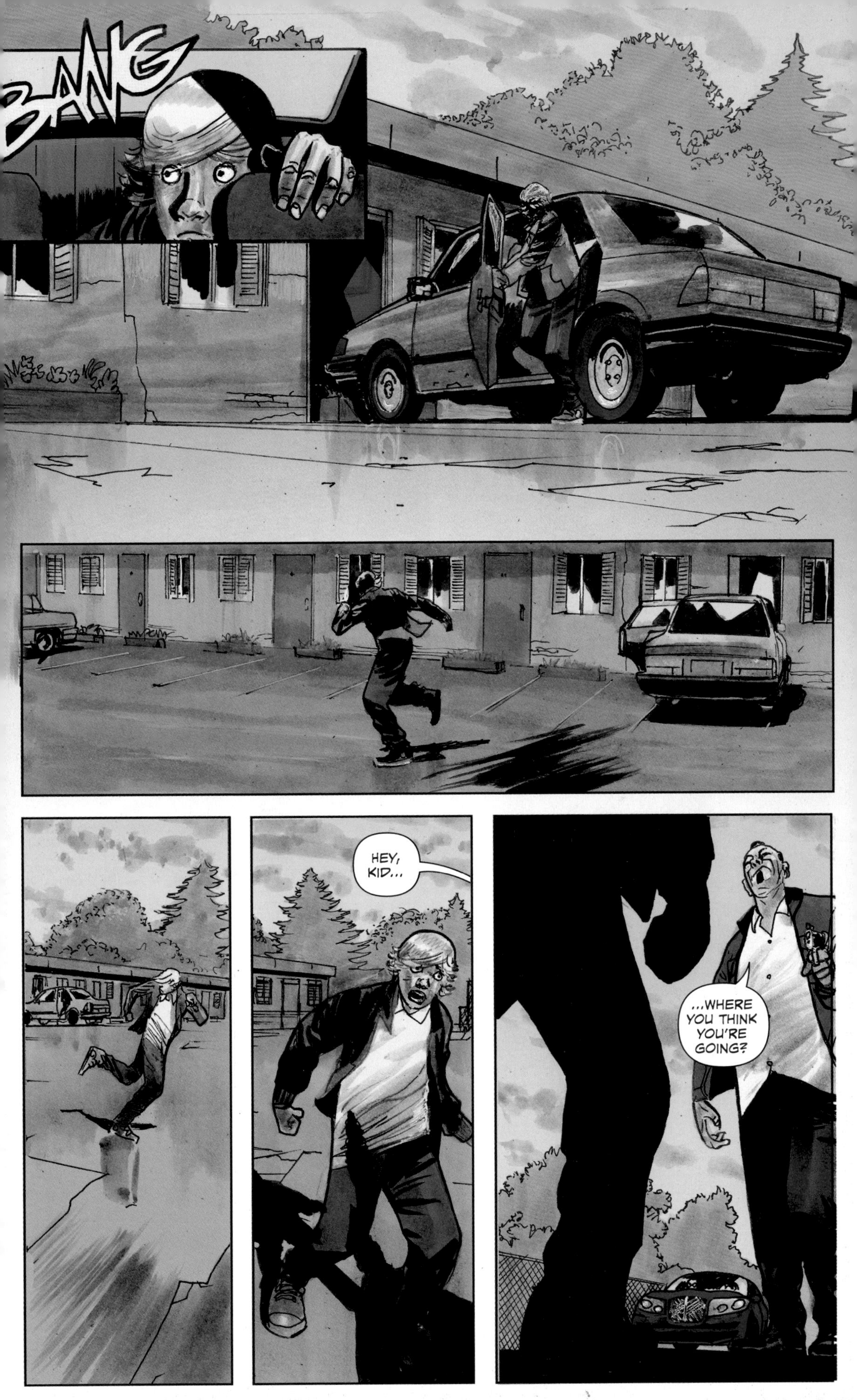
BANG
HEY, KID...
...WHERE YOU THINK YOU'RE GOING?

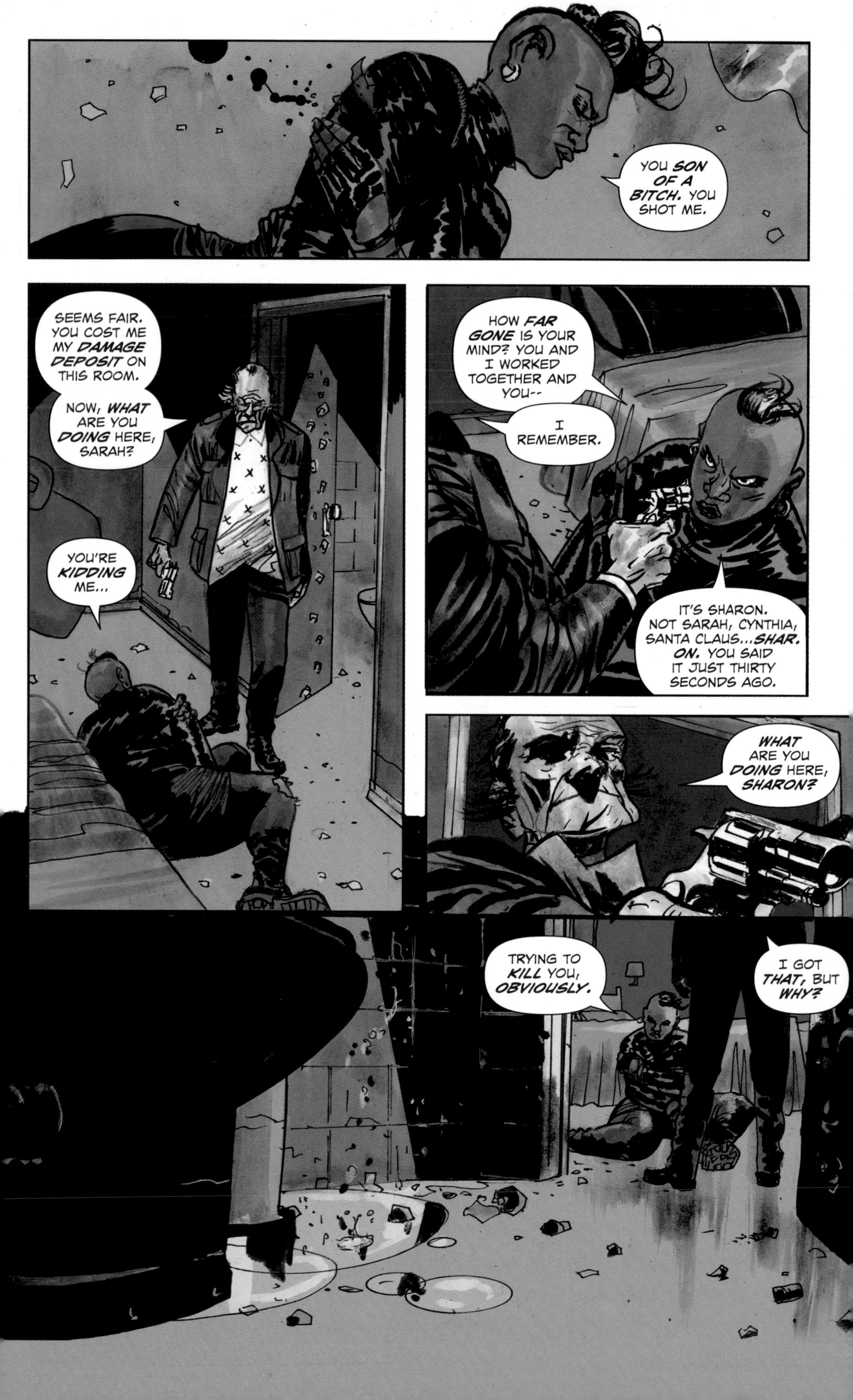
YOU SON OF A BITCH. YOU SHOT ME.
SEEMS FAIR. YOU COST ME MY DAMAGE DEPOSIT ON THIS ROOM.
NOW, WHAT ARE YOU DOING HERE, SARAH?
YOU'RE KIDDING ME...
HOW FAR GONE IS YOUR MIND? YOU AND I WORKED TOGETHER AND YOU--
I REMEMBER.
IT'S SHARON. NOT SARAH, CYNTHIA, SANTA CLAUS...SHAR. ON. YOU SAID IT JUST THIRTY SECONDS AGO.
WHAT ARE YOU DOING HERE, SHARON?
TRYING TO KILL YOU, OBVIOUSLY.
I GOT THAT, BUT WHY?

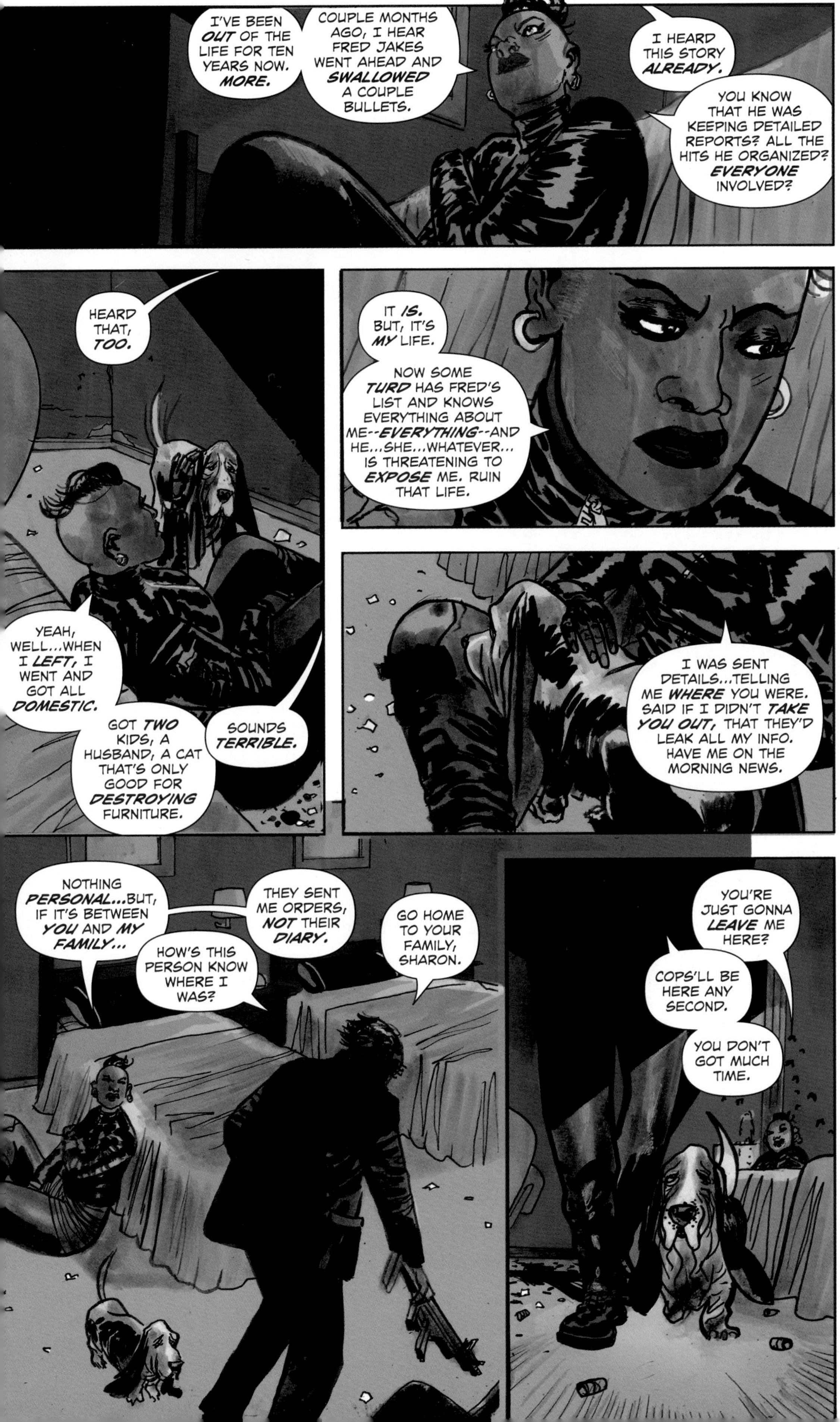
I'VE BEEN OUT OF THE LIFE FOR TEN YEARS NOW. MORE.
COUPLE MONTHS AGO, I HEAR FRED JAKES WENT AHEAD AND SWALLOWED A COUPLE BULLETS.
I HEARD THIS STORY ALREADY.
YOU KNOW THAT HE WAS KEEPING DETAILED REPORTS? ALL THE HITS HE ORGANIZED? EVERYONE INVOLVED?
HEARD THAT, TOO.
IT IS. BUT, IT'S MY LIFE.
NOW SOME TURD HAS FRED'S LIST AND KNOWS EVERYTHING ABOUT ME--EVERYTHING--AND HE...SHE...WHATEVER... IS THREATENING TO EXPOSE ME. RUIN THAT LIFE.
YEAH, WELL...WHEN I LEFT, I WENT AND GOT ALL DOMESTIC.
GOT TWO KIDS, A HUSBAND, A CAT THAT'S ONLY GOOD FOR DESTROYING FURNITURE.
SOUNDS TERRIBLE.
I WAS SENT DETAILS...TELLING ME WHERE YOU WERE. SAID IF I DIDN'T TAKE YOU OUT, THAT THEY'D LEAK ALL MY INFO. HAVE ME ON THE MORNING NEWS.
NOTHING PERSONAL...BUT, IF IT'S BETWEEN YOU AND MY FAMILY...
THEY SENT ME ORDERS, NOT THEIR DIARY.
HOW'S THIS PERSON KNOW WHERE I WAS?
GO HOME TO YOUR FAMILY, SHARON.
YOU'RE JUST GONNA LEAVE ME HERE?
COPS'LL BE HERE ANY SECOND.
YOU DON'T GOT MUCH TIME.

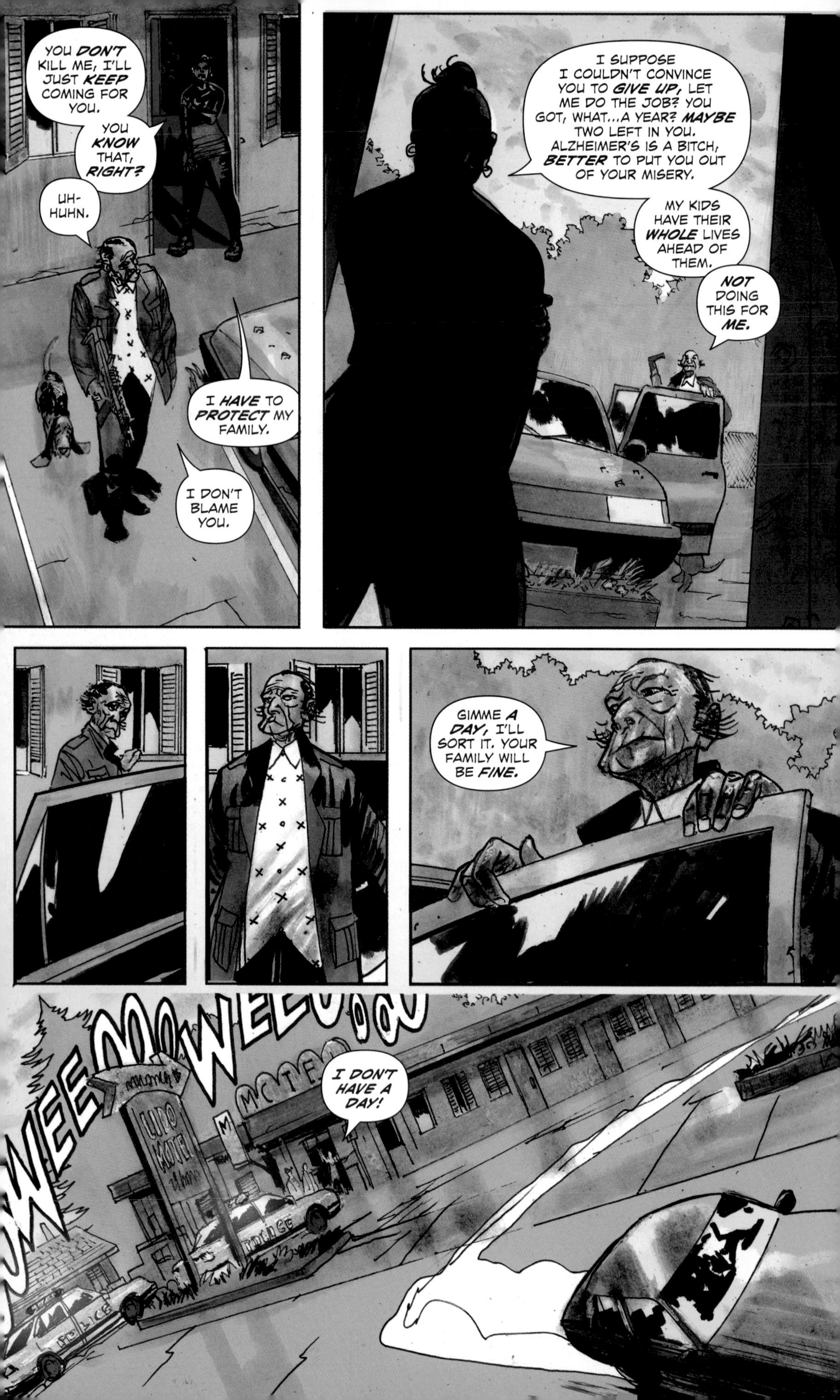
YOU DON'T KILL ME, I'LL JUST KEEP COMING FOR YOU.
YOU KNOW THAT, RIGHT?
UH-HUHN.
I HAVE TO PROTECT MY FAMILY.
I DON'T BLAME YOU.
I SUPPOSE I COULDN'T CONVINCE YOU TO GIVE UP, LET ME DO THE JOB? YOU GOT, WHAT...A YEAR? MAYBE TWO LEFT IN YOU. ALZHEIMER'S IS A BITCH, BETTER TO PUT YOU OUT OF YOUR MISERY.
MY KIDS HAVE THEIR WHOLE LIVES AHEAD OF THEM.
NOT DOING THIS FOR ME.
GIMME A DAY, I'LL SORT IT. YOUR FAMILY WILL BE FINE.
WEEOOWEEOOOO
I DON'T HAVE A DAY!

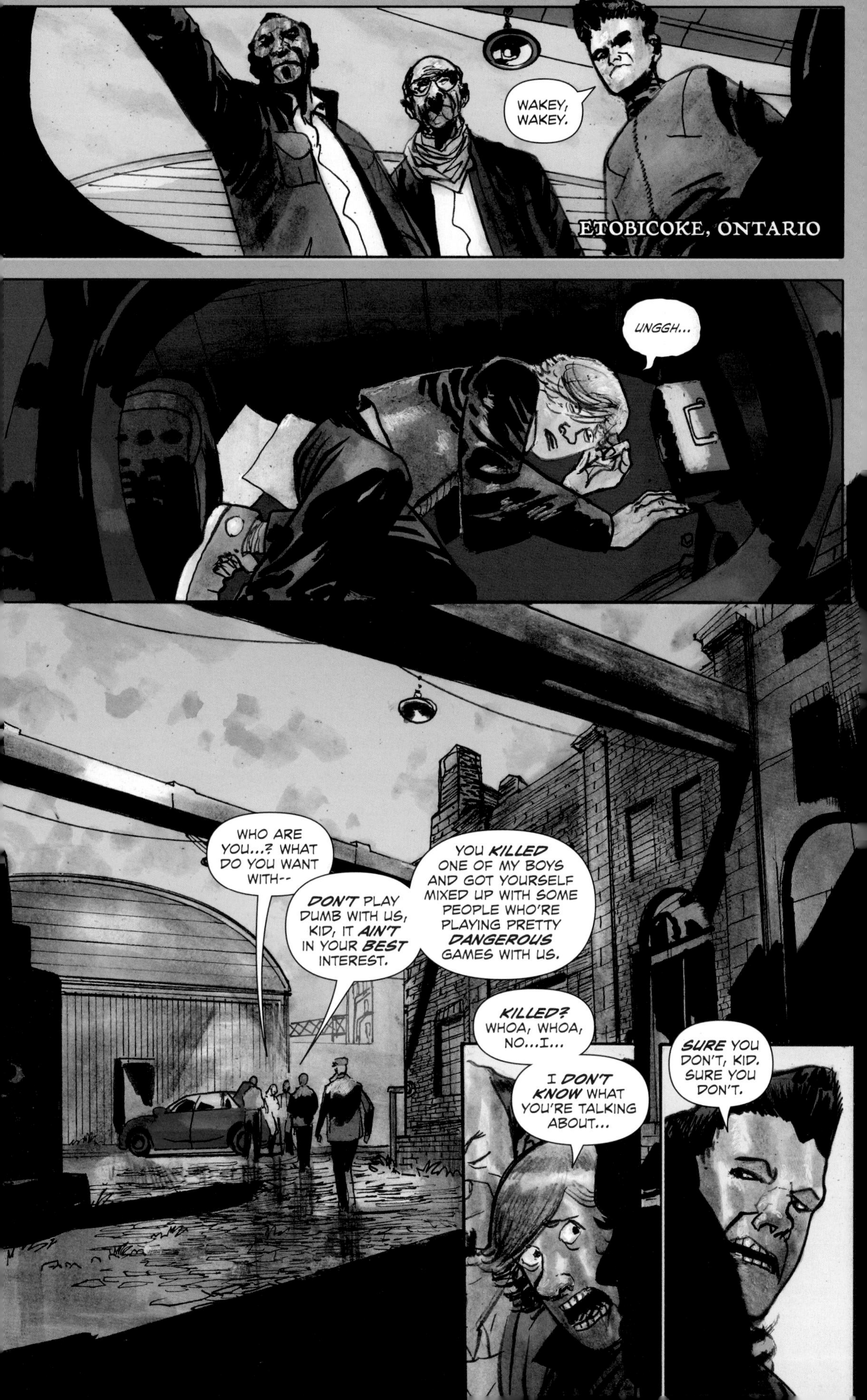
WAKEY, WAKEY.
ETOBICOKE, ONTARIO
UNGGH...
WHO ARE YOU...? WHAT DO YOU WANT WITH--
DON'T PLAY DUMB WITH US, KID, IT AIN'T IN YOUR BEST INTEREST.
YOU KILLED ONE OF MY BOYS AND GOT YOURSELF MIXED UP WITH SOME PEOPLE WHO'RE PLAYING PRETTY DANGEROUS GAMES WITH US.
KILLED? WHOA, WHOA, NO...I...
I DON'T KNOW WHAT YOU'RE TALKING ABOUT...
SURE YOU DON'T, KID. SURE YOU DON'T.

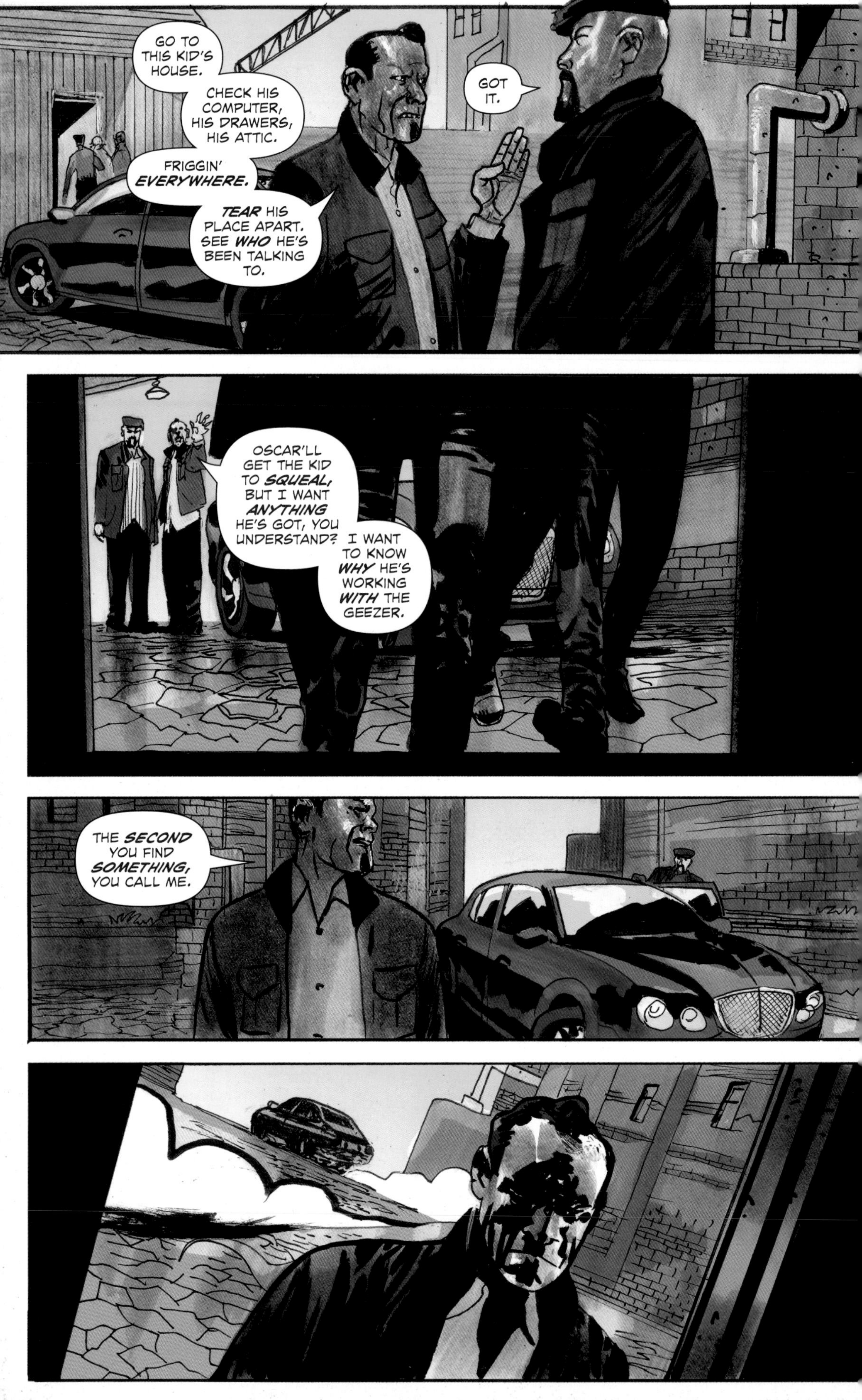
GO TO THIS KID'S HOUSE.
CHECK HIS COMPUTER, HIS DRAWERS, HIS ATTIC.
FRIGGIN' EVERYWHERE.
TEAR HIS PLACE APART. SEE WHO HE'S BEEN TALKING TO.
GOT IT.
OSCAR'LL GET THE KID TO SQUEAL, BUT I WANT ANYTHING HE'S GOT, YOU UNDERSTAND?
I WANT TO KNOW WHY HE'S WORKING WITH THE GEEZER.
THE SECOND YOU FIND SOMETHING, YOU CALL ME.

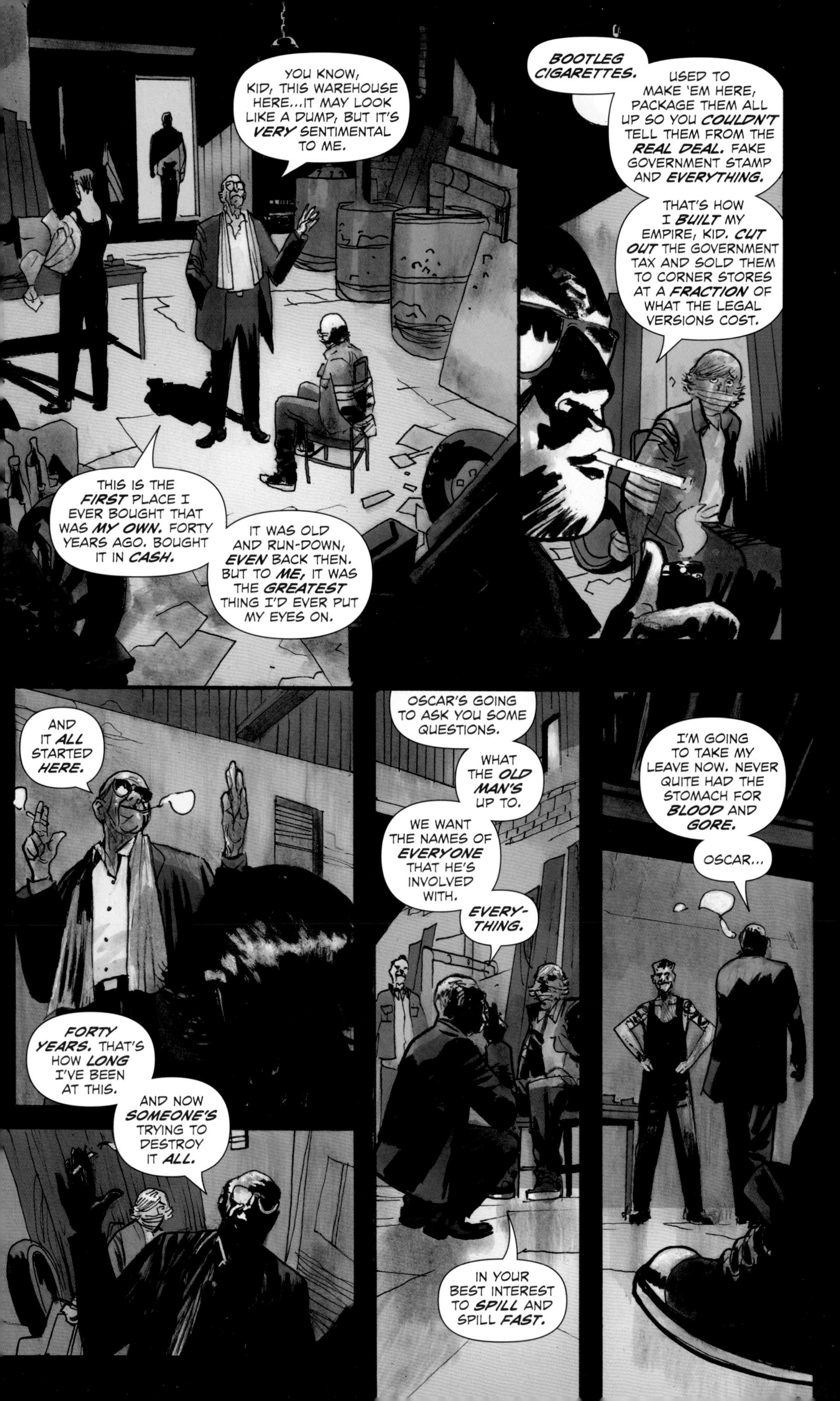
YOU KNOW, KID, THIS WAREHOUSE HERE...IT MAY LOOK LIKE A DUMP, BUT IT'S VERY SENTIMENTAL TO ME.
THIS IS THE FIRST PLACE I EVER BOUGHT THAT WAS MY OWN. FORTY YEARS AGO. BOUGHT IT IN CASH.
IT WAS OLD AND RUN-DOWN, EVEN BACK THEN. BUT TO ME, IT WAS THE GREATEST THING I'D EVER PUT MY EYES ON.
BOOTLEG CIGARETTES.
USED TO MAKE 'EM HERE, PACKAGE THEM ALL UP SO YOU COULDN'T TELL THEM FROM THE REAL DEAL. FAKE GOVERNMENT STAMP AND EVERYTHING.
THAT'S HOW I BUILT MY EMPIRE, KID. CUT OUT THE GOVERNMENT TAX AND SOLD THEM TO CORNER STORES AT A FRACTION OF WHAT THE LEGAL VERSIONS COST.
AND IT ALL STARTED HERE.
FORTY YEARS. THAT'S HOW LONG I'VE BEEN AT THIS.
AND NOW SOMEONE'S TRYING TO DESTROY IT ALL.
OSCAR'S GOING TO ASK YOU SOME QUESTIONS.
WHAT THE OLD MAN'S UP TO.
WE WANT THE NAMES OF EVERYONE THAT HE'S INVOLVED WITH.
EVERY-THING.
IN YOUR BEST INTEREST TO SPILL AND SPILL FAST.
I'M GOING TO TAKE MY LEAVE NOW. NEVER QUITE HAD THE STOMACH FOR BLOOD AND GORE.
OSCAR...

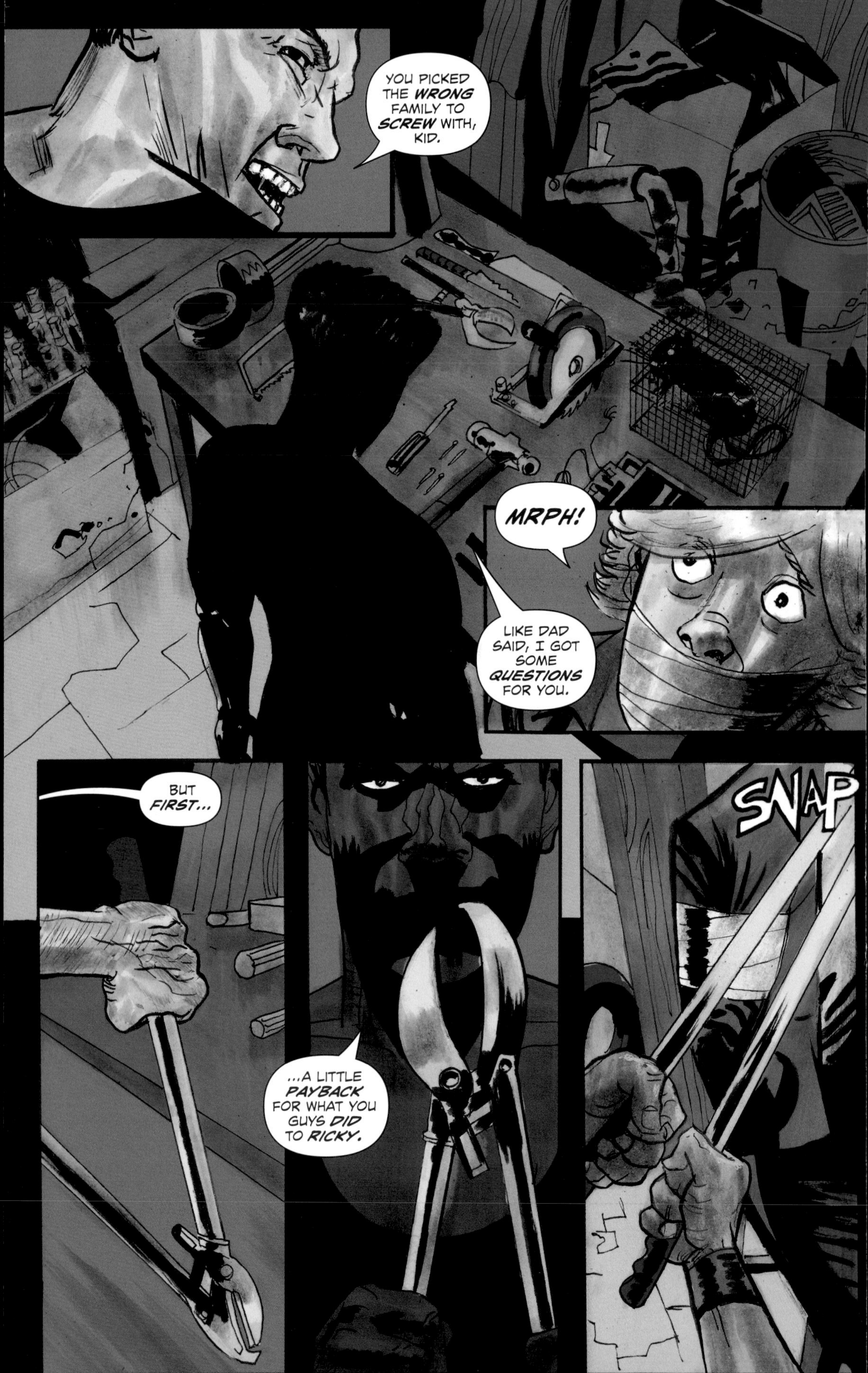
YOU PICKED THE WRONG FAMILY TO SCREW WITH, KID.
MRPH!
LIKE DAD SAID, I GOT SOME QUESTIONS FOR YOU.
BUT FIRST...
...A LITTLE PAYBACK FOR WHAT YOU GUYS DID TO RICKY.
SNAP

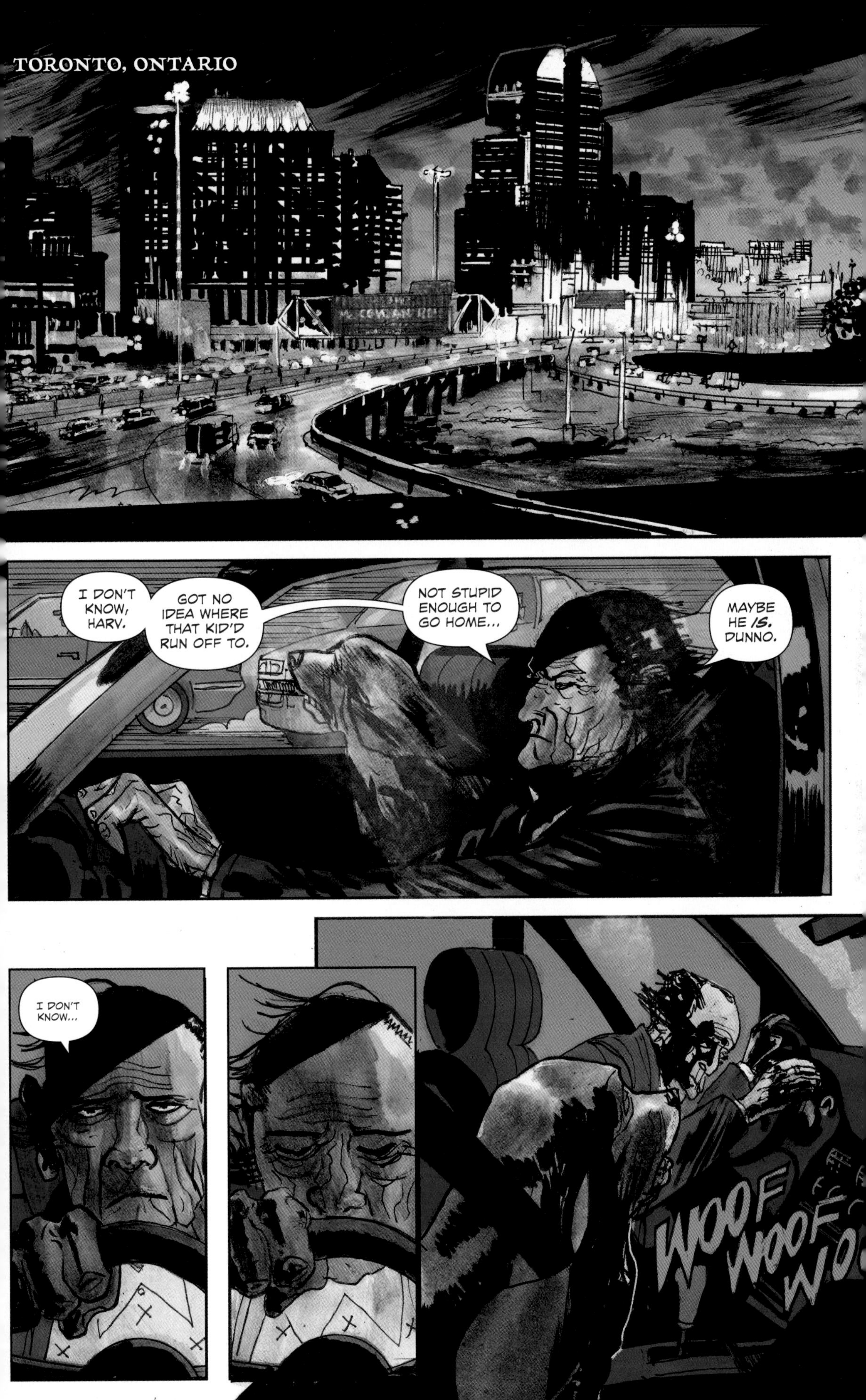
TORONTO, ONTARIO
I DON'T KNOW, HARV.
GOT NO IDEA WHERE THAT KID'D RUN OFF TO.
NOT STUPID ENOUGH TO GO HOME...
MAYBE HE *IS.* DUNNO.
I DON'T KNOW...
WOOF WOOF WO

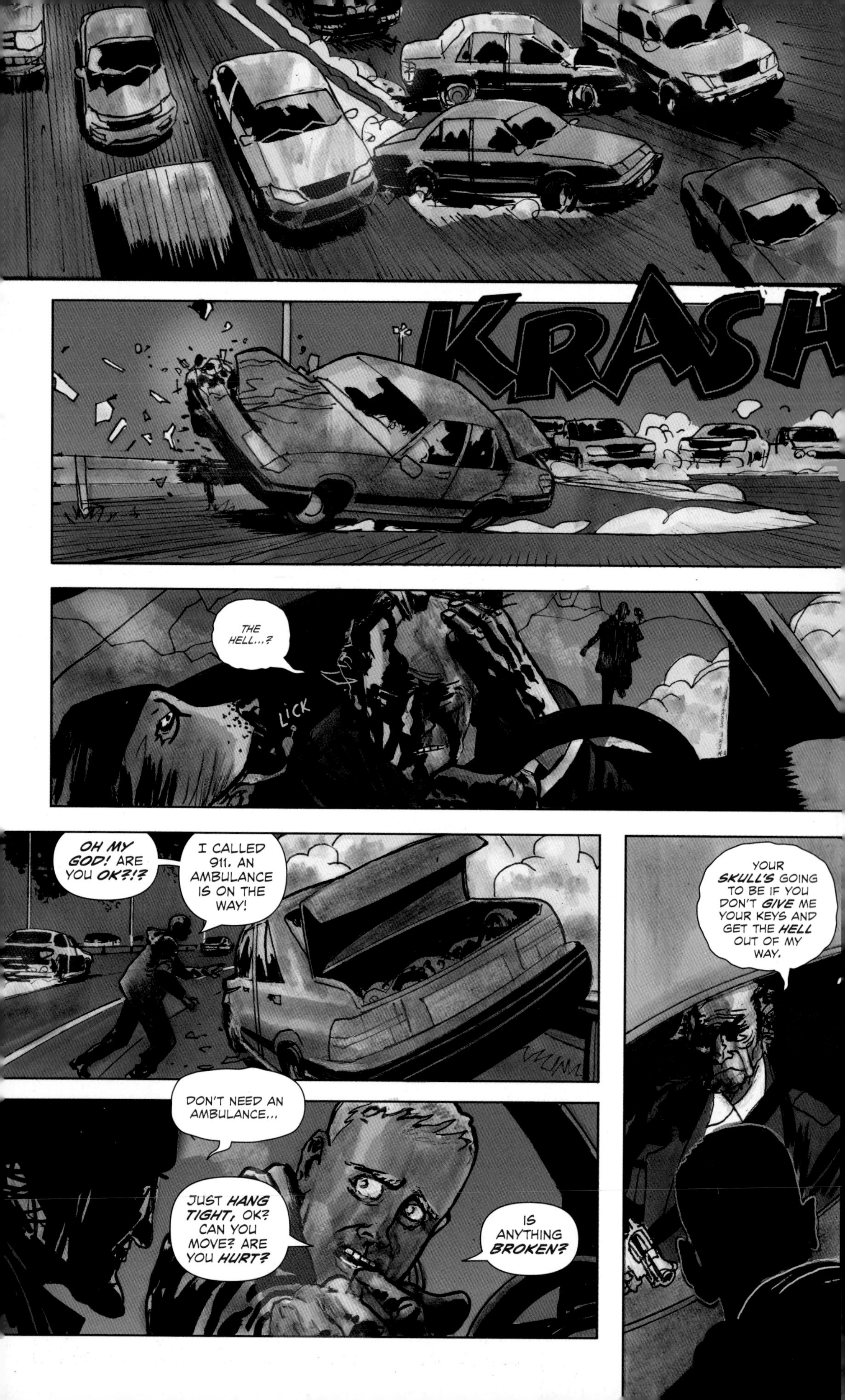
KRASH
THE HELL...?
OH MY GOD! ARE YOU OK?!?
I CALLED 911. AN AMBULANCE IS ON THE WAY!
DON'T NEED AN AMBULANCE...
JUST HANG TIGHT, OK? CAN YOU MOVE? ARE YOU HURT?
IS ANYTHING BROKEN?
YOUR SKULL'S GOING TO BE IF YOU DON'T GIVE ME YOUR KEYS AND GET THE HELL OUT OF MY WAY.

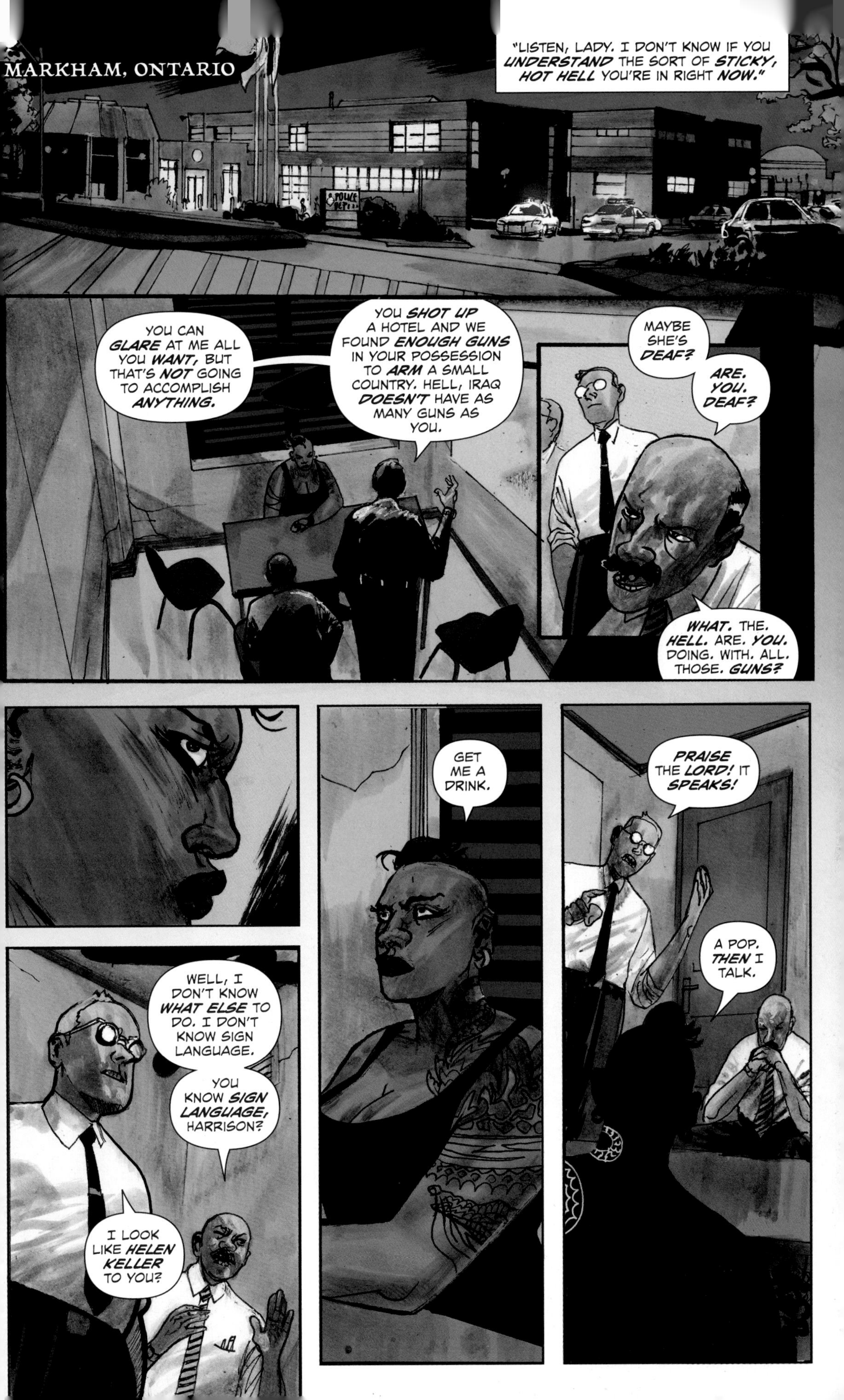
MARKHAM, ONTARIO
"LISTEN, LADY. I DON'T KNOW IF YOU UNDERSTAND THE SORT OF STICKY, HOT HELL YOU'RE IN RIGHT NOW."
YOU CAN GLARE AT ME ALL YOU WANT, BUT THAT'S NOT GOING TO ACCOMPLISH ANYTHING.
YOU SHOT UP A HOTEL AND WE FOUND ENOUGH GUNS IN YOUR POSSESSION TO ARM A SMALL COUNTRY. HELL, IRAQ DOESN'T HAVE AS MANY GUNS AS YOU.
MAYBE SHE'S DEAF?
ARE. YOU. DEAF?
WHAT. THE. HELL. ARE. YOU. DOING. WITH. ALL. THOSE. GUNS?
WELL, I DON'T KNOW WHAT ELSE TO DO. I DON'T KNOW SIGN LANGUAGE.
YOU KNOW SIGN LANGUAGE, HARRISON?
I LOOK LIKE HELEN KELLER TO YOU?
GET ME A DRINK.
PRAISE THE LORD! IT SPEAKS!
A POP. THEN I TALK.

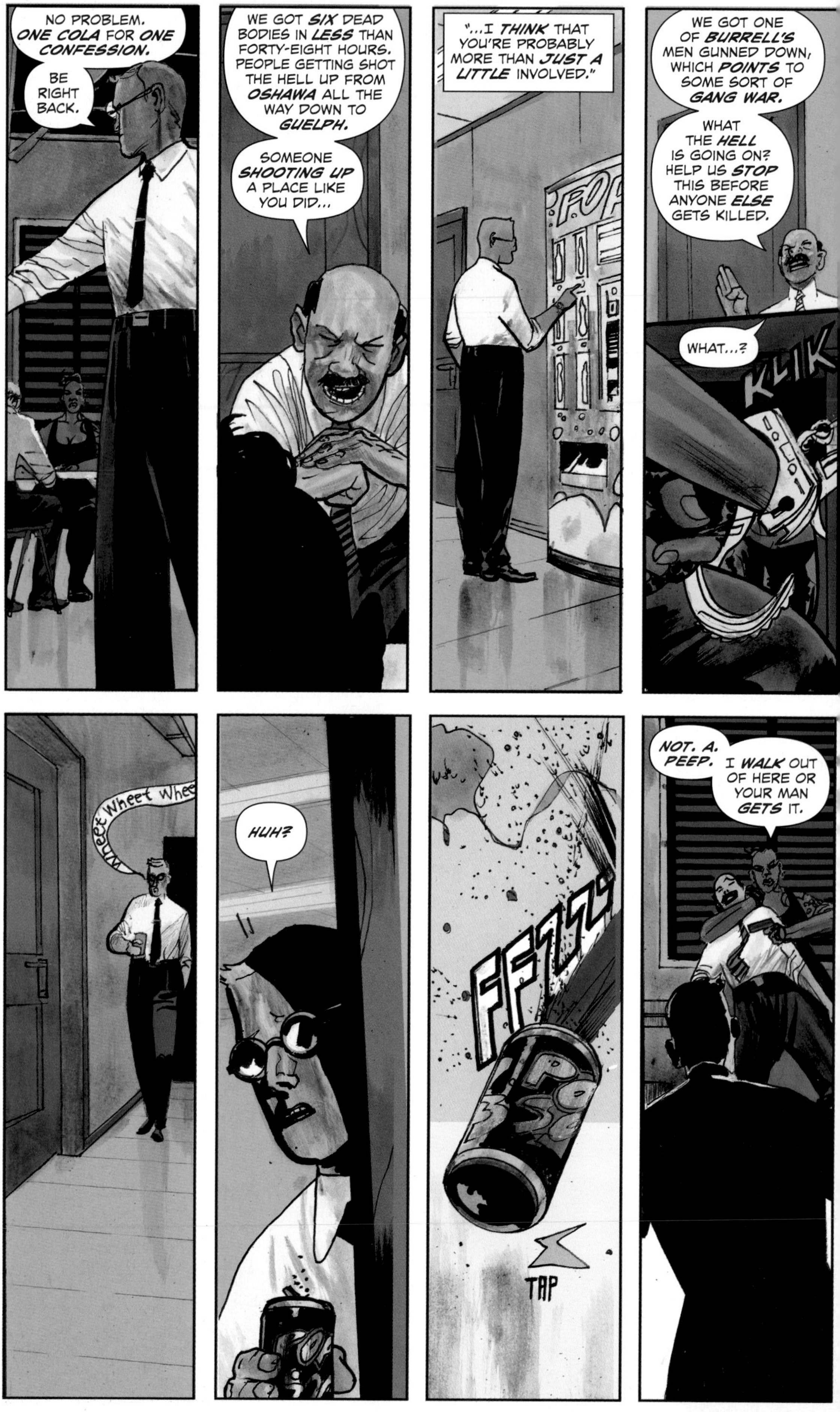
NO PROBLEM. ONE COLA FOR ONE CONFESSION.
BE RIGHT BACK.
WE GOT SIX DEAD BODIES IN LESS THAN FORTY-EIGHT HOURS. PEOPLE GETTING SHOT THE HELL UP FROM OSHAWA ALL THE WAY DOWN TO GUELPH.
SOMEONE SHOOTING UP A PLACE LIKE YOU DID...
"...I THINK THAT YOU'RE PROBABLY MORE THAN JUST A LITTLE INVOLVED."
WE GOT ONE OF BURRELL'S MEN GUNNED DOWN, WHICH POINTS TO SOME SORT OF GANG WAR.
WHAT THE HELL IS GOING ON? HELP US STOP THIS BEFORE ANYONE ELSE GETS KILLED.
WHAT...?
KLIK
Wheet Wheet Whee
HUH?
FFZZZ
TAP
NOT. A. PEEP.
I WALK OUT OF HERE OR YOUR MAN GETS IT.

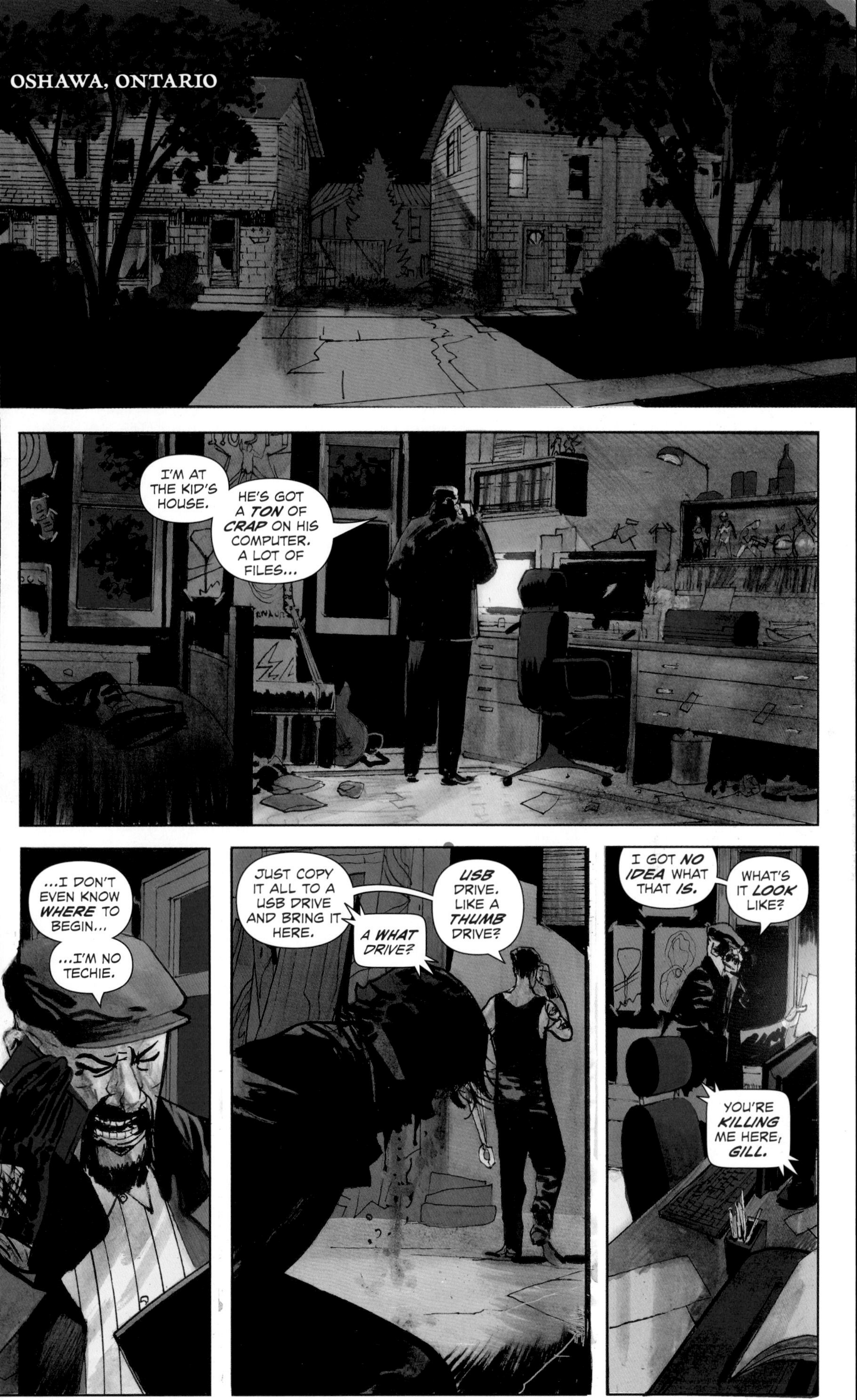

OSHAWA, ONTARIO
I'M AT THE KID'S HOUSE.
HE'S GOT A TON OF CRAP ON HIS COMPUTER. A LOT OF FILES...
...I DON'T EVEN KNOW WHERE TO BEGIN...
...I'M NO TECHIE.
JUST COPY IT ALL TO A USB DRIVE AND BRING IT HERE.
A WHAT DRIVE?
USB DRIVE. LIKE A THUMB DRIVE?
I GOT NO IDEA WHAT THAT IS.
WHAT'S IT LOOK LIKE?
YOU'RE KILLING ME HERE, GILL.

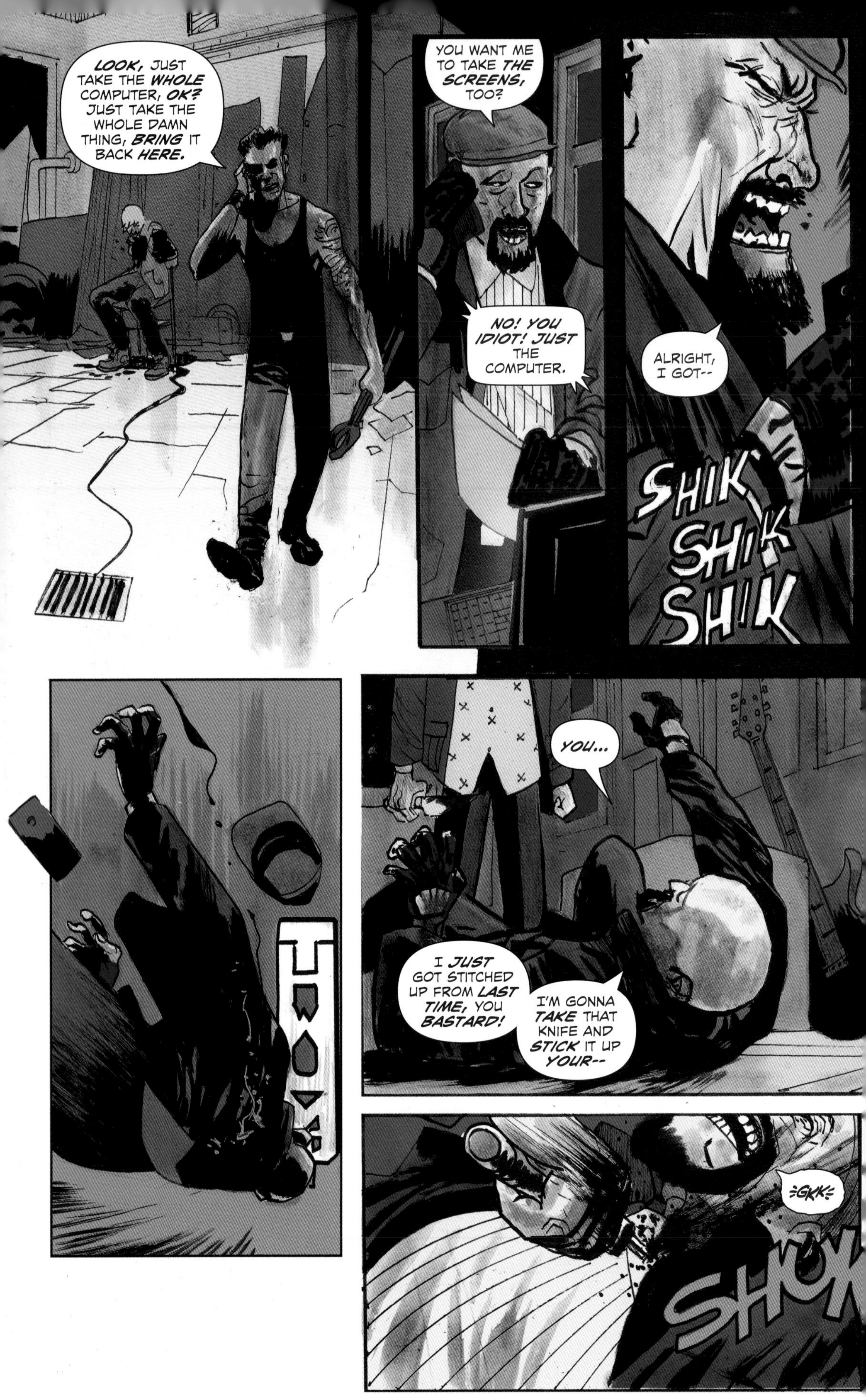
LOOK, JUST TAKE THE WHOLE COMPUTER, OK? JUST TAKE THE WHOLE DAMN THING, BRING IT BACK HERE.
YOU WANT ME TO TAKE THE SCREENS, TOO?
NO! YOU IDIOT! JUST THE COMPUTER.
ALRIGHT, I GOT--
SHIK SHIK SHIK
YOU...
I JUST GOT STITCHED UP FROM LAST TIME, YOU BASTARD!
I'M GONNA TAKE THAT KNIFE AND STICK IT UP YOUR--
GKK

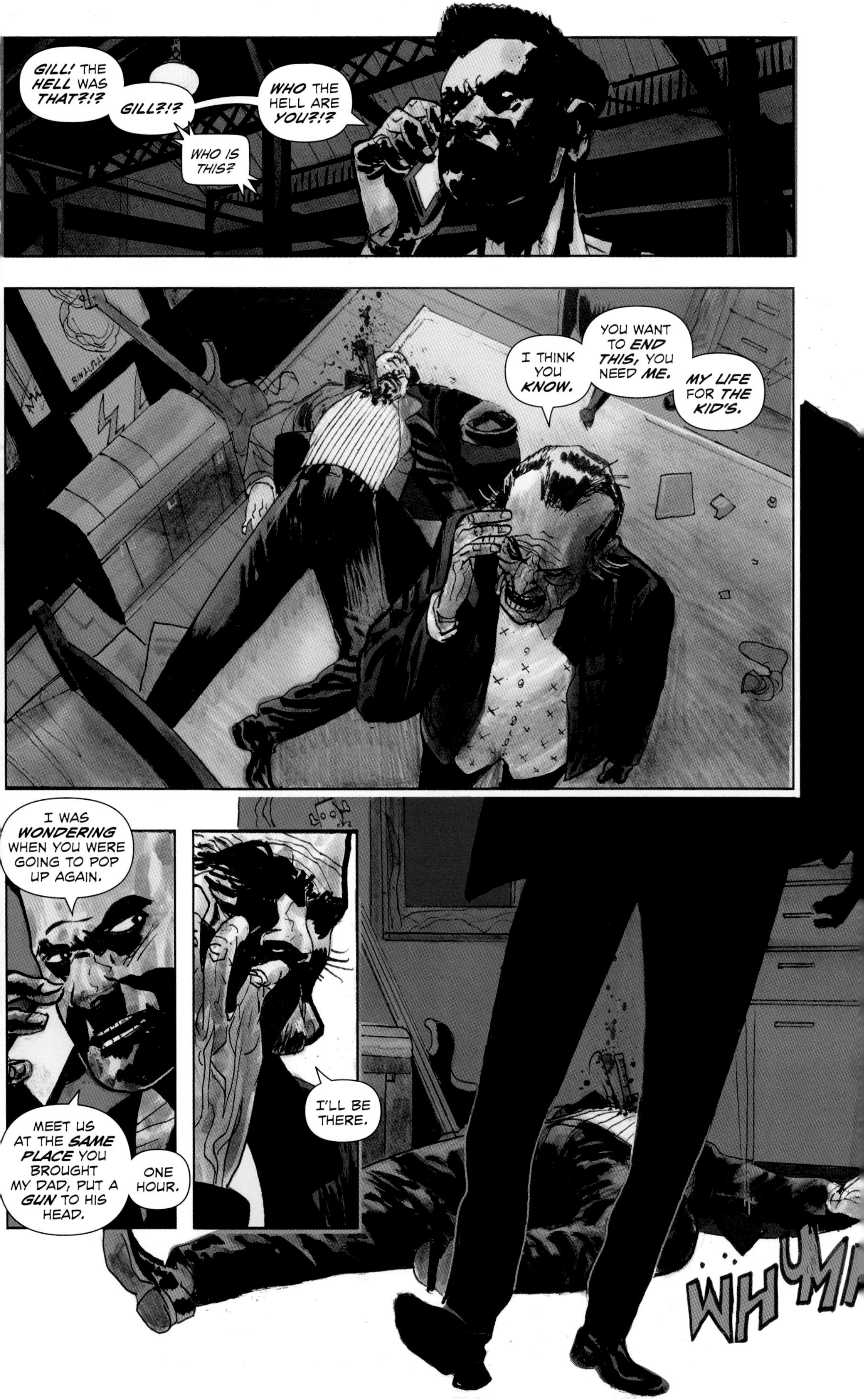
GILL! THE HELL WAS THAT?!?
GILL?!?
WHO IS THIS?
WHO THE HELL ARE YOU?!?
I THINK YOU KNOW.
YOU WANT TO END THIS, YOU NEED ME.
MY LIFE FOR THE KID'S.
I WAS WONDERING WHEN YOU WERE GOING TO POP UP AGAIN.
MEET US AT THE SAME PLACE YOU BROUGHT MY DAD, PUT A GUN TO HIS HEAD.
ONE HOUR.
I'LL BE THERE.
WHUM

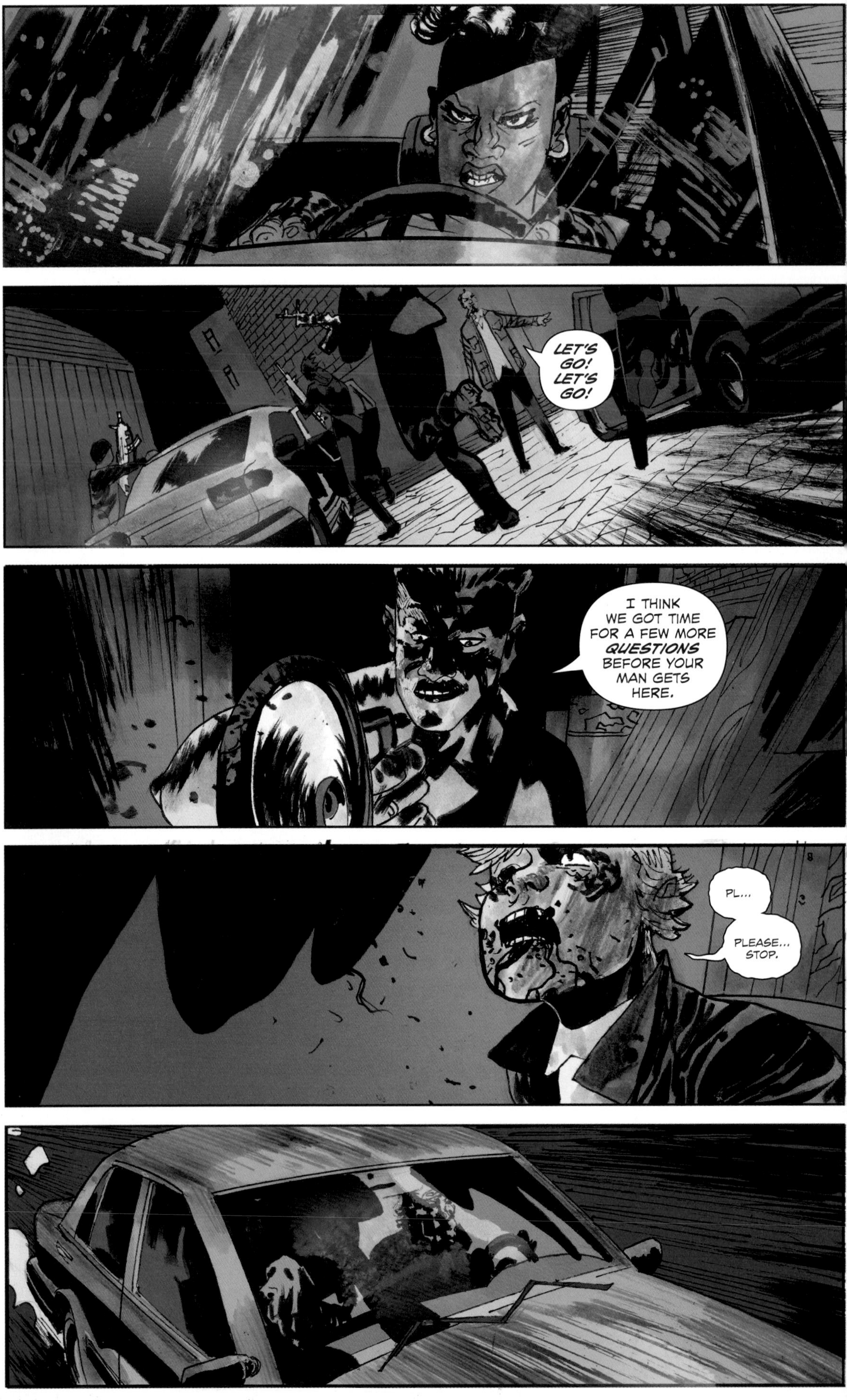
LET'S GO! LET'S GO!
I THINK WE GOT TIME FOR A FEW MORE *QUESTIONS* BEFORE YOUR MAN GETS HERE.
PL...
PLEASE... STOP.

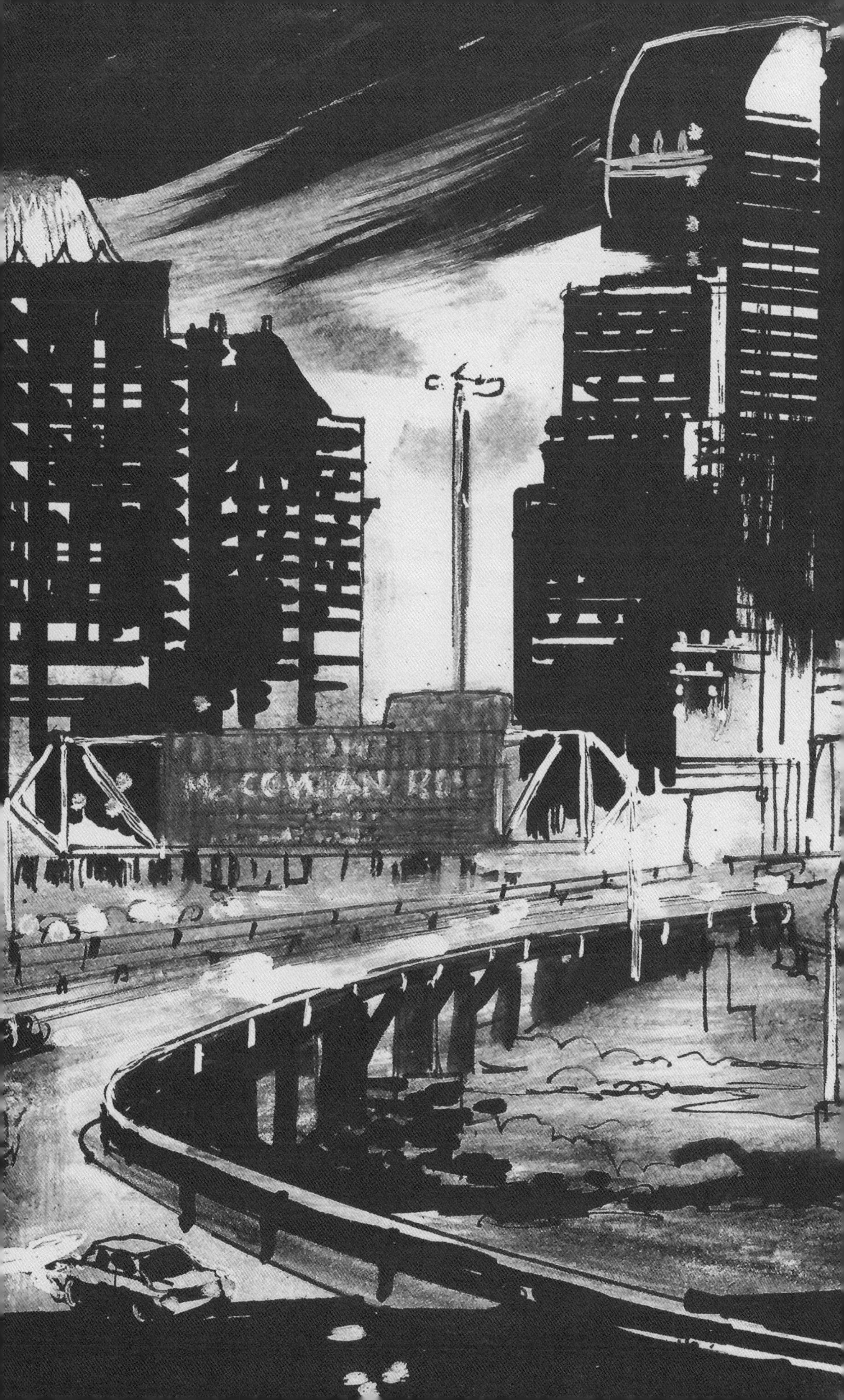

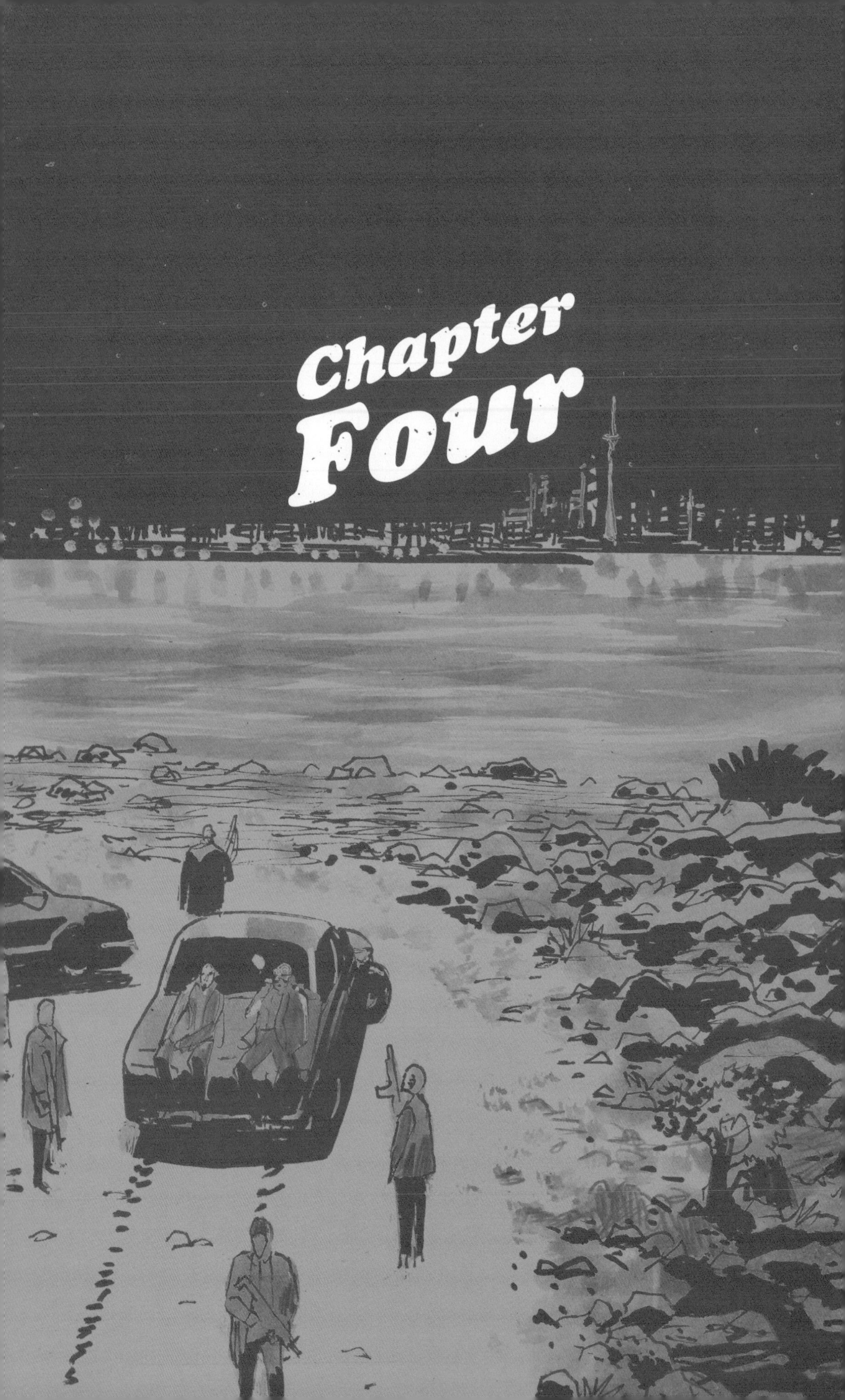
Chapter
Four

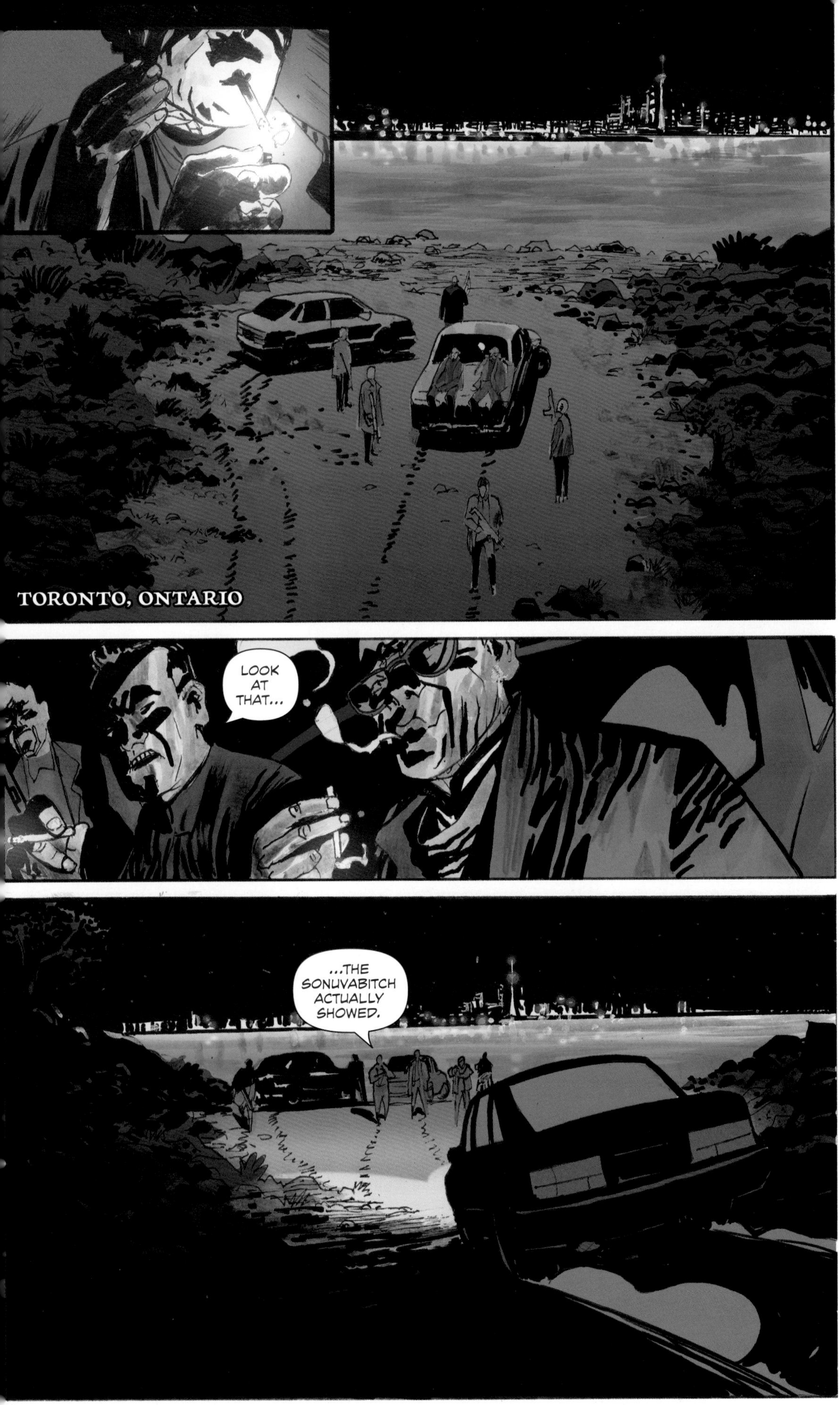
TORONTO, ONTARIO
LOOK AT THAT...
...THE SONUVABITCH ACTUALLY SHOWED.

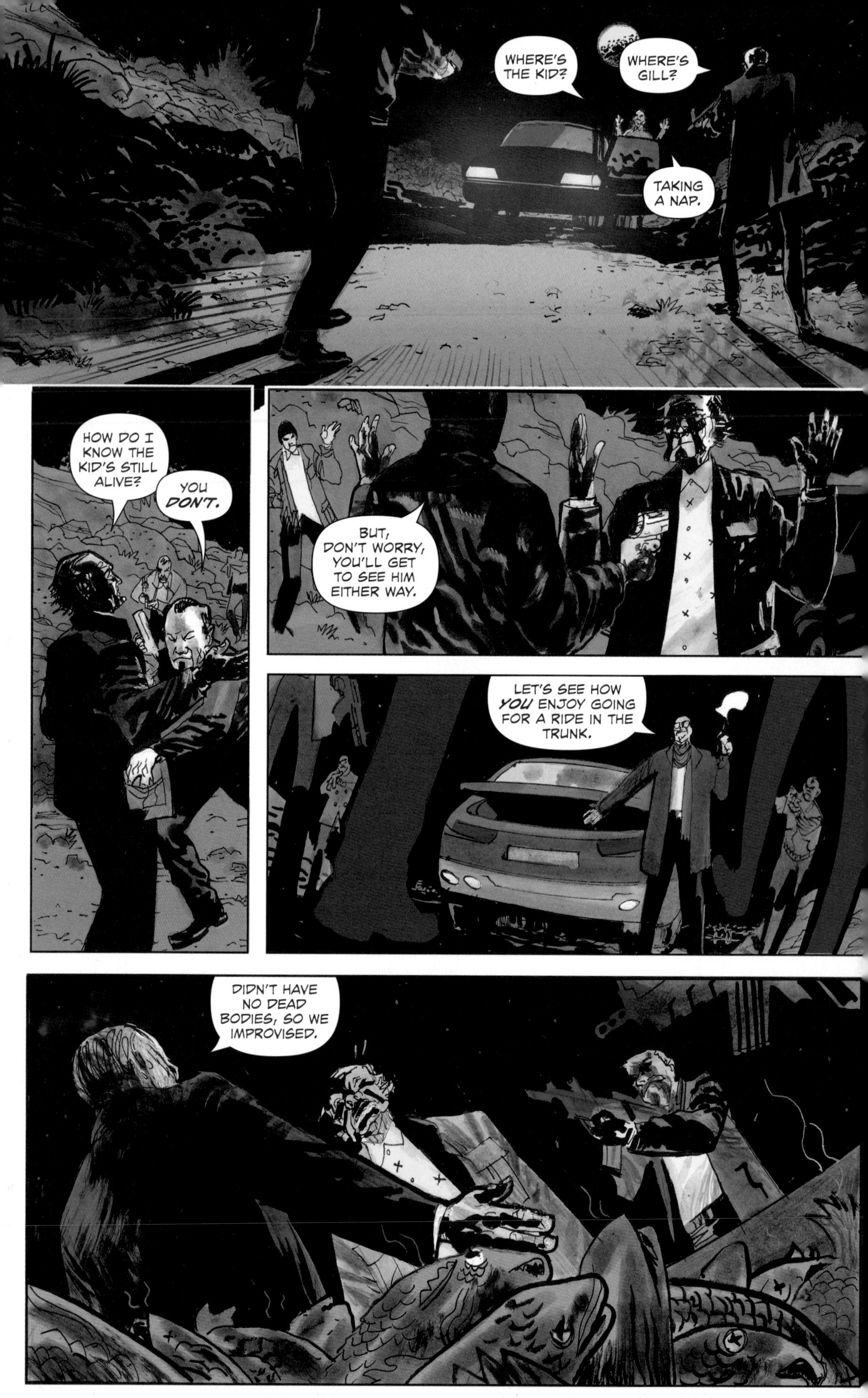
WHERE'S THE KID?
WHERE'S GILL?
TAKING A NAP.
HOW DO I KNOW THE KID'S STILL ALIVE?
YOU *DON'T.*
BUT, DON'T WORRY, YOU'LL GET TO SEE HIM EITHER WAY.
LET'S SEE HOW *YOU* ENJOY GOING FOR A RIDE IN THE TRUNK.
DIDN'T HAVE NO DEAD BODIES, SO WE IMPROVISED.

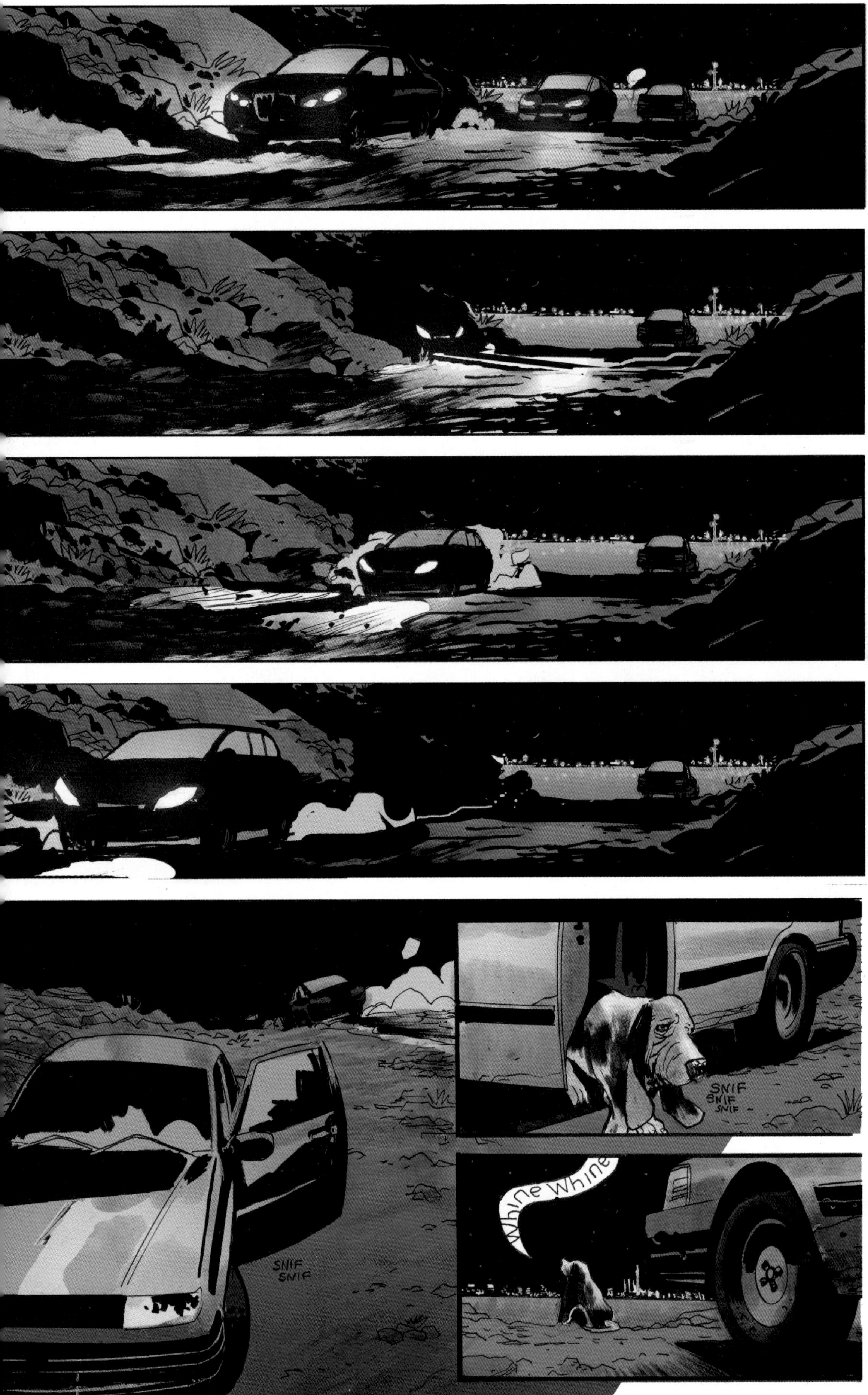
SNIF
SNIF
SNIF
SNIF
SNIF
Whine Whine

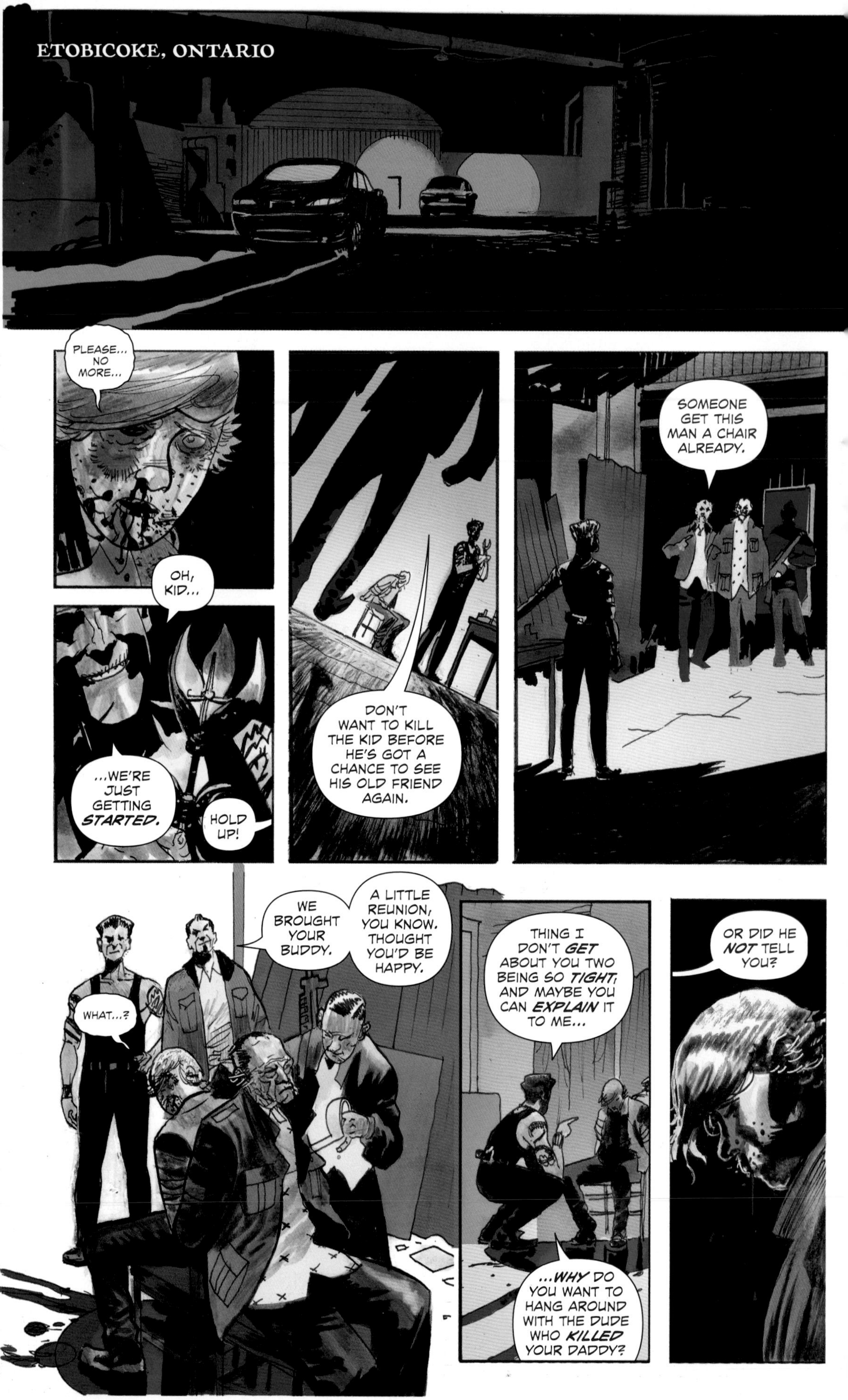

ETOBICOKE, ONTARIO
PLEASE... NO MORE...
OH, KID...
...WE'RE JUST GETTING *STARTED.*
HOLD UP!
DON'T WANT TO KILL THE KID BEFORE HE'S GOT A CHANCE TO SEE HIS OLD FRIEND AGAIN.
SOMEONE GET THIS MAN A CHAIR ALREADY.
WE BROUGHT YOUR BUDDY.
A LITTLE REUNION, YOU KNOW. THOUGHT YOU'D BE HAPPY.
WHAT...?
THING I DON'T *GET* ABOUT YOU TWO BEING SO *TIGHT,* AND MAYBE YOU CAN *EXPLAIN* IT TO ME...
...*WHY* DO YOU WANT TO HANG AROUND WITH THE DUDE WHO *KILLED* YOUR DADDY?
OR DID HE *NOT* TELL YOU?

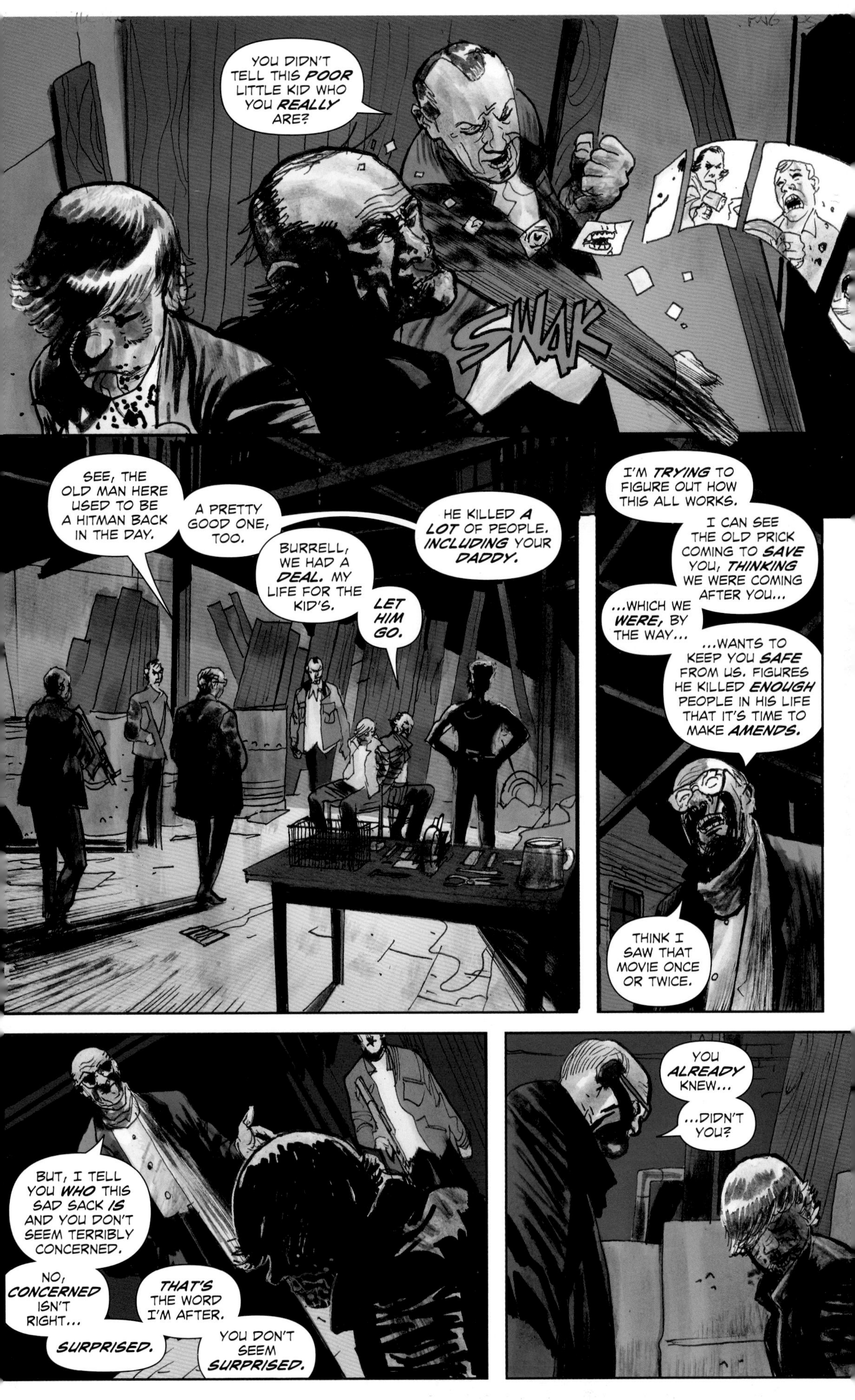
YOU DIDN'T TELL THIS POOR LITTLE KID WHO YOU REALLY ARE?
SWAK
SEE, THE OLD MAN HERE USED TO BE A HITMAN BACK IN THE DAY.
A PRETTY GOOD ONE, TOO.
HE KILLED A LOT OF PEOPLE. INCLUDING YOUR DADDY.
BURRELL, WE HAD A DEAL. MY LIFE FOR THE KID'S.
LET HIM GO.
I'M TRYING TO FIGURE OUT HOW THIS ALL WORKS.
I CAN SEE THE OLD PRICK COMING TO SAVE YOU, THINKING WE WERE COMING AFTER YOU...
...WHICH WE WERE, BY THE WAY...
...WANTS TO KEEP YOU SAFE FROM US. FIGURES HE KILLED ENOUGH PEOPLE IN HIS LIFE THAT IT'S TIME TO MAKE AMENDS.
THINK I SAW THAT MOVIE ONCE OR TWICE.
BUT, I TELL YOU WHO THIS SAD SACK IS AND YOU DON'T SEEM TERRIBLY CONCERNED.
NO, CONCERNED ISN'T RIGHT...
SURPRISED.
THAT'S THE WORD I'M AFTER.
YOU DON'T SEEM SURPRISED.
YOU ALREADY KNEW...
...DIDN'T YOU?

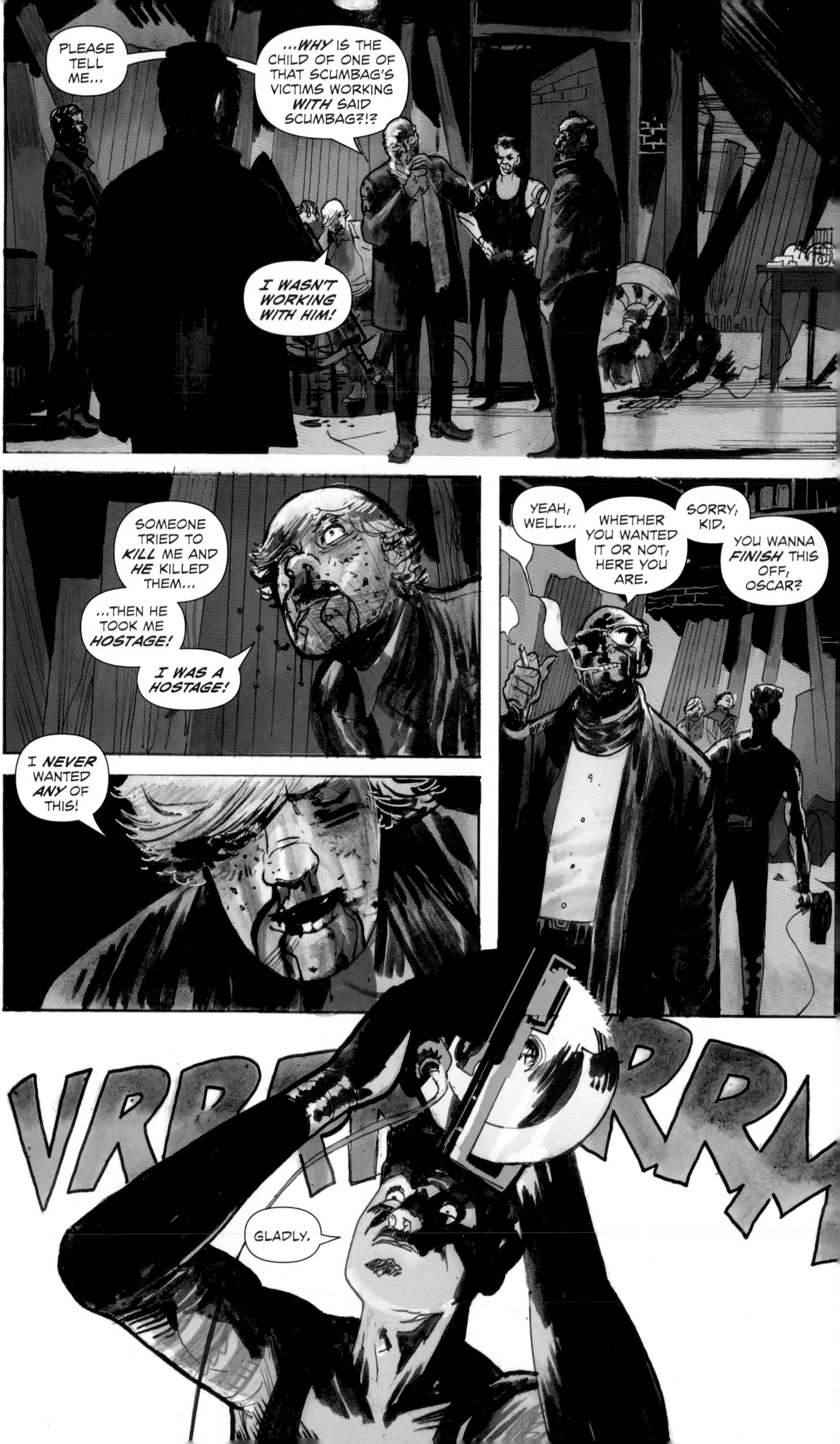
PLEASE TELL ME...
...WHY IS THE CHILD OF ONE OF THAT SCUMBAG'S VICTIMS WORKING WITH SAID SCUMBAG?!?
I WASN'T WORKING WITH HIM!
SOMEONE TRIED TO KILL ME AND HE KILLED THEM...
...THEN HE TOOK ME HOSTAGE!
I WAS A HOSTAGE!
I NEVER WANTED ANY OF THIS!
YEAH, WELL...
WHETHER YOU WANTED IT OR NOT, HERE YOU ARE.
SORRY, KID.
YOU WANNA FINISH THIS OFF, OSCAR?
GLADLY.

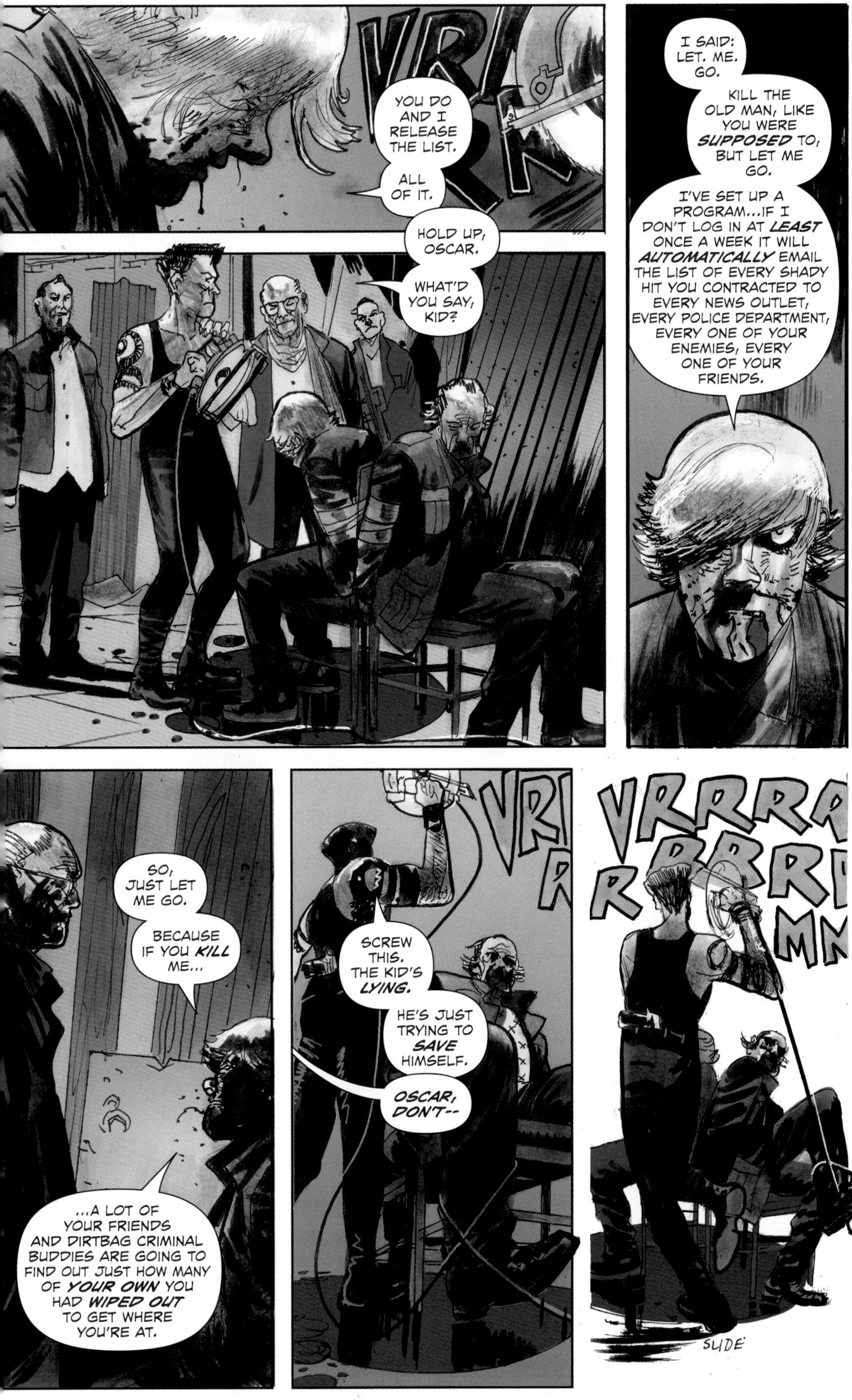
VRRR
YOU DO AND I RELEASE THE LIST.
ALL OF IT.
HOLD UP, OSCAR.
WHAT'D YOU SAY, KID?
I SAID: LET. ME. GO.
KILL THE OLD MAN, LIKE YOU WERE SUPPOSED TO, BUT LET ME GO.
I'VE SET UP A PROGRAM...IF I DON'T LOG IN AT LEAST ONCE A WEEK IT WILL AUTOMATICALLY EMAIL THE LIST OF EVERY SHADY HIT YOU CONTRACTED TO EVERY NEWS OUTLET, EVERY POLICE DEPARTMENT, EVERY ONE OF YOUR ENEMIES, EVERY ONE OF YOUR FRIENDS.
SO, JUST LET ME GO.
BECAUSE IF YOU KILL ME...
...A LOT OF YOUR FRIENDS AND DIRTBAG CRIMINAL BUDDIES ARE GOING TO FIND OUT JUST HOW MANY OF YOUR OWN YOU HAD WIPED OUT TO GET WHERE YOU'RE AT.
VRR
SCREW THIS. THE KID'S LYING.
HE'S JUST TRYING TO SAVE HIMSELF.
OSCAR, DON'T--
VRRRA RRRRR MM
SLIDE

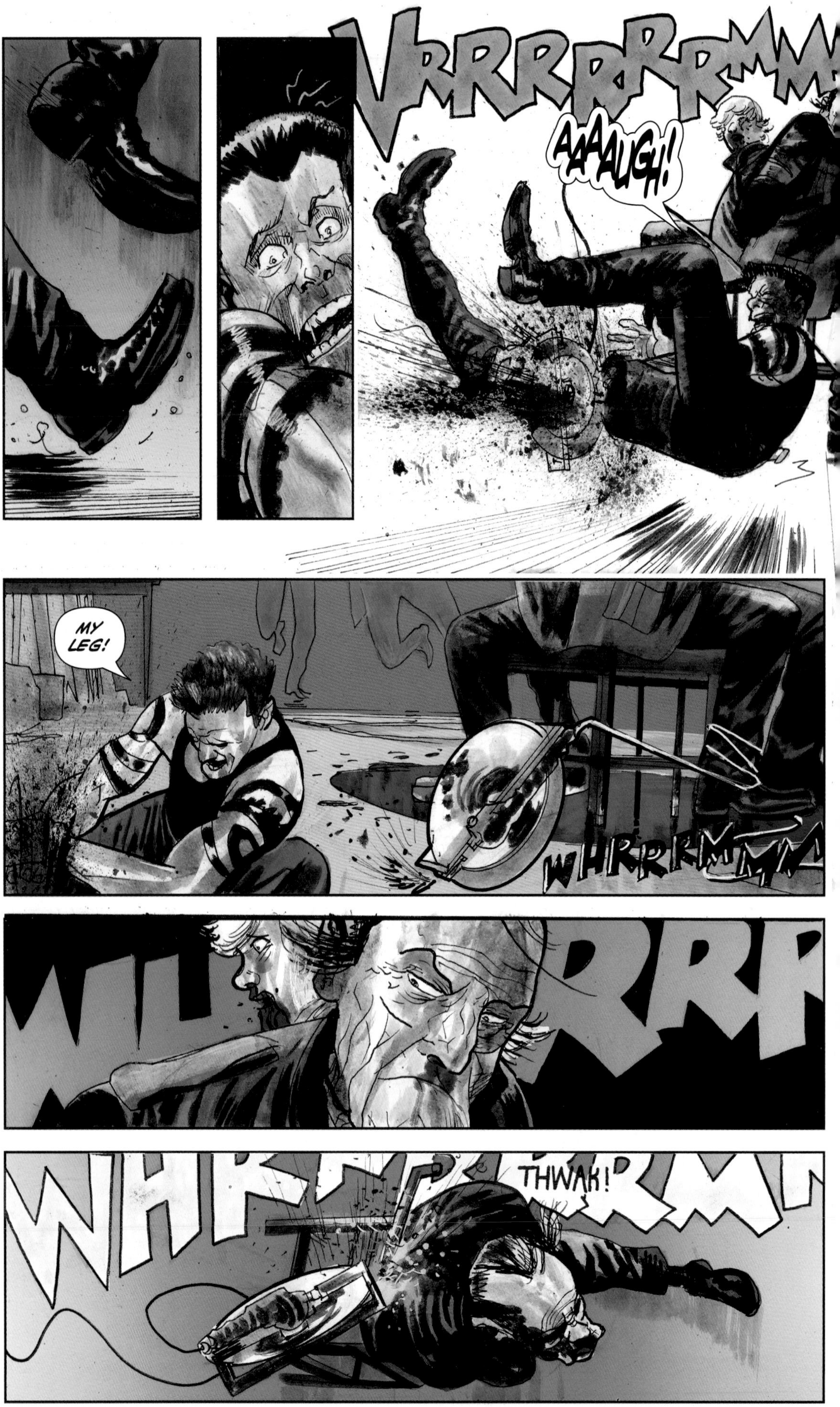
VRRRRRRMM
AAAAUGH!
MY LEG!
WHRRRMMM
WHRR
WHRRRMM
THWAK!

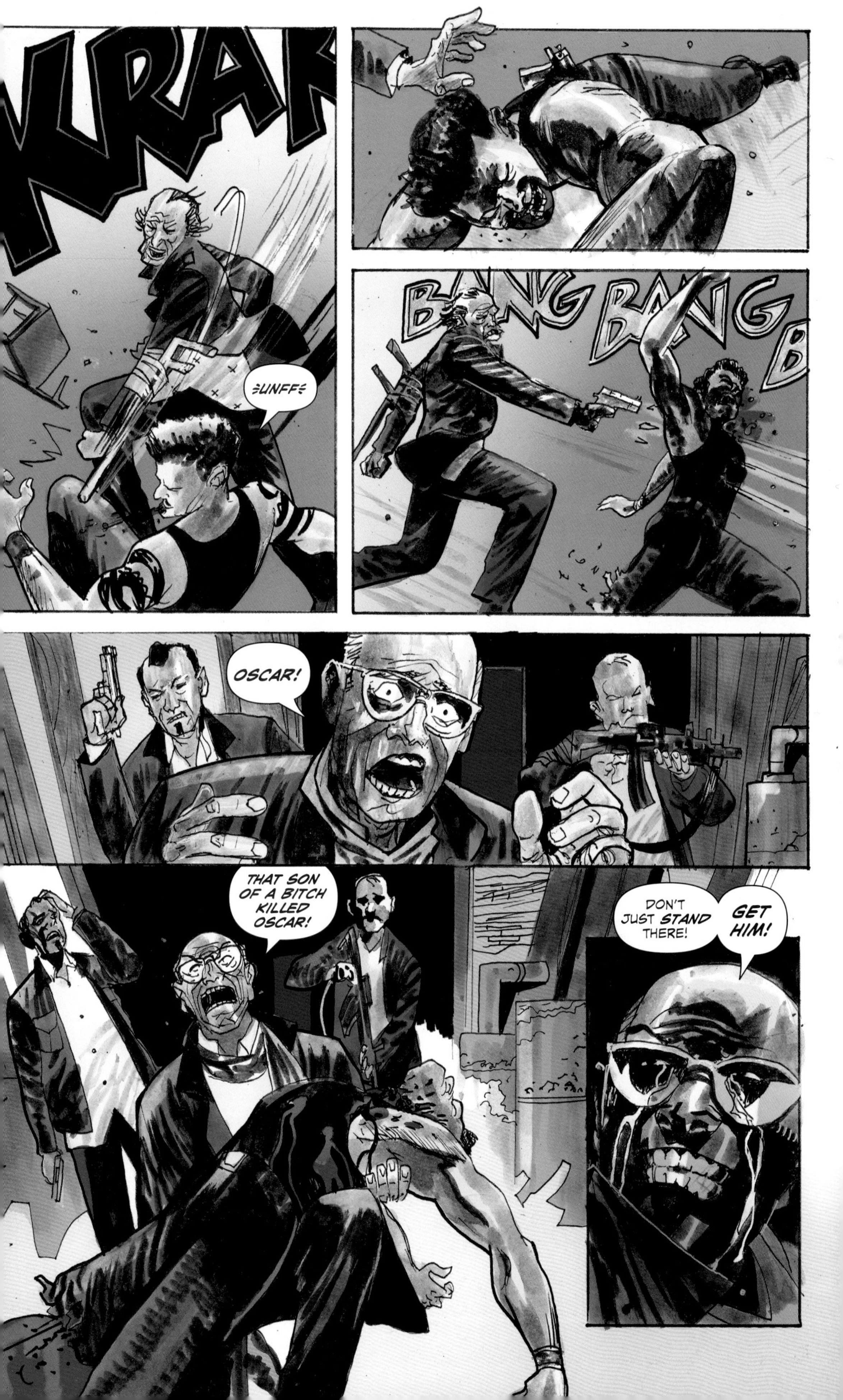
KRAK
UNFF
BANG BANG B
OSCAR!
THAT SON OF A BITCH KILLED OSCAR!
DON'T JUST STAND THERE!
GET HIM!

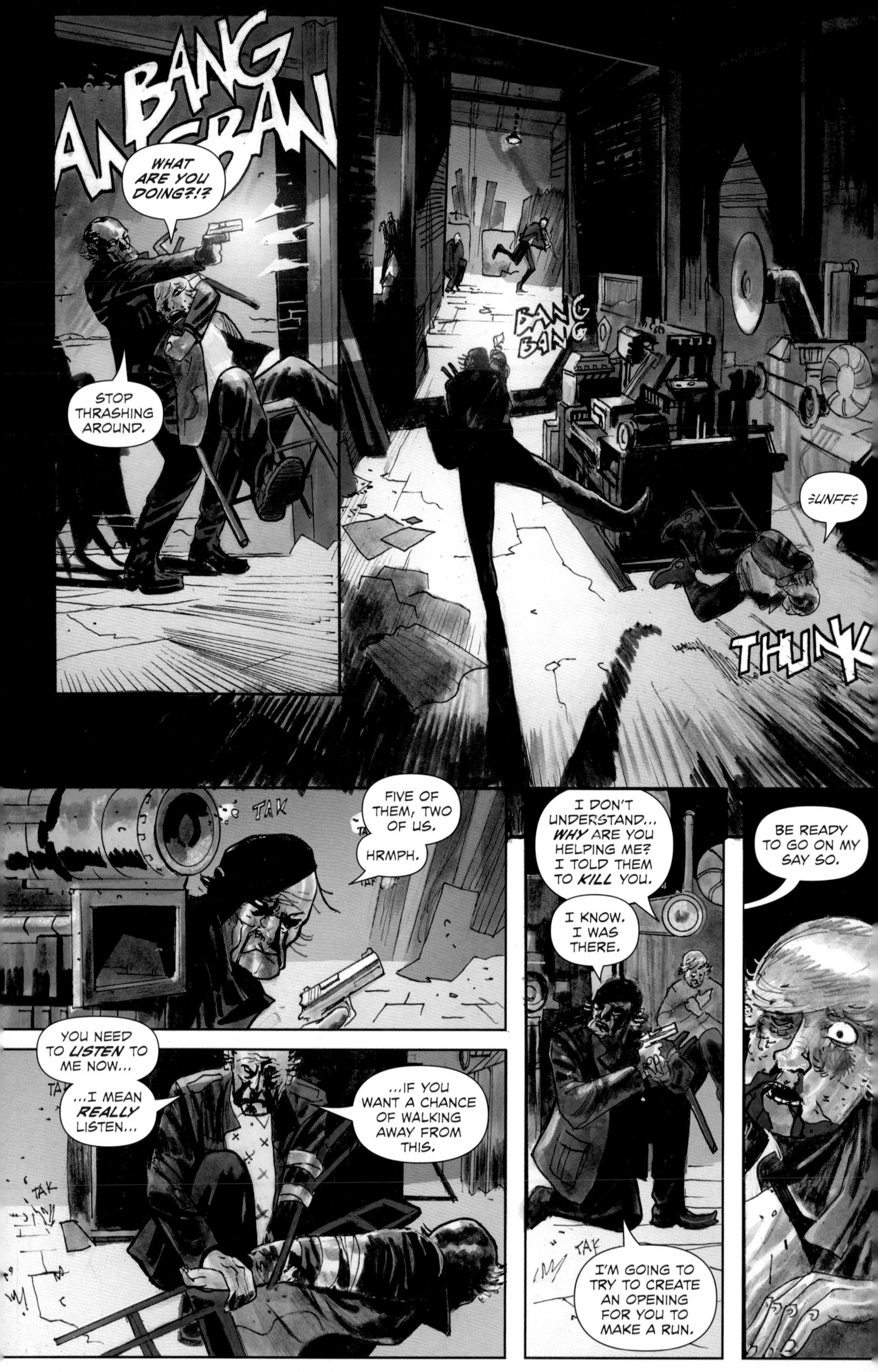
BANG
BANG
WHAT ARE YOU DOING?!?
STOP THRASHING AROUND.
BANG BANG
UNFF
THUNK
TAK
FIVE OF THEM, TWO OF US.
HRMPH.
I DON'T UNDERSTAND... WHY ARE YOU HELPING ME? I TOLD THEM TO KILL YOU.
I KNOW. I WAS THERE.
BE READY TO GO ON MY SAY SO.
YOU NEED TO LISTEN TO ME NOW...
...I MEAN REALLY LISTEN...
...IF YOU WANT A CHANCE OF WALKING AWAY FROM THIS.
TAK
TAK
I'M GOING TO TRY TO CREATE AN OPENING FOR YOU TO MAKE A RUN.

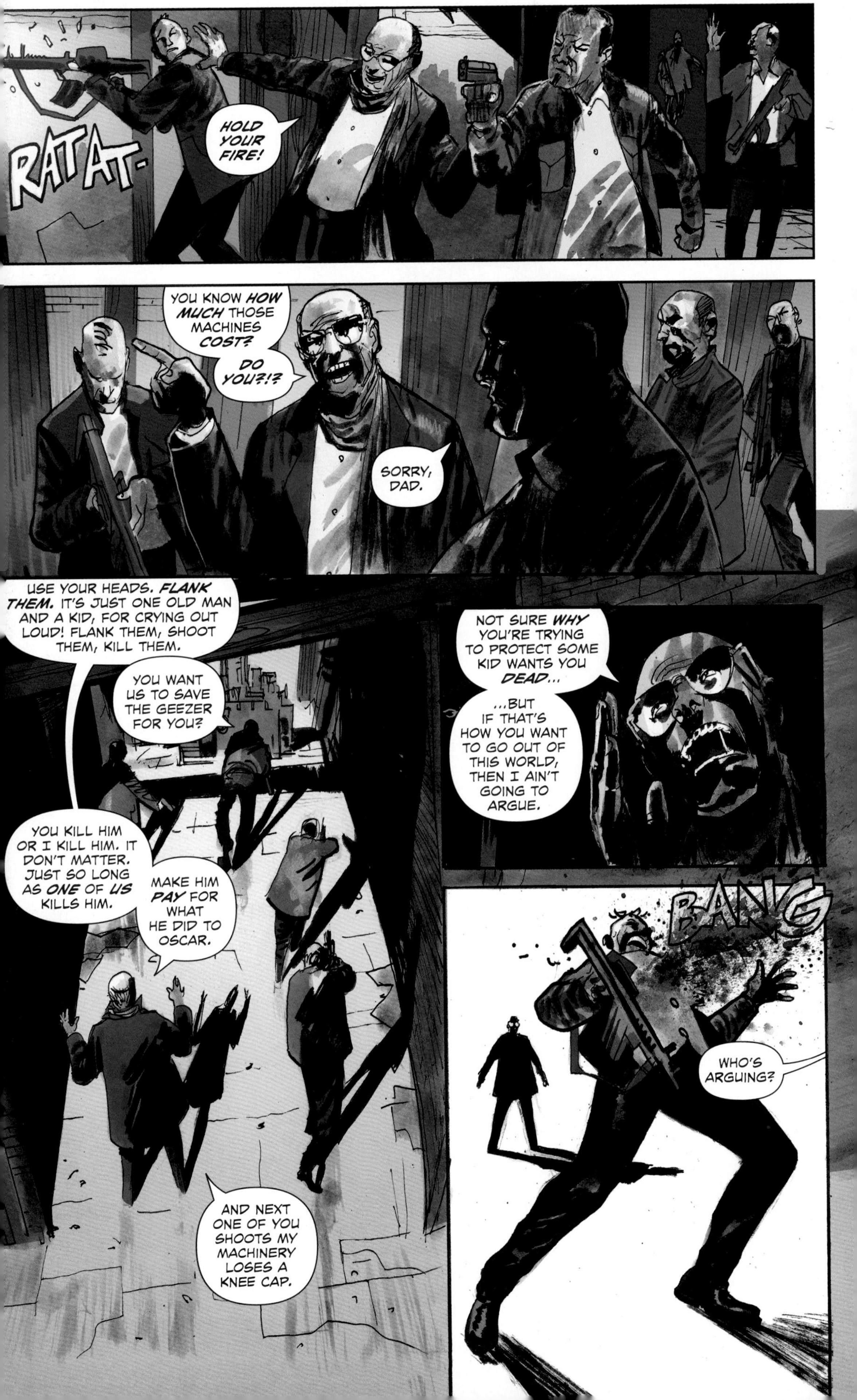
RATAT-
HOLD YOUR FIRE!
YOU KNOW HOW MUCH THOSE MACHINES COST?
DO YOU?!?
SORRY, DAD.
USE YOUR HEADS. FLANK THEM. IT'S JUST ONE OLD MAN AND A KID, FOR CRYING OUT LOUD! FLANK THEM, SHOOT THEM, KILL THEM.
YOU WANT US TO SAVE THE GEEZER FOR YOU?
YOU KILL HIM OR I KILL HIM. IT DON'T MATTER. JUST SO LONG AS ONE OF US KILLS HIM.
MAKE HIM PAY FOR WHAT HE DID TO OSCAR.
AND NEXT ONE OF YOU SHOOTS MY MACHINERY LOSES A KNEE CAP.
NOT SURE WHY YOU'RE TRYING TO PROTECT SOME KID WANTS YOU DEAD...
...BUT IF THAT'S HOW YOU WANT TO GO OUT OF THIS WORLD, THEN I AIN'T GOING TO ARGUE.
BANG
WHO'S ARGUING?

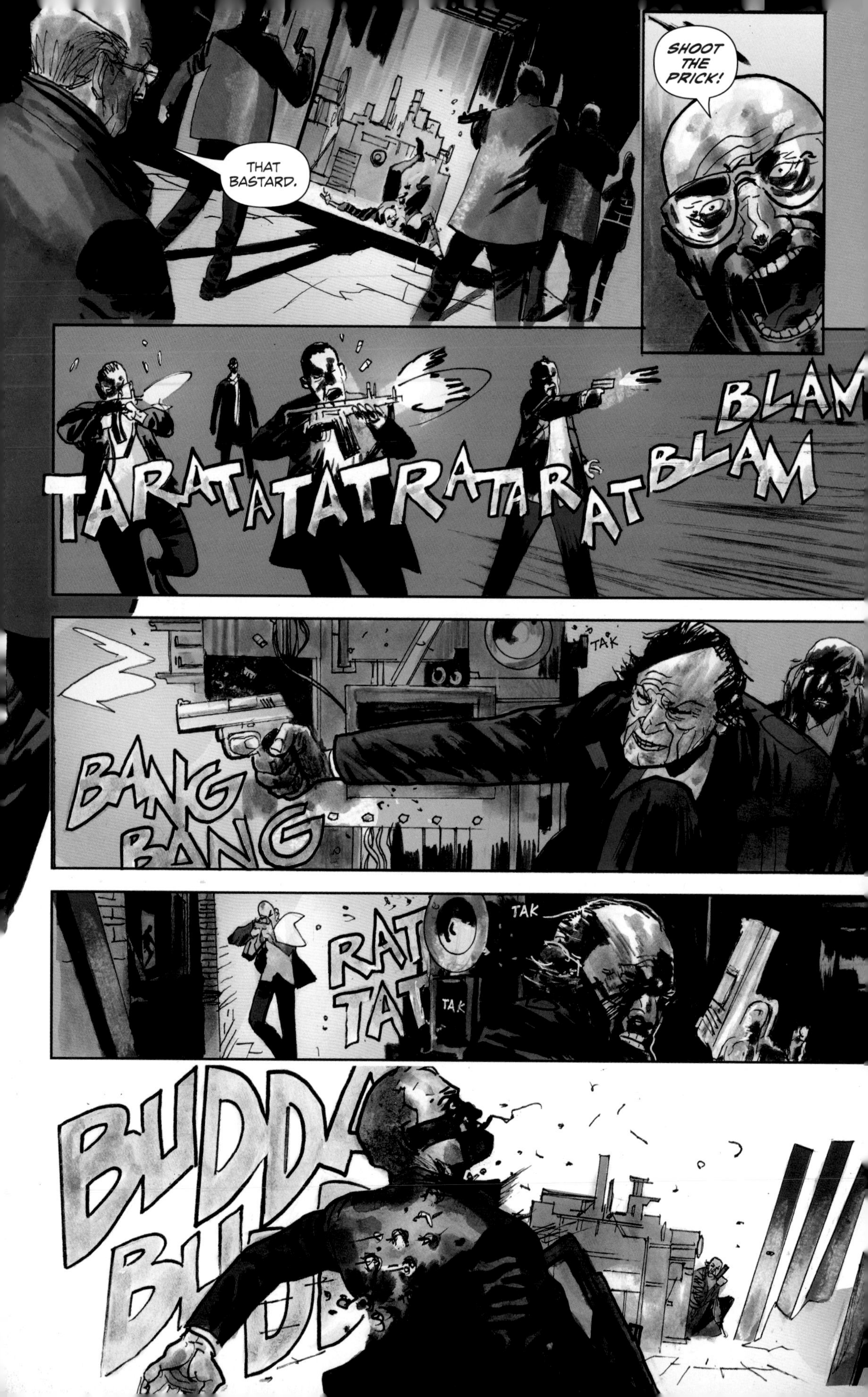
THAT BASTARD.
SHOOT THE PRICK!
TARATATATRATATARAT
BLAM
BLAM
TAK
BANG
BANG
RAT
TAT
TAK
TAK

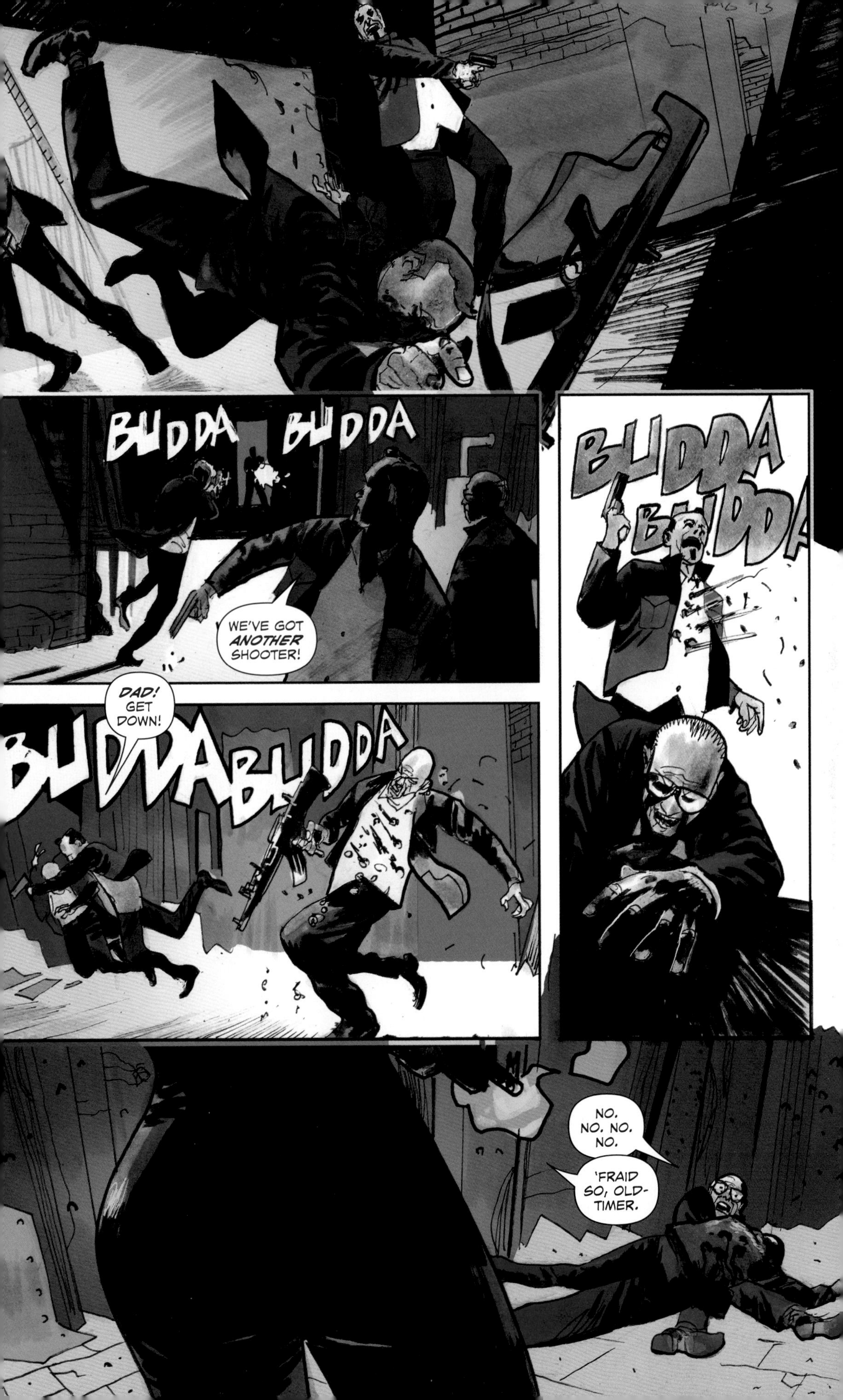
BUDDA BUDDA
WE'VE GOT ANOTHER SHOOTER!
BUDDA BUDDA
DAD! GET DOWN!
BUDDABUDDA
NO. NO. NO. NO.
'FRAID SO, OLD-TIMER.

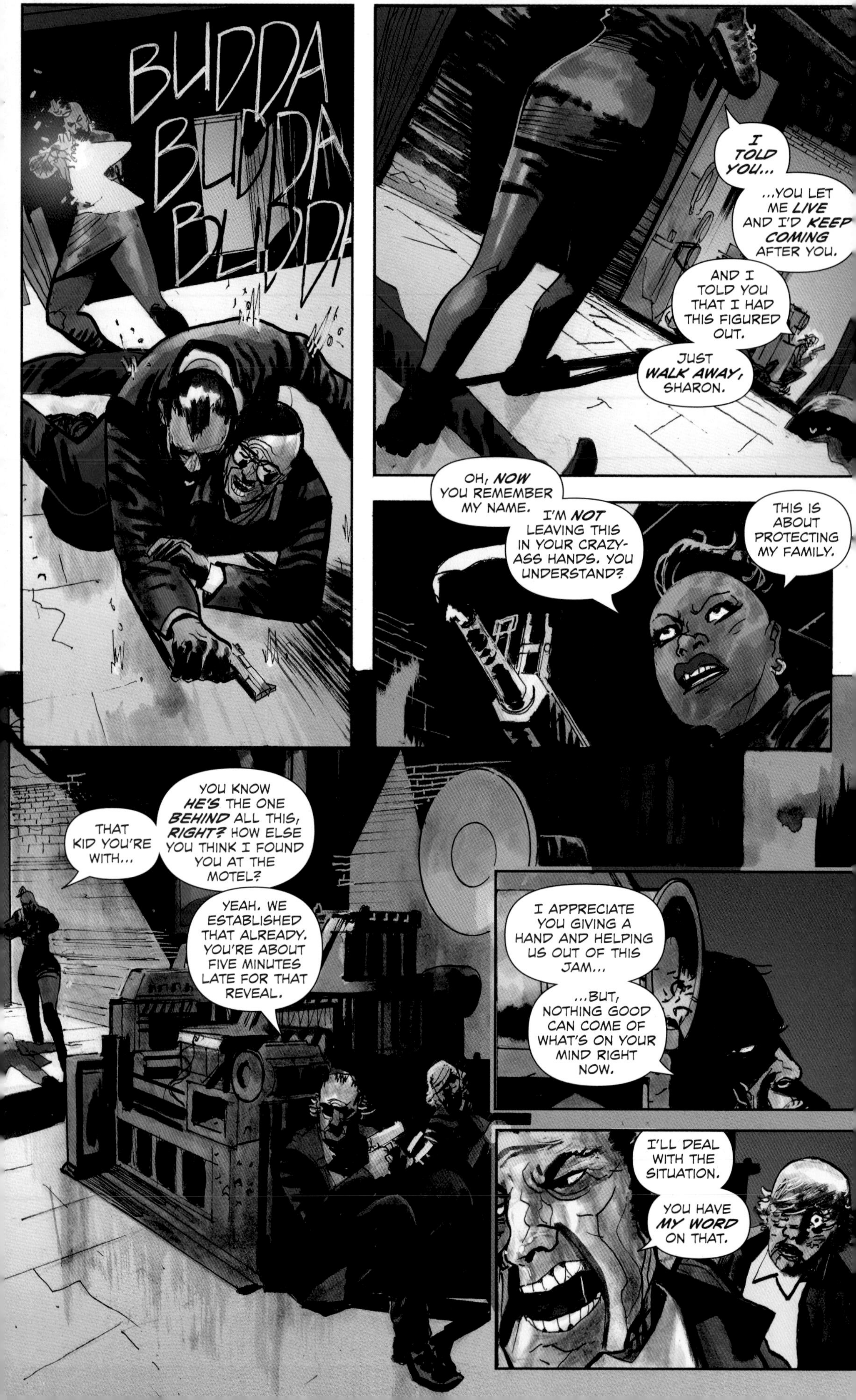
BUDDA BUDDA BUDDA
I TOLD YOU...
...YOU LET ME LIVE AND I'D KEEP COMING AFTER YOU.
AND I TOLD YOU THAT I HAD THIS FIGURED OUT.
JUST WALK AWAY, SHARON.
OH, NOW YOU REMEMBER MY NAME.
I'M NOT LEAVING THIS IN YOUR CRAZY-ASS HANDS. YOU UNDERSTAND?
THIS IS ABOUT PROTECTING MY FAMILY.
THAT KID YOU'RE WITH...
YOU KNOW HE'S THE ONE BEHIND ALL THIS, RIGHT? HOW ELSE YOU THINK I FOUND YOU AT THE MOTEL?
YEAH. WE ESTABLISHED THAT ALREADY. YOU'RE ABOUT FIVE MINUTES LATE FOR THAT REVEAL.
I APPRECIATE YOU GIVING A HAND AND HELPING US OUT OF THIS JAM...
...BUT, NOTHING GOOD CAN COME OF WHAT'S ON YOUR MIND RIGHT NOW.
I'LL DEAL WITH THE SITUATION.
YOU HAVE MY WORD ON THAT.

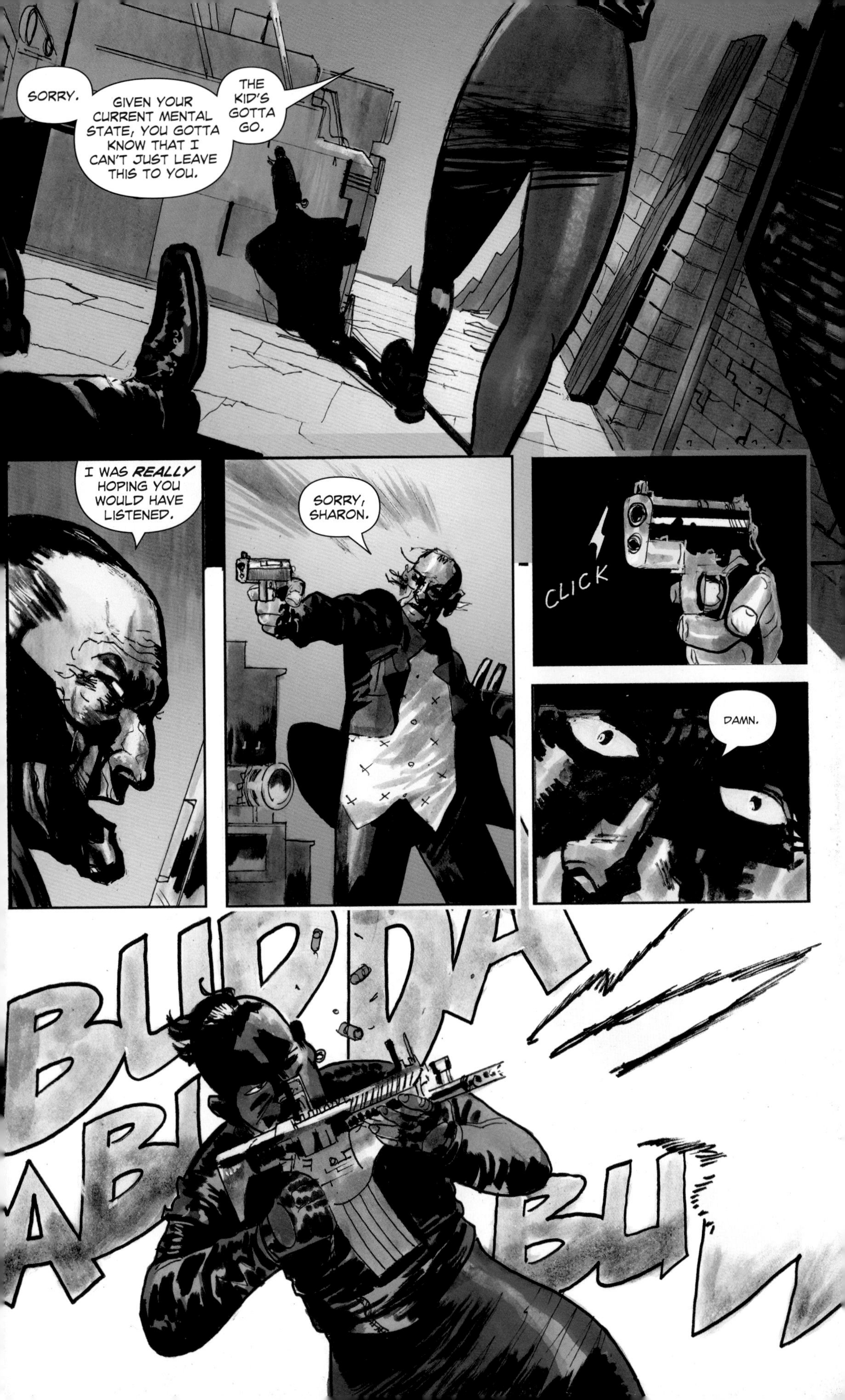
SORRY.
GIVEN YOUR CURRENT MENTAL STATE, YOU GOTTA KNOW THAT I CAN'T JUST LEAVE THIS TO YOU.
THE KID'S GOTTA GO.
I WAS REALLY HOPING YOU WOULD HAVE LISTENED.
SORRY, SHARON.
CLICK
DAMN.

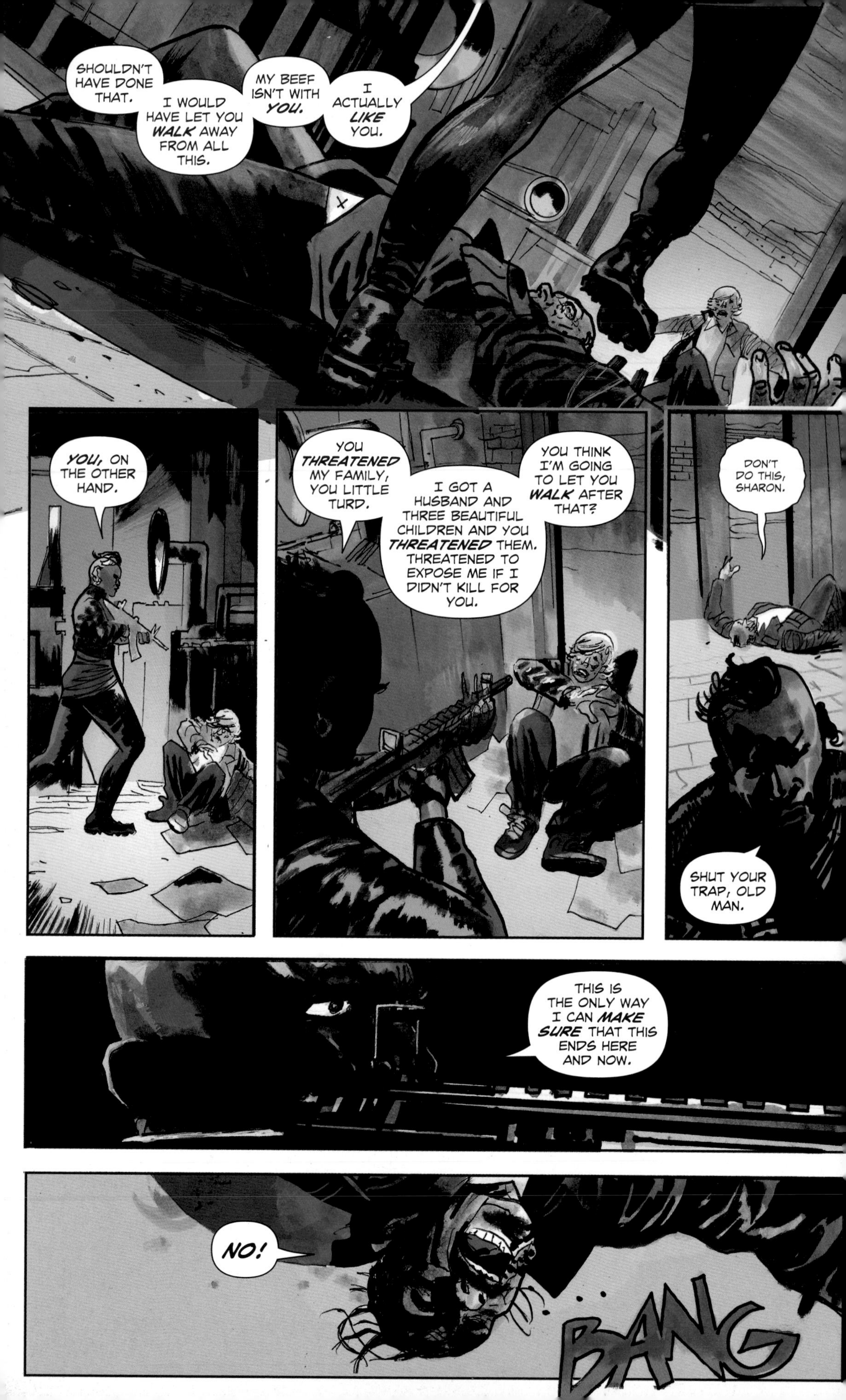
SHOULDN'T HAVE DONE THAT.
I WOULD HAVE LET YOU WALK AWAY FROM ALL THIS.
MY BEEF ISN'T WITH YOU.
I ACTUALLY LIKE YOU.
YOU, ON THE OTHER HAND.
YOU THREATENED MY FAMILY, YOU LITTLE TURD.
I GOT A HUSBAND AND THREE BEAUTIFUL CHILDREN AND YOU THREATENED THEM. THREATENED TO EXPOSE ME IF I DIDN'T KILL FOR YOU.
YOU THINK I'M GOING TO LET YOU WALK AFTER THAT?
DON'T DO THIS, SHARON.
SHUT YOUR TRAP, OLD MAN.
THIS IS THE ONLY WAY I CAN MAKE SURE THAT THIS ENDS HERE AND NOW.
NO!
BANG

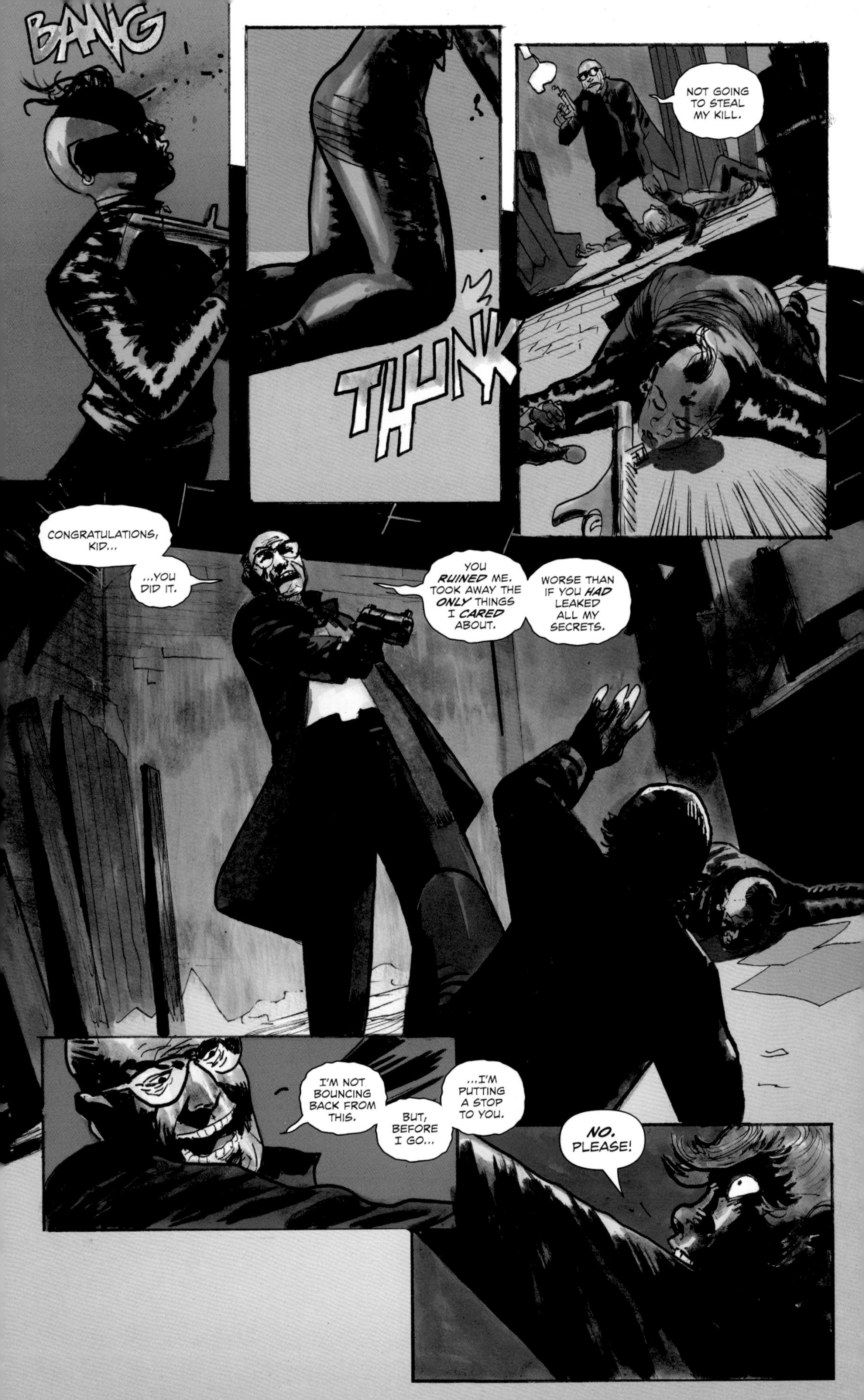
BANG
THUNK
NOT GOING TO STEAL MY KILL.
CONGRATULATIONS, KID...
...YOU DID IT.
YOU RUINED ME. TOOK AWAY THE ONLY THINGS I CARED ABOUT.
WORSE THAN IF YOU HAD LEAKED ALL MY SECRETS.
I'M NOT BOUNCING BACK FROM THIS.
BUT, BEFORE I GO...
...I'M PUTTING A STOP TO YOU.
NO. PLEASE!

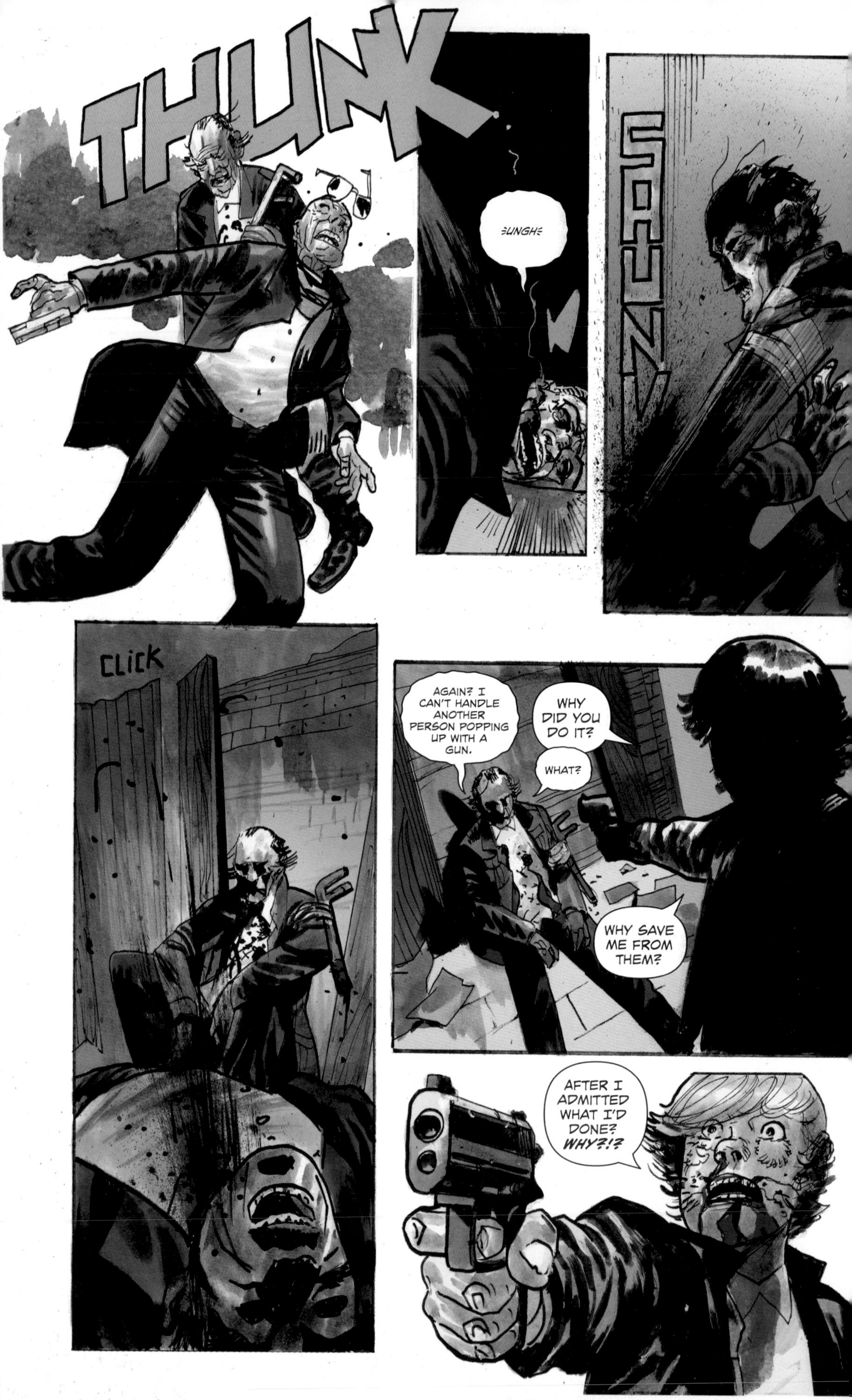
THUNK
UNGH
SQUNCH
CLICK
AGAIN? I CAN'T HANDLE ANOTHER PERSON POPPING UP WITH A GUN.
WHY DID YOU DO IT?
WHAT?
WHY SAVE ME FROM THEM?
AFTER I ADMITTED WHAT I'D DONE? *WHY?!?*

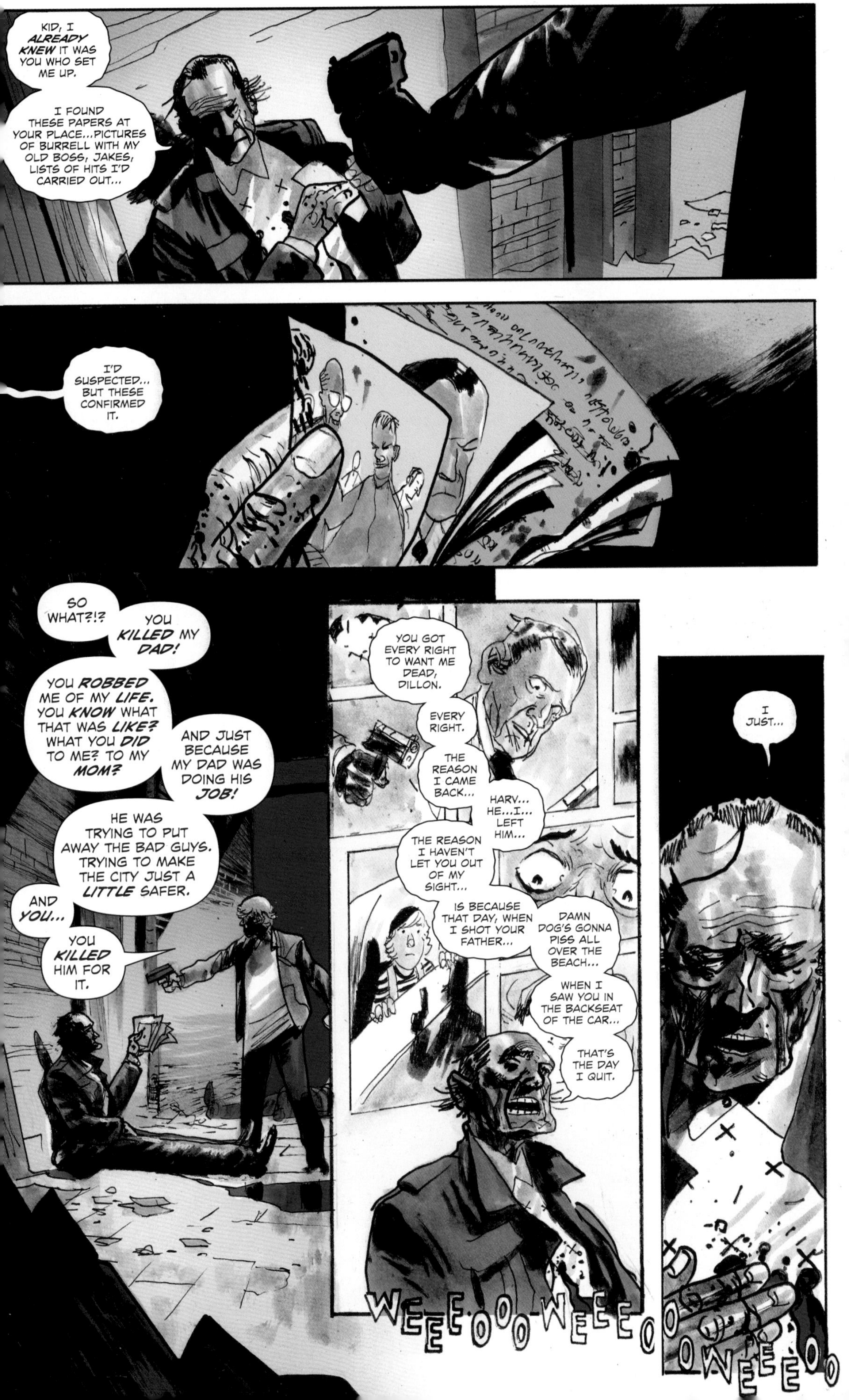

KID, I ALREADY KNEW IT WAS YOU WHO SET ME UP.
I FOUND THESE PAPERS AT YOUR PLACE...PICTURES OF BURRELL WITH MY OLD BOSS, JAKES, LISTS OF HITS I'D CARRIED OUT...
I'D SUSPECTED... BUT THESE CONFIRMED IT.
SO WHAT?!?
YOU KILLED MY DAD!
YOU ROBBED ME OF MY LIFE. YOU KNOW WHAT THAT WAS LIKE? WHAT YOU DID TO ME? TO MY MOM?
AND JUST BECAUSE MY DAD WAS DOING HIS JOB!
HE WAS TRYING TO PUT AWAY THE BAD GUYS. TRYING TO MAKE THE CITY JUST A LITTLE SAFER.
AND YOU...
YOU KILLED HIM FOR IT.
YOU GOT EVERY RIGHT TO WANT ME DEAD, DILLON.
EVERY RIGHT.
THE REASON I CAME BACK...
HARV... HE...I... LEFT HIM...
THE REASON I HAVEN'T LET YOU OUT OF MY SIGHT...
IS BECAUSE THAT DAY, WHEN I SHOT YOUR FATHER...
DAMN DOG'S GONNA PISS ALL OVER THE BEACH...
WHEN I SAW YOU IN THE BACKSEAT OF THE CAR...
THAT'S THE DAY I QUIT.
I JUST...
WEEEOOO WEEEOO
OWEEEOO

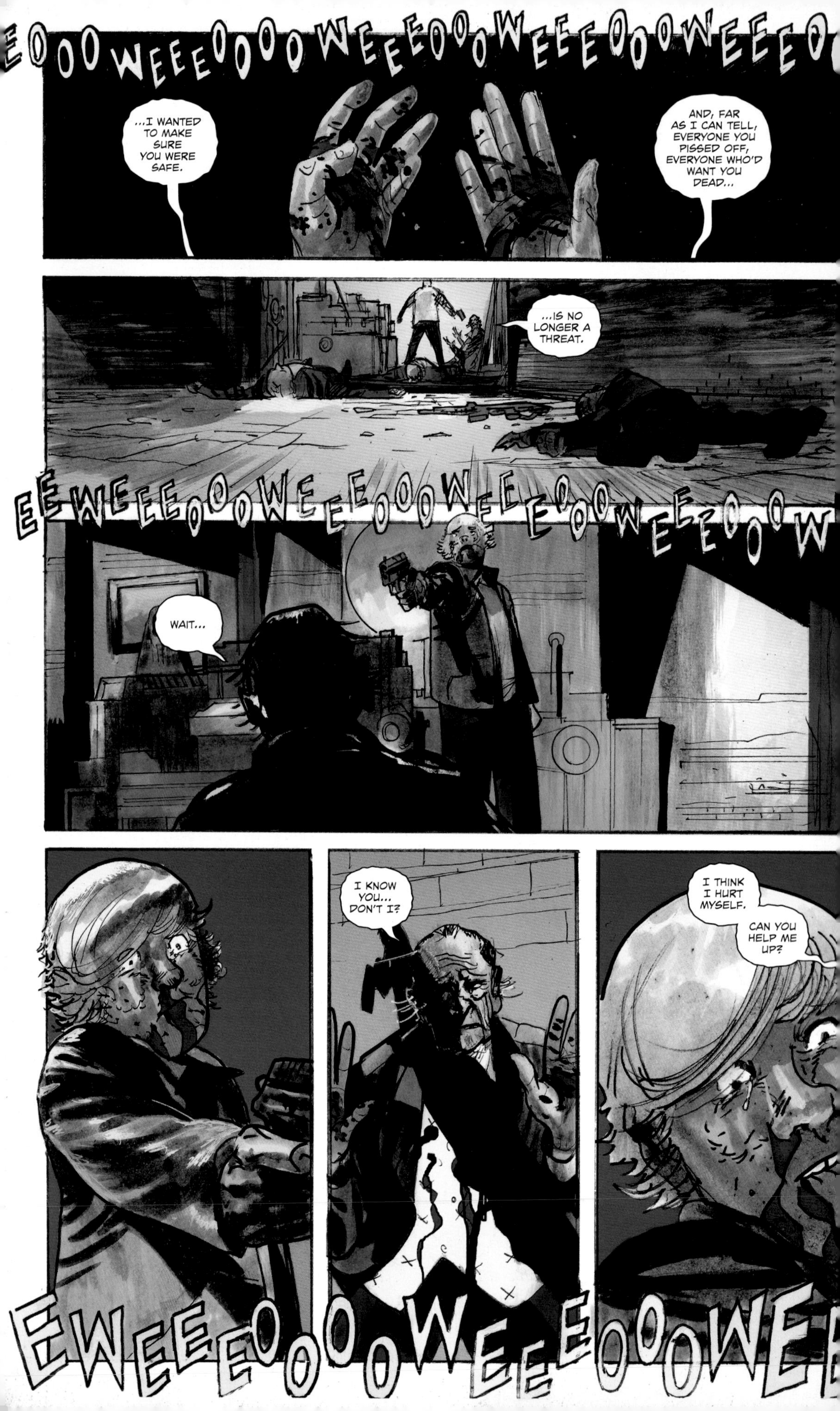
EOOWEEEOOOWEEEOOOWEEEOOOWEEEO
...I WANTED TO MAKE SURE YOU WERE SAFE.
AND, FAR AS I CAN TELL, EVERYONE YOU PISSED OFF, EVERYONE WHO'D WANT YOU DEAD...
...IS NO LONGER A THREAT.
EEWEEEOOOWEEEOOOWEEEOOOWEEEOOOW
WAIT...
I KNOW YOU... DON'T I?
I THINK I HURT MYSELF.
CAN YOU HELP ME UP?
EWEEEOOOWEEEOOOWE

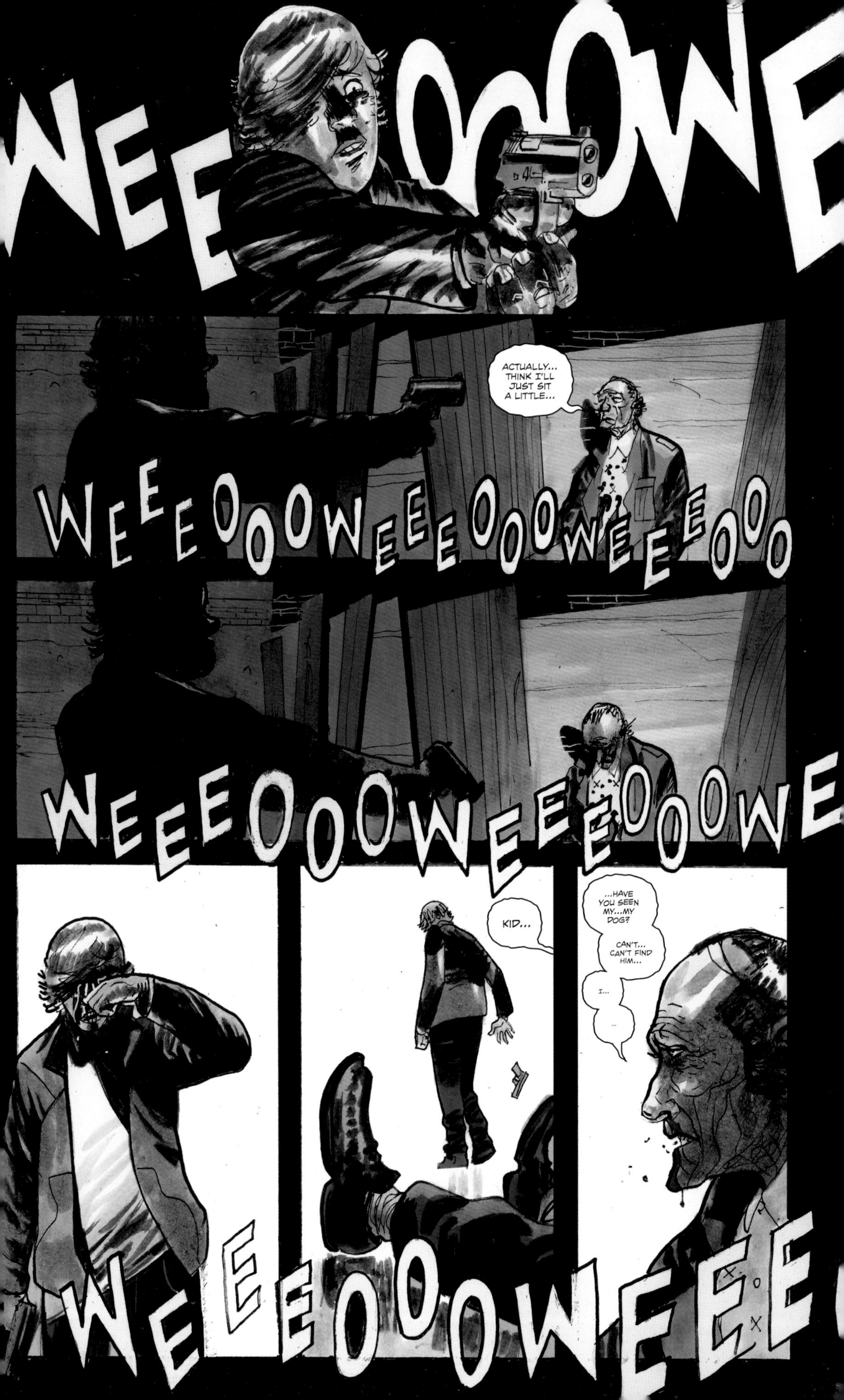
WEEOOOWE
ACTUALLY... THINK I'LL JUST SIT A LITTLE...
WEEEOOOWEEEOOOWEEEOOO
WEEEOOOWEEEOOOWE
KID...
...HAVE YOU SEEN MY...MY DOG?
CAN'T... CAN'T FIND HIM...
I...
...
WEEEOOOWEEE

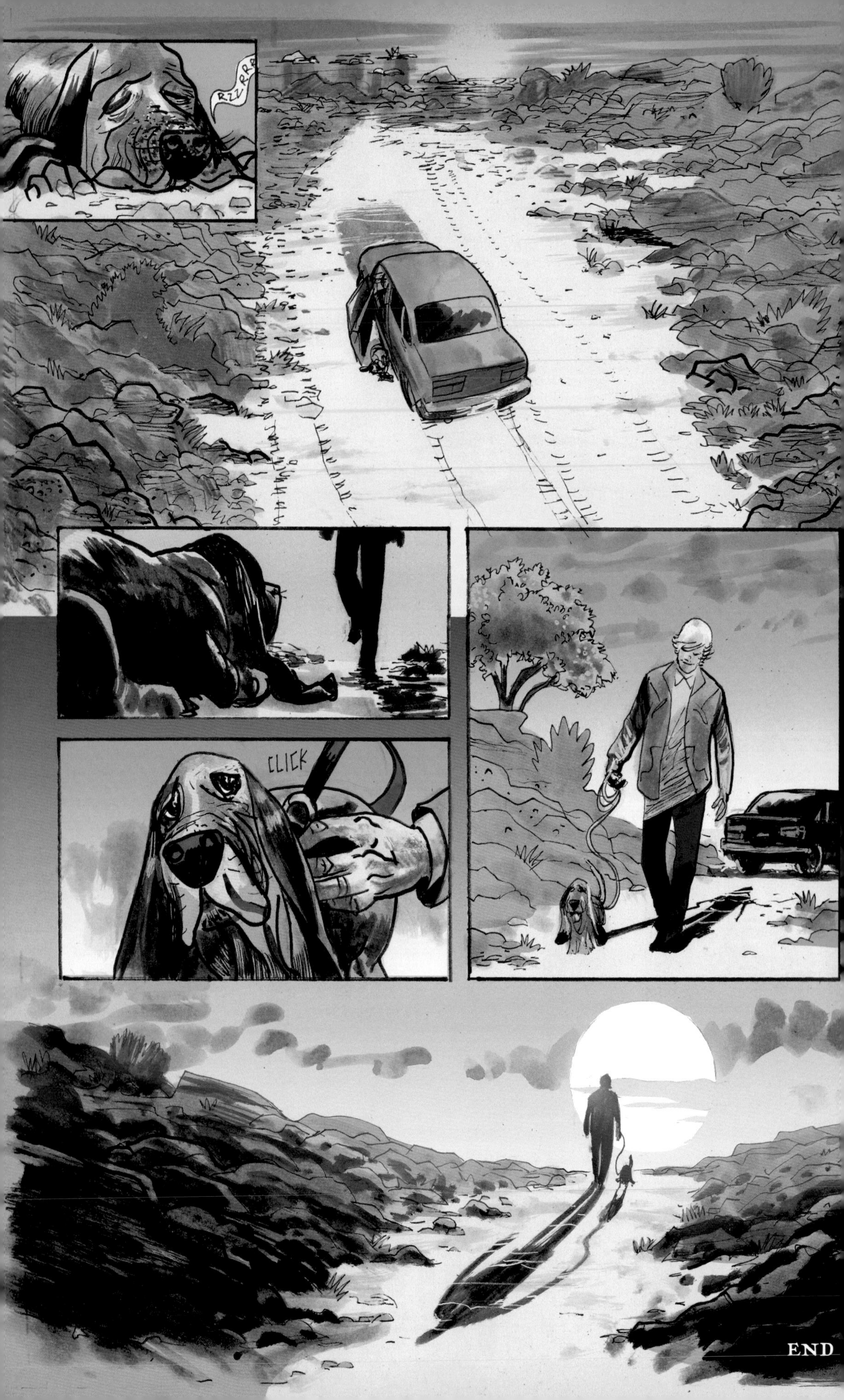
RZZRRR
CLICK
END

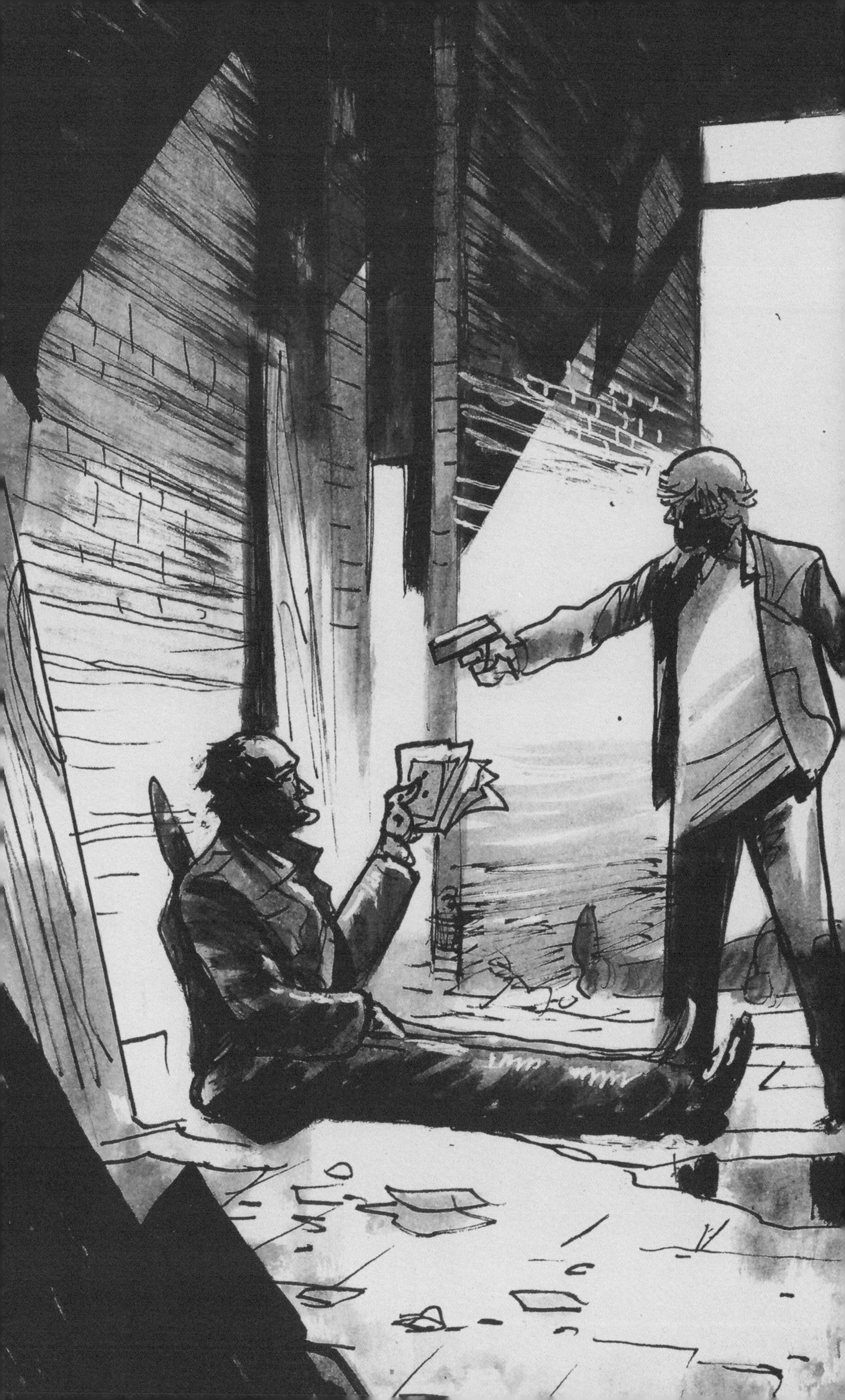

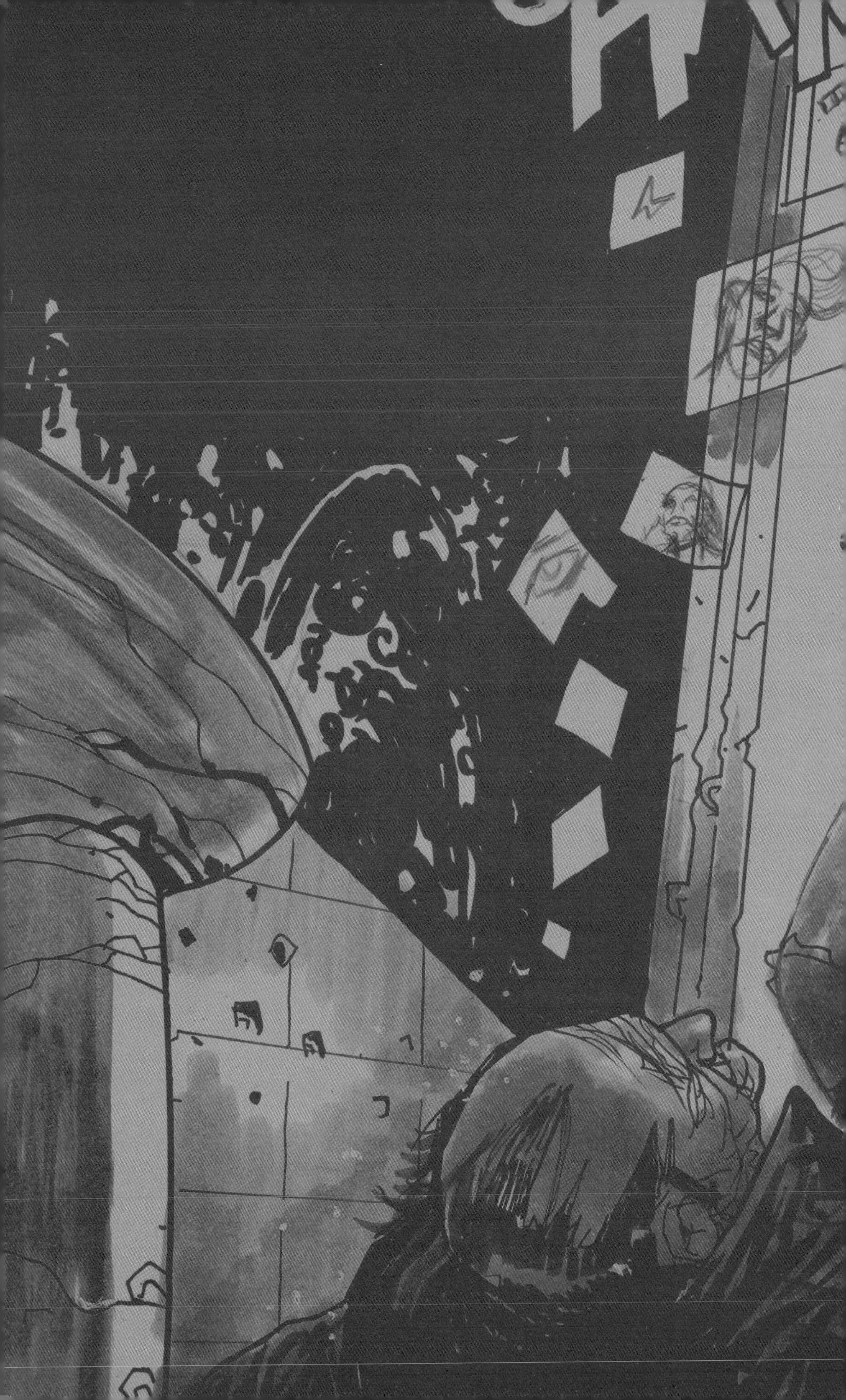

# Cover Gallery

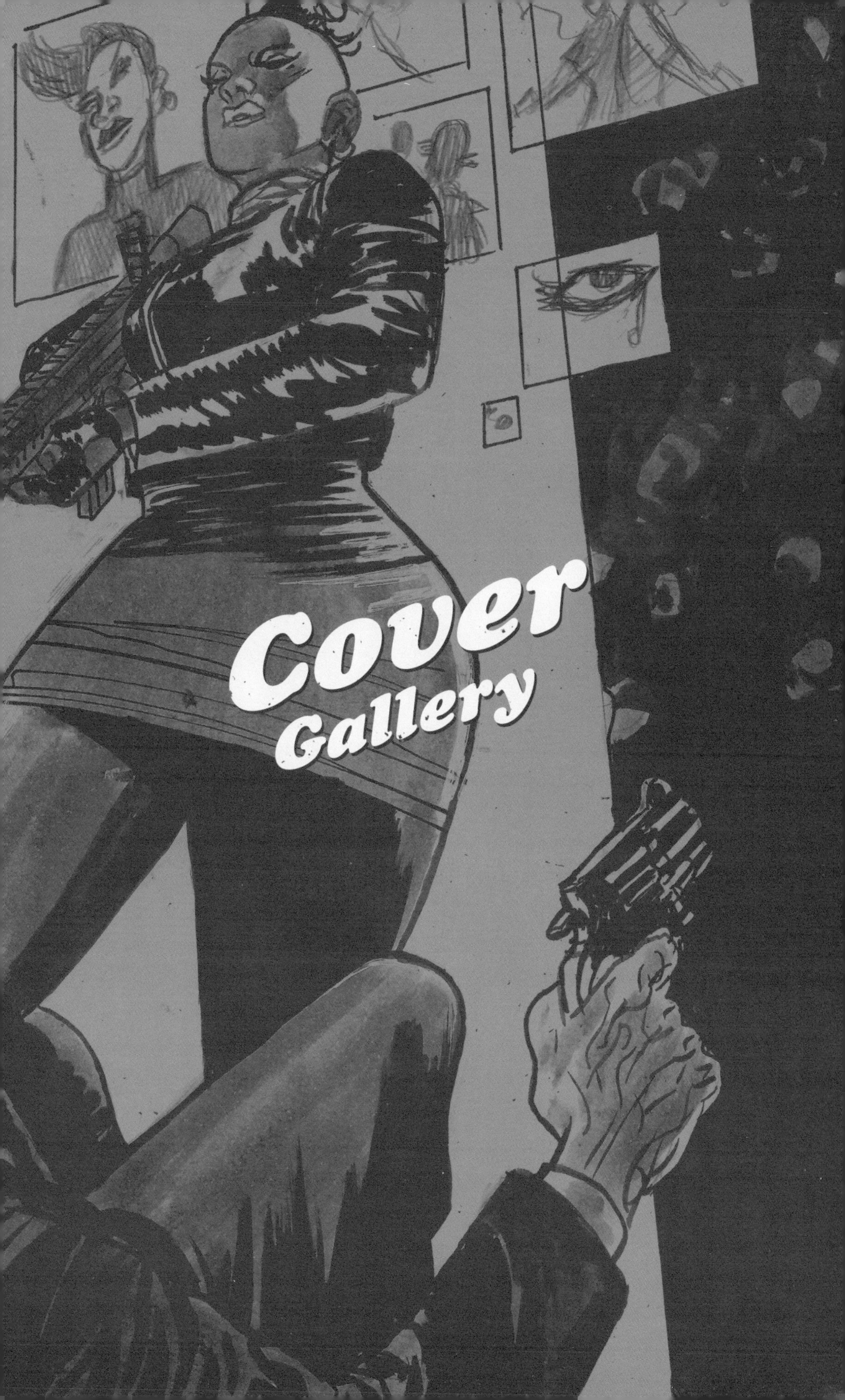

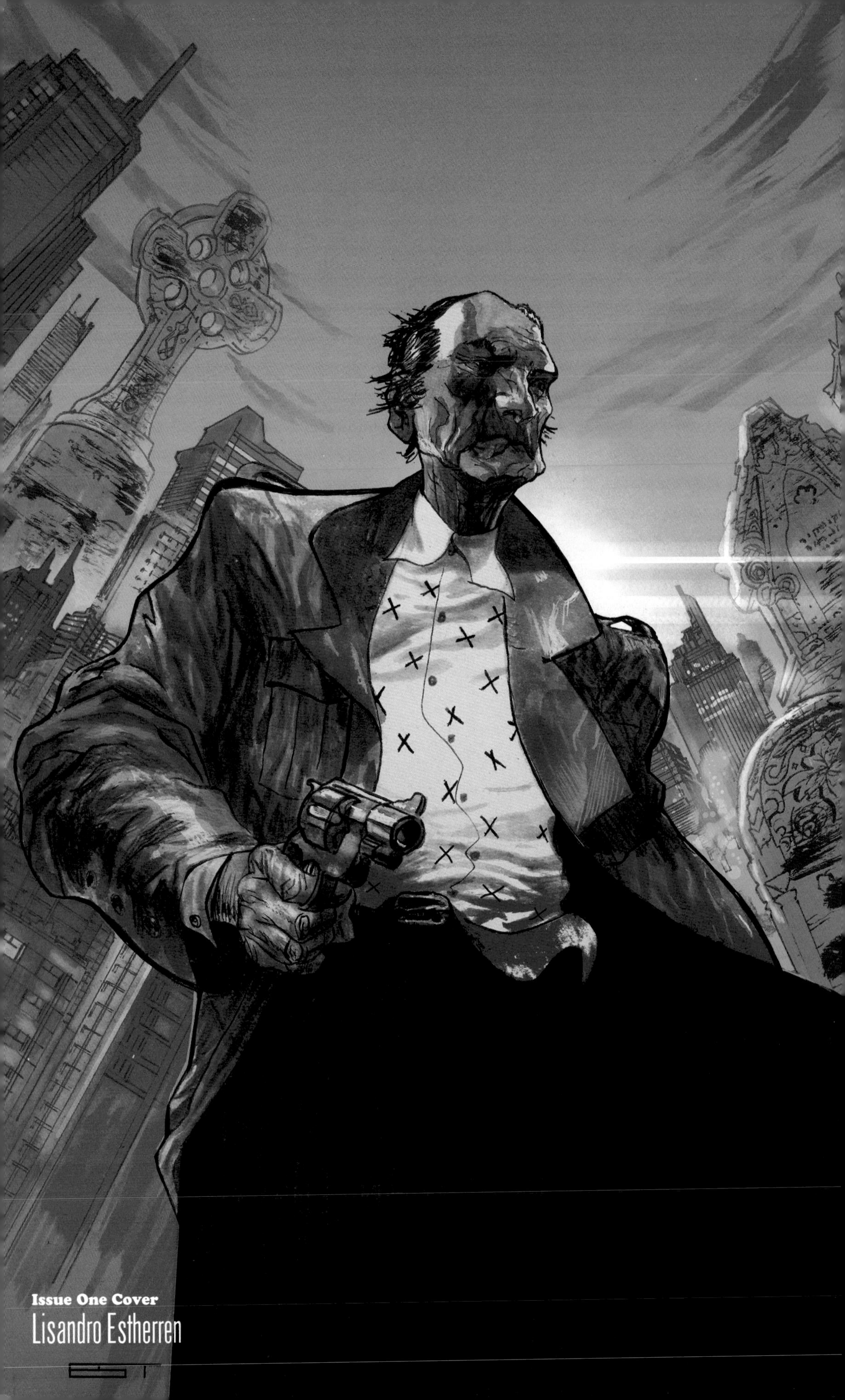

**Issue One Cover**
Lisandro Estherren

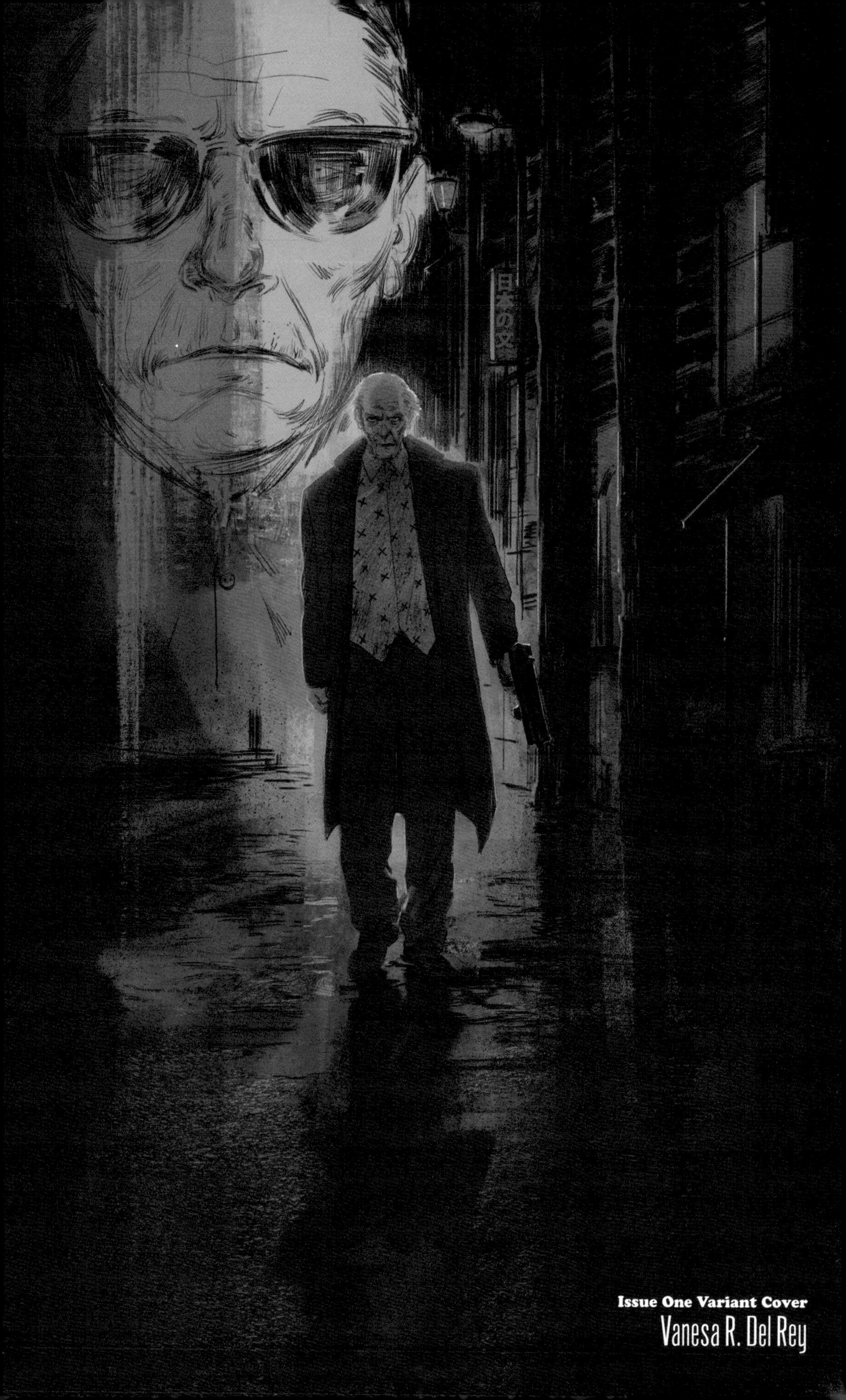
日本の文

**Issue One Variant Cover**
Vanesa R. Del Rey

**Issue Two Cover**

Lisandro Estherren

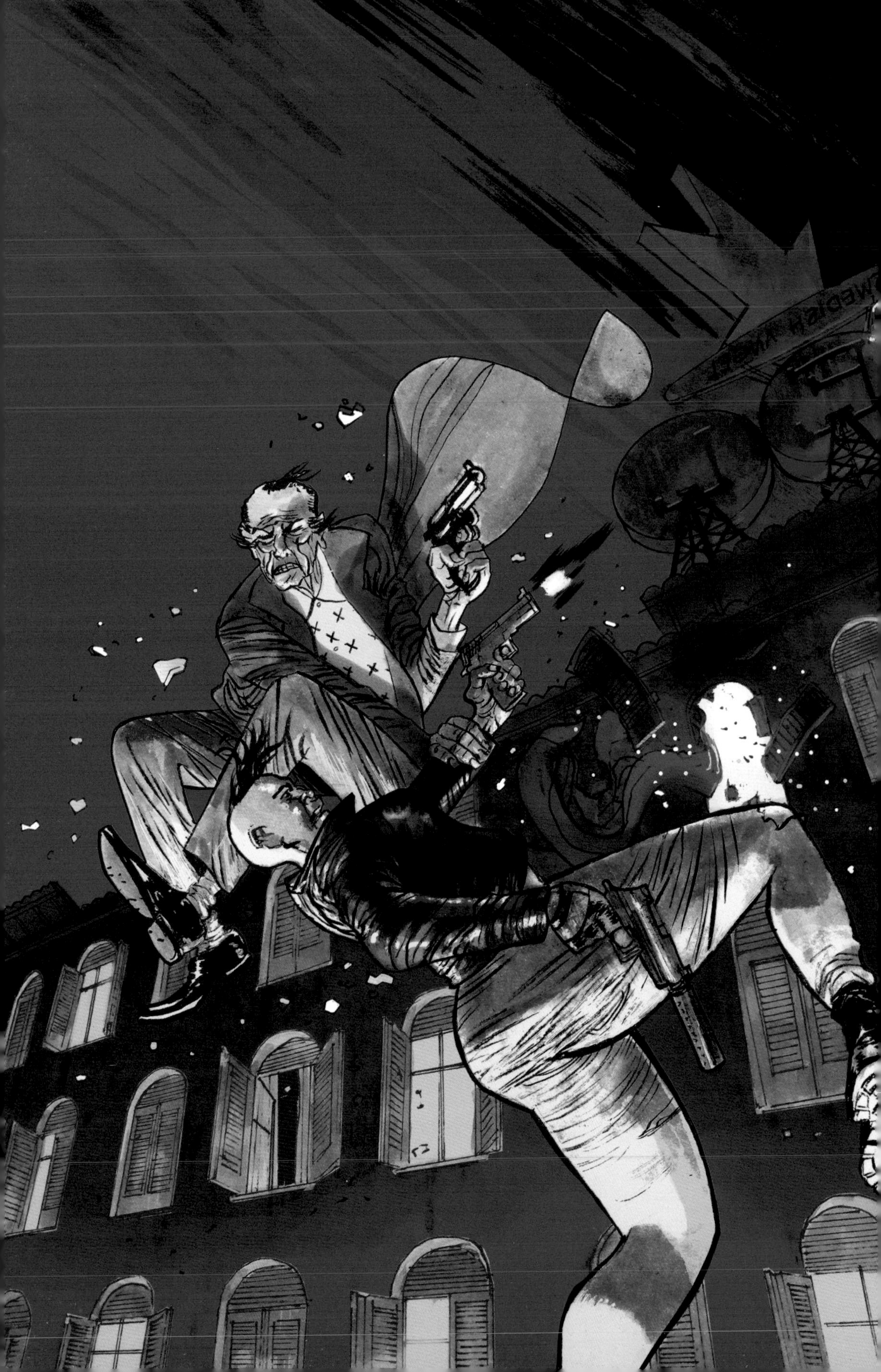

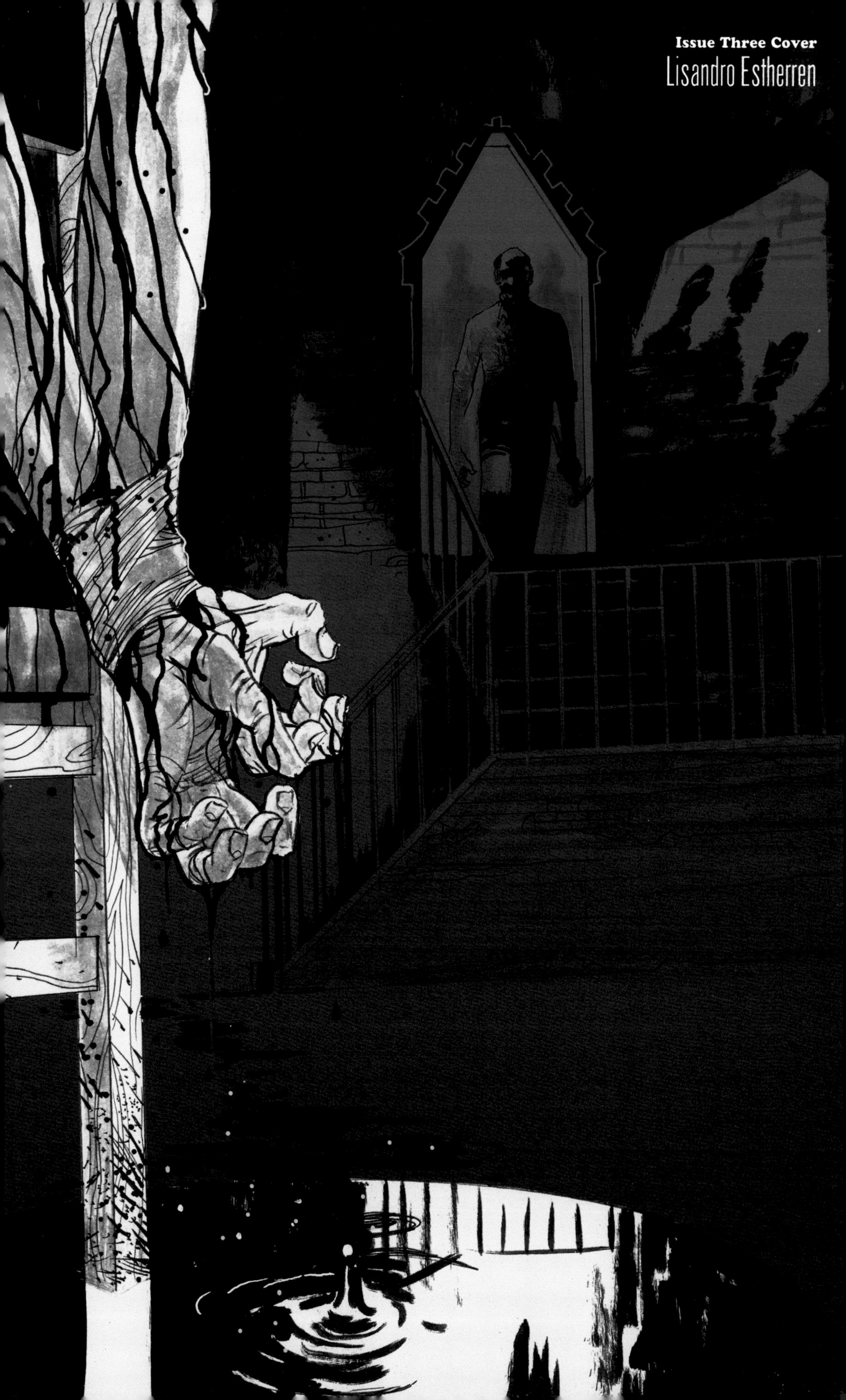

**Issue Three Cover**
Lisandro Estherren

**Issue Four Cover**
Lisandro Estherren

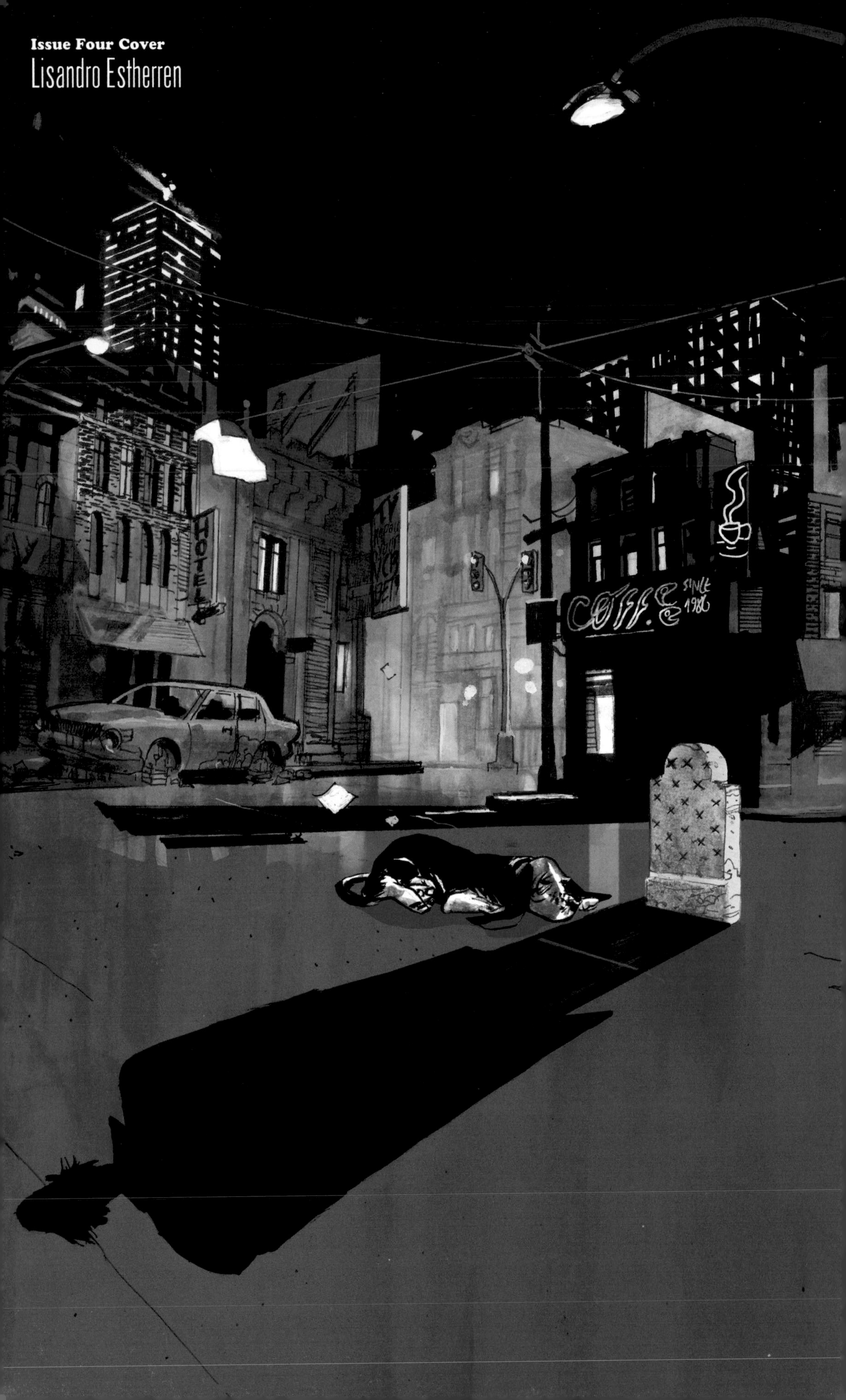
HOTEL

Lisandro Estherren

# Ink Gallery

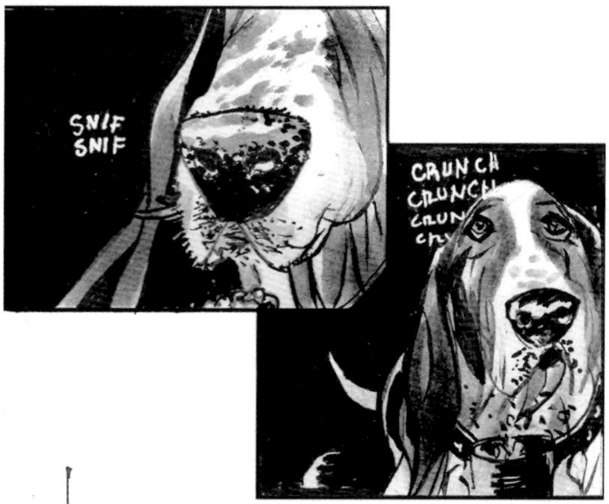
SNIF
SNIF
CRUNCH
CRUNCH

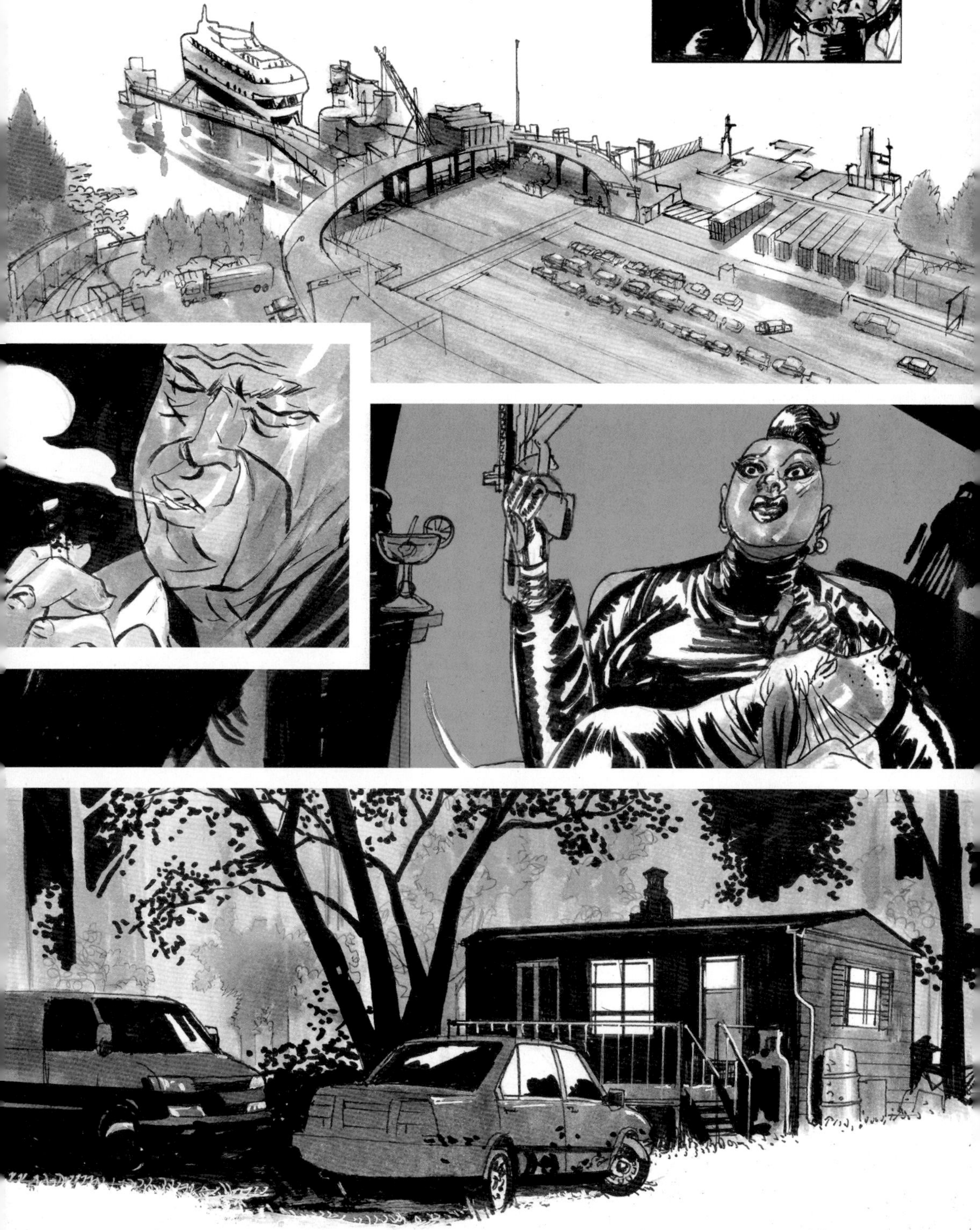

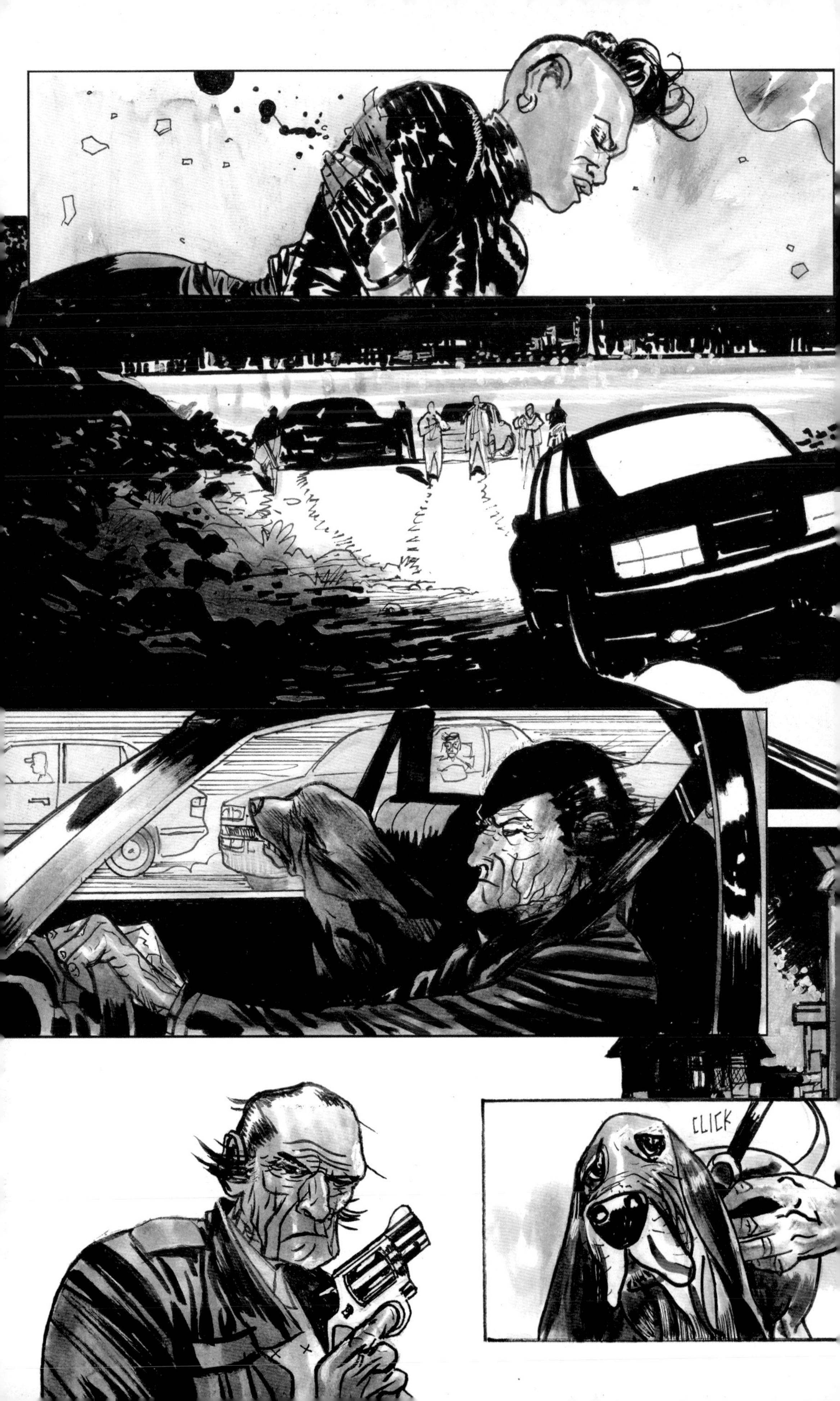
CLICK

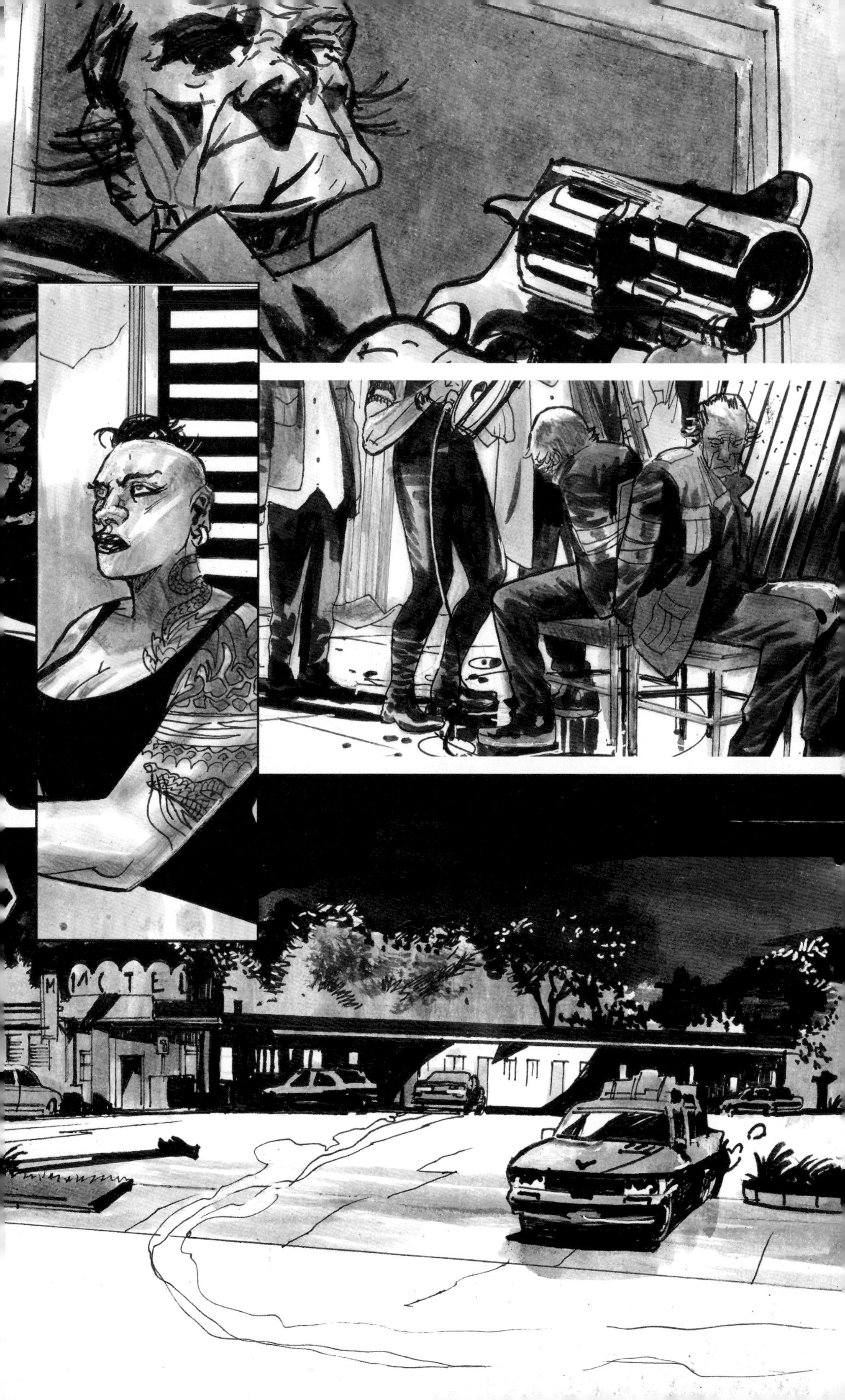

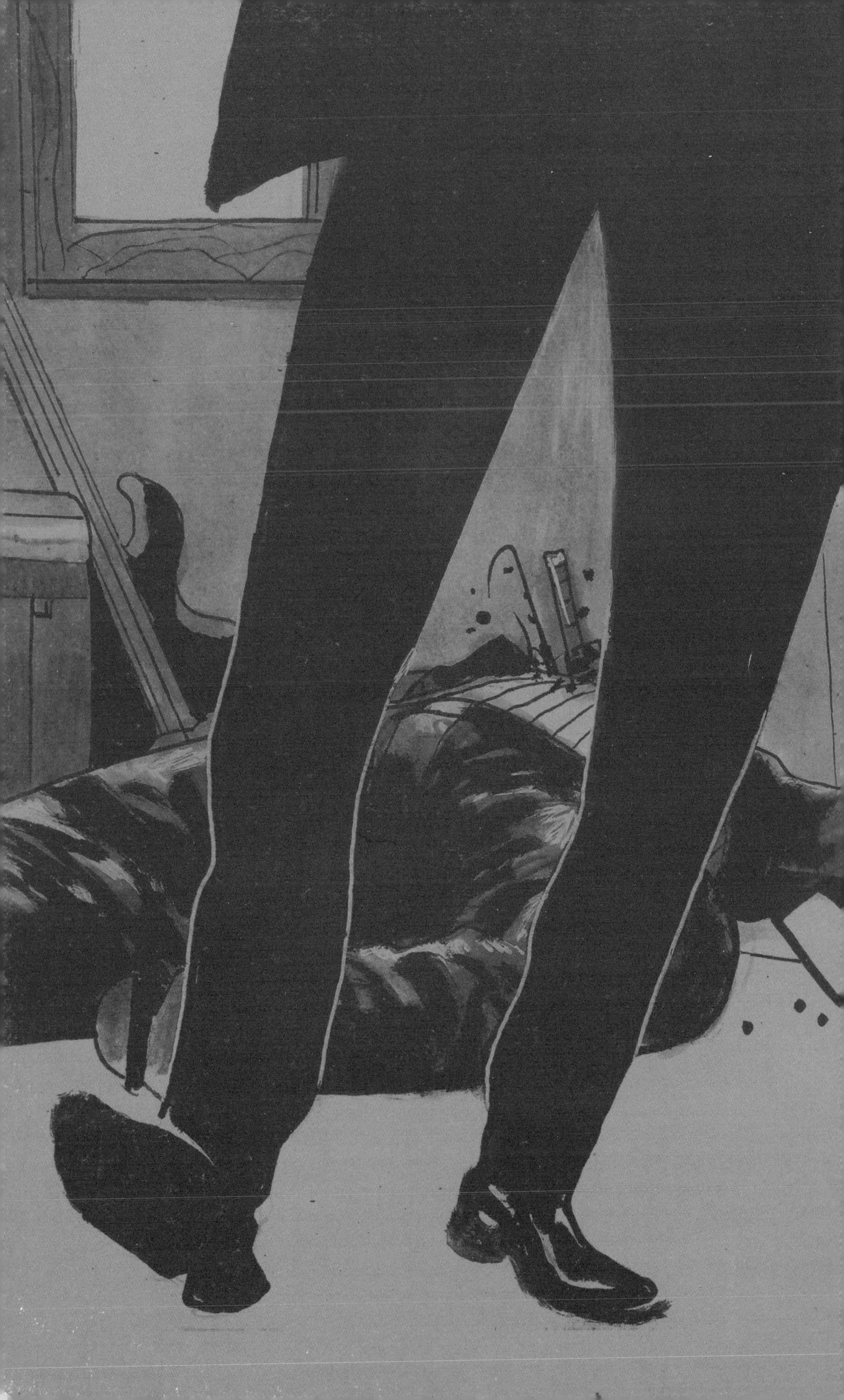